C.W.Friedmann

The Modern Language Association of America
GENERAL SERIES
VIII

PROBLEMS IN GERMAN LITERARY
HISTORY OF THE FIFTEENTH
AND SIXTEENTH CENTURIES

*Approved for publication in the General Series of the
Modern Language Association of America*

Ernest Bernbaum
Joseph E. Gillet
George L. Hamilton
H. M. Jones
William Kurrelmeyer
Kemp Malone
*Committee on
Research Activities*

Published under a grant awarded by the American Council of Learned
Societies from a fund provided by the Carnegie Corporation
of New York.

PROBLEMS IN GERMAN LITERARY HISTORY OF THE FIFTEENTH AND SIXTEENTH CENTURIES

BY

ARCHER TAYLOR

Multum adhuc restat
operis, multumque restabit, nec
ulli . . . praecludetur occasio
aliquid adicendi.
—Sen. *Epist*. VII. 2.

NEW YORK: MODERN LANGUAGE ASSOCIATION OF AMERICA
LONDON: OXFORD UNIVERSITY PRESS
1939

Copyright 1939

by the

MODERN LANGUAGE ASSOCIATION OF AMERICA

PRINTED IN U.S.A. BY GEORGE BANTA PUBLISHING COMPANY, MENASHA, WISCONSIN

TO
MY TEACHER
JOHN A. WALZ

PREFACE

IN the fifteenth and sixteenth centuries, German literature reflects movements profoundly affecting mankind. An older world imbued with the religious and social ideas of the Middle Ages was breaking up, and modern industrial and urban life was developing. Humanism brought new attitudes in thinking and living. Religious theories of every complexion fundamentally modified prevailing ethical and social principles. In the hands of the rising bourgeoisie, the ideas, themes, and literary conventions of the Middle Ages survived partly as conventional materials and partly as effective forces in a changing age. Close to the common man as it was, the German literature of this period reached its artistic perfection in folksong.

Apart from the cultural and historical importance of post-medieval German literature, this field is attractive because research in it can be undertaken and carried to a successful conclusion with simple means. In many instances, a single text in the form of a reprint or photographic copy and the ordinary reference works available in any college library are the only tools needed to attack a problem. It is hard to say whether reprinting and editing texts, compiling bibliographies, or writing essays in literary history is the most important. In the study of any epoch, these tasks comprise the business of the historian of literature. They are so interdependent that no one of them can be undertaken without some progress in the other two. Without a literary history we cannot know what texts deserve reprinting. Without a bibliography we cannot know what editions, old or new, exist or how these editions are related among themselves, or what value we should attach to a particular edition. Without access to the texts we cannot write a history of literature or compile a bibliography. Advances have been made in all three directions, but we still do not possess suitable texts, general and special reference works, and interpretative, critical, or evaluating accounts of literary movements sufficient to give us a good understanding of the characteristic literary movements and genres of the fifteenth and sixteenth centuries. In the following introduction to problems in the literary history of this period, I treat the tasks of the editor and bibliographer as subsidiary to those of the historian of literature; moreover, I endeavor to suggest tasks within the resources and abilities of American scholars and students. I have not sought to survey the entire literature of the fifteenth and sixteenth centuries. I have not sought to enumerate many problems which a historian of literature might try to solve. Finally, I have in general avoided religious topics still conducive to controversy and particularly those about which a large literature has grown up. The study of historical and philosophical currents demands wide reading and a large background of information. Although the student will do well to begin by investigating a clearly limited and narrowly defined problem, he should keep his eyes open in order to remain aware of the wider implications of his studies. I have tried to make clear the significance of the problems described, but I have not cited problems merely because they are traditionally regarded as important. I have rather considered first the possibility of an American student's solving the problem with the means at his disposal. Wolfgang Stammler, for example, cites the problem of the influence of monastic reforms on the literature of the fourteenth and fifteenth centuries.[1] This problem is too vaguely stated; it demands a greater familiarity than most students would claim with social, political, and ecclesiastical affairs, as well as with literature. In the main, I have indicated problems which can be undertaken with fair hope of success by a student who has comparatively few tools of research. The following essay purports to be no more than a superficial survey of a vast field. I hope that it will lead the earnest student to a larger view and deeper knowledge of a very interesting period in literary history.

The manner of outlining and stating the problem is intentionally varied from example to example. In one instance, the problem is stated in the form of an essay with mention of scarcely a name, date, or place. In another, a series of documents is systematically arranged, with abundant bibliographical detail and comment on the specific problems of each document. In still another, a tabulation in chronological order is given without comment. This variety in the manner of presentation is intended to appeal to differing tastes or to suggest various modes of attack. Casual illustrations are given from periods earlier and later than the fifteenth and sixteenth centuries. Free use is made of the help afforded by comparison with literary studies in allied fields. In preparing to attack a problem, one will do well to study the methods employed by others.

I have tried to introduce in a natural manner the chief works of reference, such as bibliographical tools. In general, I have not repeated citations in every instance where they might have been made. The index will facilitate reference. I have given the information which was at my

[1] *Von der Mystik zum Barock* ("Epochen der deutschen Literatur", II, i; Stuttgart, 1927), p. 461.

disposal and which suggested the problem to me. Since it has not been my intention to solve the problems, I have not striven for completeness in references. The problems are those which have occurred to me in the course of my work at the University of Chicago, and the references are those which were available to me there. I have not hesitated to cite "popular" books in the hope of arousing interest. Although I have usually mentioned studies deserving of imitation, I have cited some which show "how not to do it." A preliminary consultation with an older scholar will ordinarily help the beginner to avoid embarrassing errors. In the interest of succinctness, many of the problems mentioned below have been described so briefly that difficulties which might easily arise in their solution have not been named. My emphasis is on method rather than on completeness.

Some of the investigations described here can be attacked only by one who has at his disposal the resources of a large library. Others—particularly those discussed in the first chapter—can be begun anywhere but as they progress will tax the resources of even the largest libraries. Still others—and to these I have given special attention—can be begun in small libraries and continued by interlibrary loans or by visits to larger collections. Most problems can be undertaken more efficiently with limited resources than with free access to a large collection of books. A large library often overwhelms one by its very abundance. When one has carried an investigation beyond its initial stages, the resources of a large library become a foundation instead of an avalanche. After the plan of the investigation has been clearly formulated and has been tested by the preliminary studies possible in the smallest library, one can so organize one's time in a large library that every moment is devoted to books available only there. A scholar should not wait to attack a problem until he has at his disposal months of free time or funds for a trip to a great library. Let him do what lies to his hand. In many cases only very modest resources and very small expenditures are necessary. Goedeke's *Grundriss* will suggest an unprinted text; Götze's *Frühneuhochdeutsches Glossar* will provide the indispensable "first aid" in its interpretation; and a small expenditure for books, dissertations, and *programme* will supply the scholarly background. The cost of a comprehensive collection dealing with a particular subject is rarely excessive, particularly if we use ordinary common sense in selecting a subject. Most of us cannot seriously think of buying an adequate collection on the Reformation, on Martin Luther, or on saints' lives, but almost anyone can acquire a satisfactory library on a small subject or a definitely limited aspect of a larger one. A practically complete collection of publications on Meistergesang, including such unusual minor items as a *programm* published in 1807, a volume of a Moravian agricultural society, and a pamphlet issued by a society for the study of German music in Bohemia, cost less than a hundred dollars. On the other hand, a working collection of Johannes Geiler von Kaisersberg, whose works have not been reprinted since 1525, and are therefore rare, actually cost more than fifteen hundred dollars and needs considerable additional expenditures to be entirely satisfactory. One must cut one's coat according to the cloth. A collection of photographs of the manuscript books of rules of Meistergesang could be assembled for perhaps fifty or seventy-five dollars. It would be an arsenal for studies in the interrelations of texts, the technical vocabulary of the art, the changes occurring in the art, and so on. For even smaller expenditures one can get access to the material necessary for prosecuting a study. Interlibrary loans have developed to a point where no one is shut off from the tools of scholarship. Photography is an ever-helpful aid and, if used wisely, not unduly costly. Even problems which seem extensive can be safely undertaken in spite of onerous limitations. To make a historical dictionary of the language of German hunters, one can begin with the *Nibelungenlied*—which ought to be in the private library of every Germanist—and excerpt the pertinent words. In collecting even this small stock of words, one will meet and necessarily solve many problems fundamental to the prosecution of the investigation. What words are to be chosen? Which ones are to be excluded? What form shall the excerpts take? In thinking about such matters, one has no need for the resources of a large library. When the plan of the investigation has been worked out, one can borrow Gottfried von Strassburg's *Tristan und Isolde*. Book by book—and the cost of an interlibrary loan is not excessive—one can borrow the pertinent texts. I need not go farther to demonstrate the feasibility of undertaking even with limited resources a problem so complicated as that of making a dictionary.

For convenience I have standardized such spellings as *Literatur* and *16. Jahrhundert,* and for clarity I have introduced single quotation marks to set off the titles of books and the words forming the subject of a discussion. I have taken particular pains to indicate the series in which the books cited have appeared. This I have done because many libraries have not "analyzed" their series. Furthermore, the student will do well to post himself as to the nature and contents of these series. I have given dates for the publication of German works of the fifteenth and sixteenth centuries, but in doing so I have often given the date of the edition before me or of the edition to which I was referred. This date does not always refer to the first edition. Except when it was pertinent to the discussion, I have not indicated the place of publication or the publisher of German works of the fifteenth and sixteenth centuries. This procedure is designed to guide the student to the standard works of reference. In citing works published outside Germany, and German works issued after 1700, I have given the usual bibliographical details.

The publication of this book by the Modern Language Association has been made possible by the generosity of the American Council of Learned Societies. Without the efficient and competent assistance of the staff of the University of Chicago Library I could not have verified the references. I am happy to acknowledge the assistance of many friends. John G. Kunstmann has warned me against many a slip. Gustave Otto Arlt, Roland H. Bainton, C. R. Baskervill, Ernst Beutler, Leonard Bloomfield, Leicester Bradner, Hardin Craig, Robert Herndon Fife, William Hammer, Millett Henshaw, Rudolf Hirsch, and Hilda Norman have given me substantial aid and encouragement. From almost its beginning John W. Spargo has watched the growth of this essay with a friendly eye. His generous and unsparing criticism has left its mark on every page. The dedication intimates—in the nature of things, it can do no more—my debt to John A. Walz. I thank all who have helped me. "The indulgence of the learned reader must be solicited, to pardon errors or omissions, which, notwithstanding anxious and repeated perusal of the proofs, may have escaped detection."

Chicago, March 4, 1939.

TABLE OF CONTENTS

CHAPTER I

GENERAL PROBLEMS

Problems Involving a Survey of the Whole Period

1. *A Comprehensive History of German Literature in the Fifteenth and Sixteenth Centuries.*—The need of a history of post-medieval German literature is obvious; the undertakings proposed in the following pages are preparatory to such a history. Wolfgang Stammler's *Von der Mystik zum Barock,*[1] the only recent volume devoted to this period, is a praiseworthy effort, but its author would be the first to concede the desirability of a new survey. Gustav Ehrismann's excellent account[2] is bibliographical rather than interpretative and deals only with the beginning of the period. Although Günther Müller's review[3] of post-medieval German literature contains insufficient bibliographical details and deals with too few writers and works to be entirely satisfactory, it is valuable for its abundant use of illustrative materials from history and art. Finally, the many general histories of German literature give scant space to this period—perhaps because its problems seem remote from those of our day. To be sure, Josef Nadler's history of German literature on tribal lines contains much more than most general histories, but even it cannot take the place of a comprehensive account. Such an account would have to be based on firsthand knowledge of the literature and on a wide survey of its connections with the history, philosophy, religion, and culture of the age.

The history of post-medieval German literature is complicated by the fact that scholars have not agreed in their appraisals of many works of this age. In the case of Greek, Latin, or even Middle High German authors, the final estimates of literary historians have been largely established by centuries of opinion. The situation in post-medieval German

---

[1] "Epochen der deutschen Literatur," II, i; Stuttgart, 1927. This will be referred to henceforth as Stammler. Compare the reviews: Alker, *Zeitschrift für deutsche Philologie,* LIV (1929), 483-486; Gassen, *Zeitschrift für Aesthetik,* XXIV (1930), 84-91; Wiessner, *Anzeiger für deutsches Altertum,* XLVIII (1929), 35-53.

[2] *Geschichte der deutschen Literatur bis zum Ausgang des Mittelalters,* II, Schlussband ("Handbuch des deutschen Unterrichts," Munich, 1935). This volume will be referred to henceforth as Ehrismann; other volumes of this work will be described when cited.

[3] *Deutsche Dichtung von der Renaissance bis zum Ausgang des Barock* ("Handbuch der Literaturwissenschaft"; Wildpark-Potsdam, 1927).

literature is quite different. Thus the *Faustbuch* (1587), important as it is, has not been satisfactorily and definitively appraised. Wolfgang Stammler speaks well of it; other critics have loudly condemned its literary and artistic values. Such sharp differences of critical opinion show that the bases of literary history in our period are still in the making.

The importance of critical appraisal is shown by the entirely new valuations now put upon Heinrich Wittenweiler's *Ring* and the anonymous *Ackermann aus Böhmen*. The "discovery" of the *Ring* is the result of Wiessner's faithful efforts. Long after the appearance of Ludwig Bechstein's edition (1851), the *Ring* was neglected. In it Wiessner and Nadler have found a summary of the ideas of the late fourteenth century, and their line of thought has recently been followed by Pfeiffer-Belli. Possibly someone will take Niewöhner's hint[4] that an appreciation of the *Zimmerische Chronik* as a source of literary history is long overdue.

On an enormous scale, Konrad Burdach has drawn attention to *Der Ackermann aus Böhmen* as typical of the first German outburst of humanist enthusiasm. His learning has made this work available to the general reader and has deepened our knowledge of an age. The influence from Bohemia exemplified by *Der Ackermann aus Böhmen* is yet to be fully appraised and succinctly described. We must go much farther than did Rudolf Wolkan forty years ago in a meritorious study restricted to Bohemia. The literary and artistic streams rising in Bohemia bring to the whole of Northern and Northeastern Germany cultural changes of the utmost importance. Painting and sculpture, literary forms and ideas, and even the very shape of the language exhibit the influence of German culture in Bohemia. Ernst Beutler reminds me that the late fifteenth-century statue of the Madonna in Breslau is now believed to be Bohemian and not Rhenish in origin. Appreciation of these influences demands the wide vision found in such works as Huizinga's *The Waning of the Middle Ages; a study of the forms of life, thought, and art in France and the Netherlands in the fourteenth and fifteenth centuries*.[5] Although the task is more extensive and more difficult than most of those proposed in these pages, the spirit guiding Wiessner, Nadler, Burdach, and Huizinga should inspire the student, and their works should be familiar to him. Fundamental to a study of these relations is *Kulturräume und Kulturströmungen im mitteldeutschen Osten*,[6] by Wolfgang Ebert, Theodor

[4] *Anzeiger für deutsches Altertum*, XLV (1926), 20, n. 2.

[5] London, 1924. The original editions—*Herfsttij der middeleeuwen* (Haarlem, 1919, 1921, 1928, 1935)—should also be consulted; they contain references omitted in the English translation.

[6] Halle, 1936.

Frings, and others, which is primarily concerned with forces determining the Germanization of this Eastern region, and Konrad Burdach's monumental *Vom Mittelalter zur Reformation*,[7] which brings invaluable materials for the study of these problems.

Less ambitious would be an enthusiastic interpretative account of a day at Nuremberg in Hans Sachs's house or one at Augsburg in Conrad Peutinger's after the manner of Franz Joseph Delitzsch' *Ein Tag in Kapernaum*.[8] Gustave Flaubert's *Tentation de Saint-Antoine* or Philip F. W. Oertel's story of three days in Gellert's life suggests ways of dealing with such themes. Georg Buchwald's calendar[9] of Luther's activities day by day would make such a task something less than a work of the imagination. It goes without saying that the writer should avoid the pedantry which weighted down the *Professorenroman*.

2. *A Comprehensive Bibliography of German Literature in the Fifteenth and Sixteenth Centuries.*—Fundamental bibliographical work must be done before we can proceed rapidly and confidently in the study of post-medieval German literature. The essential apparatus is sadly deficient, incomplete, and inaccurate. We have no satisfactory list of books published between 1501, the date when the catalogues of incunabula close, and 1700, the date when Wilhelm Heinsius' *Allgemeines Bücherlexikon* begins.[10] It need hardly be said that a list of the books published in our period is the only safe foundation for a literary history. An invaluable bibliography lists the German and Latin publications in the first years of the sixteenth century: G. W. Panzer, *Annalen der älteren deutschen Literatur oder Anzeige und Beschreibung derjenigen Bücher, welche von der Erfindung der Buchdruckerkunst bis MDXX in deutscher Sprache gedruckt worden sind*[11] with the companion work, *An-*

---

[7] In seventeen volumes, Berlin, 1912 ff. (still appearing).

[8] 3d ed.; Leipzig, 1886.

[9] *Luther-Kalendarium* ("Schriften des Vereins für Reformationsgeschichte," CXLVII; Leipzig, 1929). Compare also R. Poser, *Synoptisches Inhaltsverzeichnis der gebräuchlichsten Luther-Ausgaben* published with B. Woerner, *Wegweiser in Buchwalds Luther-Kalendarium* ("Schriften" etc., CLVIII; Leipzig, 1935). I have not seen Gusta Mix, "Ein Tag aus Luthers Leben," *Die Wartburg*, II (1903), 502-505, as cited in Schottenloher, *Bibliographie zur deutschen Geschichte im Zeitalter der Glaubensspaltung*, I, 477, no. 11,215.

[10] See some indispensable suggestions on ways and means in R. F. Arnold, *Allgemeine Bücherkunde zur neueren deutschen Literaturgeschichte* (3d ed.; Berlin, 1931), pp. 209-210, 212. I refer henceforth to this work by the author's name. Compare also the instructive remarks in T. Besterman, *The Beginnings of Systematic Bibliography* (Oxford, 1935; 2d ed., 1936).

[11] Nuremberg, 1788. A second volume (Nuremberg, 1805) extends to 1526. Compare also the *Zusätze zu den Annalen* (Leipzig, 1802). Emil Weller's *Repertorium*

nales typographici ab artis inventae origine ad annum MD,[12] which
are continued in supplementary volumes down to 1536. Excellent as these
works are, the dates of their publication are a sufficient commentary:
much water has flowed under the bridge in five generations. Furthermore, neither Panzer nor anyone else tries to list completely what came
from German presses between 1536 and 1700. Contemporary efforts
to collect such bibliographical information are so rare that they are
virtually inaccessible.[13] They are perforce incomplete and difficult to use.
The trade-catalogues (*Messbücher*) of annual local fairs on which Wil-
lerus and Clessius based their lists are inaccessible to most American
scholars, as well as inconvenient, unreliable, and confusing.[14] Notwithstanding these disadvantages and the fact that sixteenth-century citations fall short of modern bibliographical standards, such works contribute a great deal of very useful information which is not to be found else-

---

and other works cited below replace Panzer in large measure. See also Arnold,
p. 209.

[12] In eleven volumes; Nuremberg, 1793-1803.

[13] See, e.g., [Georgius Willerus], *Collectio in unum corpus, omnium librorum
hebraeorum, graecorum, latinorum necnon germanice, italice, et hispanice scriptorum, qui in nundinis Francofurtensibus ab anno 1564 usque ad nundinas Autum-
nales anni 1592, partim nova forma et diversis in locis editi, venales extiterunt*
(Frankfurt a.M., 1592); Johannes Clessius, *Unius seculi eiusque virorum
literatorum monumentis tum florentissimi tum fertilisimi: ab anno Dom. 1500 ad
1602. Nundinarum autumnalium inclusive, Elenchus consumatissimus librorum;
Hebraei, Graeci, Latini, Germani, aliorumque Europae idiomatum. Desumptis
partim ex singularum nundinarum catalogis partim ex . . . bibliothecis* (Frankfurt
a. M., 1602), of which the second part entitled *Catalogi librorum Germanicorum
alphabetici, das ist: Verzeichnis der Teutschen Bücher u. Schriften, . . . so anno
1500 bis auf . . . 1602 ausgegangen* is especially important for us. On Clessius see
J. Petzholdt, *Bibliotheca bibliographica: kritisches Verzeichniss der das Gesammt-
gebiet der Bibliographie betreffenden Literatur des In- und Auslandes* (Leipzig,
1866), p. 70. See T. Besterman, *The Beginnings of Systematic Bibliography* (Oxford, 1935; 2d ed., 1936), *passim;* K. Schottenloher, "Die Anfänge der neueren
Bibliographie," *Festschrift für Georg Leidinger* (Munich, 1930), pp. 233-240.

[14] See Arnold, pp. 209-10; G. Schwetzke, *Codex nundinarius Germaniae literatae
bisecularis.—Mess-Jahrbücher des deutschen Buchhandels von dem Erscheinen
des ersten Mess-Katalogs im J. 1564 bis einschliesslich des Jahres 1846* (Halle,
1850-77); Georg Witkowski, "Die Leipziger Messrelationen," *Mitteilungen der
Deutschen Gesellschaft zur Erforschung vaterländischer Sprache . . . in Leipzig,*
XII (1927), 56-63. This volume was also issued separately under the title *Beiträge
zur deutschen Bildungsgeschichte: Festschrift zur Zweihundertjahrfeier der
Deutschen Gesellschaft.* See also F. C. Dahlmann and G. Waitz, *Quellenkunde
der deutschen Geschichte* (9th ed. by H. Haering; Leipzig, 1931), p. 698, nos.
11173-77, and especially the *Archiv für Geschichte des deutschen Buchhandels,* I
(1878 ff.), and its continuations.

where. It is regrettable that our knowledge of sixteenth- and seventeenth-century bibliographies is altogether inadequate. Besterman gives an incomplete and unsatisfactory notion of the number and value of such bibliographies.

Compiling an exhaustive bibliography of German publications in the sixteenth century is too big a job for any one man. To be sure, Emil Weller, Karl Goedeke, Wendelin Freiherr von Maltzahn, and more recently, Conrad Borchling in collaboration with Bruno Claussen, and Karl Schottenloher have shown what surprising results the diligence of a single man can achieve.[15] Emil Weller includes primarily books which he considers rare or important for their literary or cultural value in the *Annalen,* books which offer bibliographical complications in *Die falschen und fingirten Druckorte* and the *Lexicon pseudonymorum,* and books printed in the first quarter of the sixteenth century in the *Repertorium typographicum.* Karl Goedeke chooses titles of literary significance, but sets very wide limits. Wendelin Freiherr von Maltzahn lists rare and "interesting" titles. Conrad Borchling and Bruno Claussen seek to collect everything printed in Low German. Finally, Karl Schottenloher gathers materials for the historian of political, economic, religious, and cultural conditions. Two recent compilations[16] do not pretend

---

[15] Emil Weller, *Annalen der poetischen Nationalliteratur der Deutschen im XVI. und XVII. Jahrhundert* (Freiburg i. Br., 1862-64), *Die falschen und fingirten Druckorte* (Leipzig, 1864), *Lexicon pseudonymorum* (2d ed.; Ratisbon, 1886), and *Repertorium typographicum. Die deutsche Literatur im ersten Viertel des sechzehnten Jahrhunderts* (Nördlingen, 1864) with a supplement (*ibid.,* 1874-85), a revision of the corresponding portion of Panzer's *Annalen.*—Karl Goedeke, *Grundriss zur Geschichte der deutschen Dichtung* (2d ed.; Dresden, 1884 ff.). This work will be referred to henceforth as Goedeke. See the instructive analysis in Arnold, pp. 2-7. The portion of the first edition which has not yet been reissued in the second edition—except for the bibliography of translations into German—and the third edition, so far as it has appeared, do not deal with our period.—Wendelin Freiherr von Maltzahn, *Deutscher Bücherschatz des 16., 17. und 18. bis um die Mitte des 19. Jahrhunderts* (Jena, 1875), with an index (Frankfurt a.M., 1882) by G. Völcker.—Conrad Borchling and Bruno Claussen, *Niederdeutsche Bibliographie; Gesamtverzeichnis der niederdeutschen Drucke bis zum Jahre 1800* (Neumünster, 1931 ff.).—Karl Schottenloher, *Bibliographie zur deutschen Geschichte im Zeitalter der Glaubensspaltung 1517-1585* (Leipzig, 1933 ff.).

[16] Wilhelm Kosch, *Deutsches Literaturlexikon* (Halle, 1927-30); Hugh William Davies, *Catalogue of a Collection of Early German Books in the Collection of Charles Fairfax Murray* (London, 1913). The collection belonging to Charles Fairfax Murray includes primarily illustrated works printed in the first half of the sixteenth century. The catalogue is a superb example of care in bibliography and skill in printing.

to completeness, but deserve mention here. Although often incomplete
and inaccurate in the sections dealing with the literature of the fifteenth
and sixteenth centuries, Wilhelm Kosch's companion and supplement to
Goedeke's *Grundriss* is convenient for quick reference, and the Murray
catalogue, though very rich and admirable in its bibliographical detail,
is naturally not exhaustive.

A comprehensive bibliography of post-medieval German literature,
essential for all effective study of the period, is being prepared by competent hands, but it will not be finished for many years. The staff of
the British Museum is revising the catalogue of that great collection,
and the staffs of the various Prussian libraries together with the author-
ities in Munich and Vienna are compiling a union catalogue of German
books. These two catalogues will be the foundation of future literary
scholarship in our field. To be sure, even these extensive catalogues will
not include every book.[17] Some books exist now only in single copies,
e.g., an edition of Joachim Greff's early sixteenth-century play about
Jacob preserved in the University of Chicago Library.[18] Others have
disappeared entirely, although their former existence is sufficiently
authenticated. About 1750 or so, Gottsched had in his hands Wolfhart
Spangenberg's *Kurtzer Bericht vom uralten Herkommen, Fortpflanzung
und Nutzen des alten deutschen Meistergesangs (ca.* 1630 ?), but no
one has seen it since then.[19] The peculiar situation which obtains in
the cases of books mentioned in the trade-catalogues, although they
may never have been issued, is a bibliographical annoyance which need
not concern us greatly. Lists of books actually owned by various libraries[20] are the indispensable foundation of a comprehensive bibliography of post-medieval German literature, and we shall find our resources ample when the catalogue of the British Museum and the German union catalogue are finished.

We are so well supplied with lists of books printed before 1500 that
someone might undertake to review publications in a particular field

[17] See L. M. Price's instructive article, "Der deutsche Gesamtkatalog," *Germanic Review,* XII (1937), 203-208.

[18] This edition is of uncertain date; the title-page is lacking. It appears to differ
from the three copies of *Ein lieblich und nützbarlich Spil von dem Patriarchen
Jacob und seinen zwelf sönen* in the British Museum; see *Catalogue of Books
in the British Museum, s.v.* "Jacob, the patriarch." See also Goedeke, II, 357,
no. 121.

[19] H. Ellenbeck, *Die Sage vom Ursprung des deutschen Meistergesangs* (Diss.;
Bonn, 1911), p. 61.

[20] For comment on the uses to which catalogues of sixteenth-century libraries
can be put see below pp. 12-14.

and attempt to draw some inferences regarding cultural and other currents.[21] No one has yet surveyed the publications in German from the beginning of printing down to 1500 with the aims of determining what sorts of books were issued in German, where they were published, what audiences they appealed to, and what developments occurred in the course of two generations. The problem is not difficult, but involves some knowledge of the period and some ability in drawing inferences. Comparison of the production in various countries might be instructive. Contrast, for example, the number of editions of the Bible in Germany with the number in England, France, or Italy.

3. *Special Bibliographies.*—In the absence of an even approximately comprehensive catalogue of post-medieval German literature, various special lists supply information of great value. Such special lists are, for example, the histories and bibliographies of printing in particular localities, or at particular presses, or the bibliographies of special classes, such as books on medicine, proverbs, broadsides, and the like.[22]

[21] As a start in this direction compare John M. Lenhart, *Pre-Reformation Printed Books; a study in statistical and applied bibliography* ("Franciscan Studies," XIV; Washington, D.C., 1935). Although Lenhart displays a laudable industry in assembling statistics, he does not draw as many inferences as he should. See further J. Benzing, *Der Buchdruck des 16. Jahrhunderts im deutschen Sprachgebiet. Eine Literaturübersicht* ("Zentralblatt für Bibliothekswesen," Beiheft LXVIII; Leipzig, 1936), which gives a valuable survey of regional and other bibliographies, and F. Eichler, "Die Renaissance des Buches im 15. Jahrhundert und ihre Nachwirkung," *Festschrift Georg Leyh* (Leipzig, 1937), pp. 1-10. Eichler's remarks (pp. 6-7) interpreting the choice of books to be printed should stimulate further investigation. An old essay which is still useful is F. Falk, *Die Druckkunst im Dienste der Kirche, zunächst in Deutschland, bis zum Jahre 1520,* "Görres-Gesellschaft, 2. Vereinsschrift für 1879" (Cologne, 1879).

[22] The following examples will serve as illustrations: G. W. Zapf, *Augsburgs Buchdruckergeschichte* (Augsburg, 1788-91) may be contrasted with modern treatises like K. Schottenloher, *Das Regensburger Buchgewerbe im 15. und 16. Jahrhundert* ("Veröffentlichungen der Gutenberg-Gesellschaft," XIV-XIX; Mainz, 1920) and the older, standard work, Charles Schmidt, *Répertoire bibliographique strasbourgeois jusque vers 1530,* I-VIII (Strassburg, 1893-96); E. Langer and W. Dolch, *Bibliographie der österreichischen Drucke des 15. und 16. Jahrhunderts,* I, i: *Trient, Wien, Schrattenthal* (Vienna, 1913).

For the history of a single printer or press see such models as K. Schottenloher, *Der Münchner Buchdrucker Hans Schobser* (Munich, 1925) or an older essay, H. Pallmann, *Sigmund Feyerabend, sein Leben und seine geschäftlichen Verbindungen* (Frankfurt a.M., 1881).

For bibliographies of special classes of writings see such works as K. Schottenloher, *Deutsche medizinische Inkunabeln* ("Studien zur Geschichte der Medizin," II-III; Leipzig, 1908); P.A. [Gratet]- Duplessis, *Bibliographie parémiologique* (Paris, 1847) and Anon., *Catalogue des livres parémiologiques composant la*

In general, the preparation of any specialized bibliography requires facilities and library resources not available in America. Furthermore, the compilation of special bibliographies for the purpose of literary historians ordinarily exceeds what can be expected of a librarian. Such bibliographies demand an understanding of the uses to which they will be put in a highly specialized field of study as well as a comprehensive knowledge of a literary movement, a literary type, or an age. Of course, bibliographers who are dealing with books of the fifteenth and sixteenth centuries must consult German libraries. Those who are compiling lists of books and articles dealing with a movement or a literary type can do much of the preliminary work in America.

The compilation of a list of sixteenth-century books owned in America is altogether feasible. A similar list of incunabula without limitation to a particular language is G. P. Winship's *Census of Fifteenth-Century Books Owned in America*.[23] *A Short-Title Catalogue of Sixteenth-Century German Books Owned in America* would be of incalculable service to American scholarship in the humanities. The task has been bravely begun by the Bibliographical Committee of the Germanic Section of the Modern Language Association, but progress has been slow. A list of the sixteenth-century books owned in any of the more important centers—Boston, New York, Philadelphia, Washington, or Chicago—is an undertaking within the powers of a single individual. Scholars would be grateful for a comprehensive list or for one restricted to a single city, and the compiler would learn much to his advantage. To be sure, the task of compiling such a list lies somewhere between the duty of a librarian and the opportunity of the scholar.

Perhaps the most obvious field for bibliographical enterprises is the drama. The bibliographical tools at the disposal of the student of English literature arouse the envy of his comrade in German studies. Maxi-

---

bibliothèque de Ignace Bernstein (Warsaw, 1900) ; F. H. Reusch, *Der Index der verbotenen Bücher; ein Beitrag zur Kirchen- und Litteraturgeschichte* (Bonn, 1883-85) and *Die Indices librorum prohibitorum des 16. Jahrhunderts* ("Bibliothek des Literarischen Vereins," CLXXVI; Tübingen, 1868) ; Anon., *Einblattdrucke des 15. Jahrhunderts; ein bibliographisches Verzeichnis* ("Sammlung bibliothekswissenschaftlicher Arbeiten," XXXV-XXXVI; Halle, 1914).

[23] New York, 1919. A new edition is greatly to be desired, since the Library of Congress has purchased the Vollbehr collection, and other large additions to incunabula owned in America have been made in the last few years. Miss Margaret Stillwell, Annmary Brown Memorial Library, Providence, R.I., has undertaken this task. A typical example of a list restricted to a single city is Pierce Butler's admirable *A Check List of Fifteenth Century Books in the Newberry Library and in Other Libraries of Chicago* (Chicago, 1933).

milian J. Rudwin's bibliography of German religious drama[24] is almost the only work which students of German literature can set beside the many English lists.

Interesting and valuable would be a list of sixteenth-century German dictionaries owned in America. Many of these dictionaries have come to America in the libraries of such scholars as Friedrich Zarncke (now at Cornell University) and Moritz Heyne (now at the University of Illinois). Several dictionaries formerly in the library of Hermann Paul are at the University of Chicago. Harvard University has made a special effort to collect such dictionaries. All in all, many of these are within easy reach of American scholars. In fact, the number is larger than one might suppose. There are, for example, three editions of Dasypodius at the University of Chicago. A catalogue giving bibliographical descriptions of these books and indicating where they may be found would be very useful. When completed, it would suggest, on the one hand, expansion to include all such dictionaries[25] and, on the other, the addition of descriptive and critical comment. Many persons whom we might not associate with the making of dictionaries were interested in words. Erasmus Alberus, the writer of fables, compiled an early German dictionary, and Erasmus Sarcerius, preacher and moralizer, made notes for a Latin-German vocabulary. Study of the connections among these dictionaries would be instructive, but difficult. It would soon lead back to the study of earlier vocabularies and glosses. These various undertakings are preliminary to a history of early German dictionaries.[26]

[24] *A Historical and Bibliographical Survey of the German Religious Drama* ("University of Pittsburgh Studies in Language and Literature"; Pittsburgh, 1924).

[25] Fundamental to these bibliographical studies is the *Quellen-Verzeichnis zum Deutschen Wörterbuch* (Göttingen, 1910, reprinted, Berlin, 1930). See also *Deutsches Rechtswörterbuch; Quellenheft* (Weimar, 1930). Hermann Hirt has a useful introduction to the bibliography of German dictionaries; see *Etymologie der neuhochdeutschen Sprache* (2d ed.; "Handbuch des deutschen Unterrichts," IV, ii; Munich, 1921), pp. 58-61, 146-147. Under the names of various writers of this period Schottenloher cites articles dealing with dictionaries compiled by these men; see, e.g., *Bibliographie zur deutschen Geschichte im Zeitalter der Glaubensspaltung*, I, 10, no. 233. Pertinent special studies in the history of sixteenth- and seventeenth-century lexicography are the collectanea of Lorenz Diefenbach cited in Ehrismann, p. 441, n. 3, and M. Lexer, *Zur Geschichte der neuhochdeutschen Lexikographie* (Würzburg, 1890). See also the histories of pedagogy, notably Johannes Müller (b. 1846), *Quellenschriften und Geschichte des deutschsprachlichen Unterrichts bis zur Mitte des 16. Jahrhunderts* (Gotha, 1882).

[26] As an example of work in this field see the brilliant studies by René Ver-

Such studies as I have just described belong primarily to the linguistic history of our period and can be touched upon here only in passing. Satisfactory linguistic apparatus, essential for the student of literature, is unfortunately lacking in this period. Although we have many monographs—good and bad—on particular aspects of linguistic history,[27] syntheses are largely unwritten. In fact, our period has often been neglected as a matter of principle. There is no dictionary of sixteenth-century German to set beside the early modern English dictionary now in progress, and none is contemplated.[28] The excellent glossary of Alfred Götze is the only vocabulary limited to our period, and it does not include citations of sources. Special dictionaries have been under an evil star. That of Luther's language reached only to the letter "H" and, having been compiled before the standard edition was thought of, is necessarily difficult to use. The promised dictionary of Hans Sachs has never appeared. As a matter of principle, the dictionaries of foreign words and technical vocabularies, e.g., Hans Schulz's *Deutsches Fremdwörterbuch* (now continued by Otto Basler)[29] and Alfred Schirmer's *Wörterbuch der deutschen Kaufmannssprache auf geschichtlichen Grundlagen*,[30] exclude words no longer in use, that is to say, just the words which we most often need to have explained. Three generations have elapsed since the publication of Joseph Kehrein's *Grammatik der deutschen Sprache des 15. bis 17. Jahrhunderts*.[31] Meritorious as it was for the time when it was written, we now know a great deal more about the language of the sixteenth century. Virgil Moser's *Frühneuhochdeutsche Grammatik*[32] is a model of accuracy and thoroughness, but includes only the first half of the phonology. A dictionary and a grammar of the language of the sixteenth century are large tasks, and the beginner must at first restrict his efforts to fields which he can cover.

An American student can compile a very useful bibliography of

deyen, *Colloquia et dictionariolum septem linguarum,* I-III ("Vereeniging der Antwerpsche bibliophilen," XXXIX, XL, XLII; Antwerp, 1925-35).

[27] See an altogether new combination of methods in Hermann Gumbel, *Deutsche Sonderrenaissance in deutscher Prosa; Strukturanalyse deutscher Prosa im 16. Jahrhundert* ("Deutsche Forschungen," XXIII; Frankfurt a.M., 1930).

[28] See Hermann Paul's admirable essay on the problems of the lexicographer: "Ueber die Aufgaben der wissenschaftlichen Lexikographie mit besonderer Rücksicht auf das deutsche Wörterbuch," *Sitzungsberichte der philosophisch-philologischen und der historischen Classe der k. b[ayerischen] Akademie der Wissenschaften* (Munich, 1894), pp. 53-91.

[29] Strassburg (now Berlin), 1913 ff.

[30] Strassburg, 1911.

[31] Leipzig, 1854-56 and reprinted *ibid.,* 1863.

[32] "Germanische Bibliothek," I, i, Vol. 17; Heidelberg, 1929.

studies in the post-medieval literature and cultural history of Germany and add references to the books necessary for filling in the background. There are already many books and articles on the introduction and development of humanistic ideas in various cities, but they have never been conveniently collected. Gustav Bauch, for example, has written admirable treatises on the acceptance of humanism in Erfurt, Frankfurt an der Oder, and elsewhere; Max Herrmann describes the rise of humanism in Nuremberg and gives a brief bibliography of humanism in Heidelberg and Augsburg,[33] others discuss humanism in the Tirol, the Palatinate, or a dozen other places.[34] Perhaps the most extensive effort of this sort is Gustav Bauch's bibliography of the Renaissance in Silesia.[35] A survey of these essays might be arranged chronologically and should contain brief critical or descriptive comment. It would disclose regions which had been incompletely studied. Comparison of the study of one region with the study of another would reveal interesting problems. The necessary annotations would be helpful in suggesting problems as well as in evaluating the works. Of course, such a study can be extensive and detailed or it can be judiciously limited. It is an obvious prerequisite to a history of post-medieval German literature and culture.

As an example of another kind of bibliographical survey—but only as

[33] *Die Reception des Humanismus in Nürnberg* (Berlin, 1898), an enthusiastic and facile book which was not received with favor by specialists in the history of Nuremberg; and *Albrecht von Eyb und die Frühzeit des deutschen Humanismus* (Berlin, 1893), pp. 2, 423. I shall refer henceforth to the second work as Herrmann. References to the studies of Bauch can be easily assembled by consulting the standard bibliographies.

[34] See a convenient bibliography of regional studies in Schottenloher, IV, 283-92, *s.v.* "Humanismus." I have cited examples to illustrate the variety of these studies. A. Zingerle, "Der Humanismus in Tirol unter Erzherzog Sigmund dem Münzreichen," *Tirolensia; Festgruss an die 42. Versammlung deutscher Philologen* (Innsbruck, 1893), pp. 147-54; Joseph Kopp, *Der Neuhumanismus in der Pfalz* ("Monumenta Germaniae paedogogica," Beiheft 3; Berlin, 1928); K. Grossmann, "Die Frühzeit des Humanismus in Wien bis zu Celtis' Berufung," *Jahrbuch für Landeskunde von Niederösterreich*, N. F., XXII (1929), 150-325. See convenient bibliographies in F. C. Dahlmann and G. Waitz, *Quellenkunde der deutschen Geschichte* (9th ed. by H. Haering; Leipzig, 1931), pp. 580-81, nos. 905-64; and Stammler, pp. 463 (note on p. 21), and 475 (note on p. 81). The first of these will be referred to henceforth as Dahlmann-Waitz. A collation of these lists will provide the foundation for a comprehensive bibliography.

[35] "Bibliographie der schlesischen Renaissance (1475-1521)," *Silesiaca: Festschrift des Vereins für Geschichte und Alterthum Schlesiens zum 70. Geburtstage seines Präses Colmar Grünhagen* (Breslau, 1898), pp. 145-186, with additions in *Zeitschrift des Vereins für Geschichte und Alterthum Schlesiens*, XXXIV (1900), 379-381.

an example which later experience will modify—I give in an Appendix I a collection of bibliographical notes on Strassburg, a center of humanistic influence in Southwestern Germany. I have chosen Strassburg for the subject of this collection because a large number of important books have been written about the extremely varied and significant aspects of social, economic, and political life there. Less varied, but no less valuable as a basis for further study would be a review of the materials for the history of Augsburg. A use to which such collections lend themselves is the expansion of such brief, interpretative descriptions of German cities as those given by Hans Rupprich.[36] I have learned a good deal from these modest descriptions and could only wish that someone might write at greater length in the same vein.

4. *The Catalogue of a Private Library as Indicative of the Cultural Background of an Individual or an Age.*—Midway between bibliography and literary history lies the problem of interpretating the catalogues of libraries as evidences of the cultural life of an individual or an age.[37]

[36] *Humanismus und Renaissance in den deutschen Städten und an den Universitäten* ("Deutsche Literatur. Humanismus und Renaissance," II; Leipzig, 1935), pp. 7-54.

[37] See in general G. A. E. Bogeng, *Die grossen Bibliophilen; Geschichte der Büchersammler und ihrer Sammlungen* (Leipzig, 1922) ; Paul Lehmann, *Mittelalterliche Bibliothekskataloge Deutschlands und der Schweiz* (Munich, 1915-28) ; K. Heilig, "Mittelalterliche Bibliotheksgeschichte als Geistesgeschichte," *Zeitschrift für deutsche Geistesgeschichte,* I (1935), 12-23. A work of fundamental importance in this field has just appeared; see H. Kramm, *Deutsche Bibliotheken unter dem Einfluss von Humanismus und Reformation* ("Zentralblatt für Bibliothekswesen," Beiheft LXX; Leipzig, 1938). A good example of an interpretative study is R. Stauber, *Die Schedelsche Bibliothek; Beitrag zur Geschichte der Ausbreitung der italienischen Renaissance, des deutschen Humanismus und der medizinischen Literatur* ("Studien und Darstellungen aus dem Gebiete der Geschichte," VI, 2-3; Freiburg i. Br., 1908). Compare the important and instructive reviews of this book; see *Jahresbericht über die Erscheinungen auf dem Gebiete der germanischen Philologie,* XXXI (1909), 131, §9, no. 3, XXXII (1910), 144, §9, no. 149, XXXIII (1911), 155, §9, no. 112; *Bibliographie der deutschen Rezensionen,* XI (1909), 277, XII (1910), 307, XIII (1911), 329. The *Jahresbericht* appears to have overlooked the important review by E. Reicke, *Mitteilungen des Vereins für die Geschichte der Stadt Nürnberg,* XIX (1911), 271-78. In general, the *Jahresbericht* and the *Bibliographie* are convenient sources for references to reviews, and I have cited them here to call attention to their merits. See also the dissertations on the Schedels, e.g. W. Höpfner, *Die Nürnberger Aerzte des 15. Jahrhunderts, DDr. Herrmann und Hartman Schedel* (Leipzig, 1915) ; Joseph Sprengler, *Hartmann Schedels Weltchronik* (Munich, 1905). Stammler thinks that a study of the *Weltchronik* in the light of Hartmann Schedel's library is needed, but see now H. L. Bullen, *The Nuremberg Chronicle* (privately printed by the Book Club of California; San Francisco, 1930). Paul

George R. Havens has achieved good results in his examination of Voltaire's library now preserved at Leningrad, and other scholars have dealt with English and French libraries of the eighteenth and early nineteenth centuries. Many catalogues of German libraries, public and private, formed in the fifteenth and sixteenth centuries, have been published, but few have been adequately interpreted. The discussions of Johannes Geiler's and Thomas Murner's reading are not very satisfactory examples of interpretative essays.[38] Hartmann Schedel's library has been competently described, and the reviews of this investigation are instructive in matters of method. The slurs cast upon Luther's reading brought forth responses in which his knowledge of books was fully described and appraised. These studies show what can be accomplished and what value they have in understanding the life of an age.

Studies dealing with private libraries of the fifteenth and sixteenth centuries have been occupied with the difficulties in identifying the books and have usually neglected to some extent the interpretation of the library. The interpretation might either add to our knowledge of an important writer or give us a better idea of the cultural interests of a book-collector, preacher, or teacher. Editing or interpreting the catalogue of a private library cannot be easily undertaken in America, unless we deal with a catalogue already in print or one that can be readily photographed. A small task would be a discussion of the few Hebrew books and manuscripts in Hartmann Schedel's library; Stauber left it undone.[39] What can be learned about the libraries of Jacob Wimpfeling,

---

Lehmann's comment on Sigmund Gotzkircher's library is instructive in matters of method; it is cited in the list below. For methods see also Ernst Beutler, *Forschungen und Texte zur frühhumanistischen Komödie* ("Mitteilungen aus der Hamburger Staats- und Universitäts-Bibliothek," II; Hamburg, 1927), p. 37; Paul Lehmann, *Johannes Sichardus und die von ihm benutzten Bibliotheken und Handschriften* ("Quellen und Untersuchungen zur lateinischen Philologie," IV, i; Munich, 1911). An old and famous book—perhaps the only treatise on a private library to have reached a second edition—is P. de Nolhac, *Pétrarque et l'humanisme d'après un essai de restitution de sa bibliothèque* ("Bibliothèque de l'école des hautes études," XCI; Paris, 1892) which was revised and reissued as *Pétrarque et l'humanisme* (Paris, 1907). Perhaps the latest important work of this sort is Pearl Kibre, *The Library of Pico della Mirandola* (New York, 1936).

[38] E. Fuchs, "Die Belesenheit Geilers von Kaisersberg," *Zeitschrift für deutsche Philologie,* LII (1927), 119-122, and "Thomas Murners Belesenheit, Bildungsgang und Wissen," *Franziskanische Studien,* IX (1922), 70-79 (also published as a Breslau diss.).

[39] *Op. cit.,* p. 50. See, however, Otto Hartig, "Die Gründung der Münchner Hofbibliothek durch Albrecht V. und Johann Jakob Fugger," *Abhandlungen der königlich bayerischen Akademie der Wissenschaften, philosophisch-philologische und historische Klasse,* XXVIII, no. 3 (1917), pp. 265-266.

Conrad Celtis, Erasmus, or Melanchthon? Melanchthon's library was scattered, and some of the volumes have come to the University of Chicago. The catalogue of the large collection which Ulrich Fugger gave to the University of Heidelberg in 1584 is still unpublished.[40] Inventories of estates occasionally contain references to books and might provide a basis for investigation. Comparative studies in the private libraries named in the appendix might enlarge our knowledge.

5. *Changes in the Meaning and Use of a Characteristic Word or Phrase.*—Study of the changes in the meaning and use of a word or phrase has much in common with the literary history of a period. It surveys a large scene, and provides a basis for the interpretation and understanding of an age. In investigating the history of a word or phrase, one must first ascertain whether it is characteristic of a period and then choose significant points in time for the beginning and end of the study. Examples of historical investigation in medieval vocabulary are rather numerous; familiarity with them will greatly aid the student. There are recent studies in the cultural history of the phrase *hoher muot* and the word *huote,* the meaning and use of *höfisch, guot, rein, sælde,* the contrast of *freude* and *truren,* and many other words.[41]

---

[40] Beutler (cited in the previous note 37), pp. 50-51. See also F. L. Hoffmann, "Ueber ein Inventarium der Bibliothek Ulrich Fuggers vom Jahre 1571," *Serapeum,* IX (1848), 289-300, 305-309. Compare Konrad Burdach, *Vorspiel,* I, 2 (Halle, 1925), 94; R. Sillib, "Zur Geschichte der grossen Heidelberger (Manessischen) Liederhandschrift," *Sitzungsberichte der Heidelberger Akademie, philosophisch-historische Klasse,* XII (1921), no. 3, passim.

[41] A valuable introduction to these problems with a survey of results achieved is J. Trier, "Deutsche Bedeutungsforschung," in *Germanische Philologie: Ergebnisse und Aufgaben; Festschrift für Otto Behaghel* ("Germanische Bibliothek," Abt. I, Reihe I, XIX; Heidelberg, 1934), pp. 173-200. For examples of investigations compare August Arnold, *Studien über den 'hohen mut'* ("Von deutscher Poetery," IX; Leipzig, 1930) and the important remarks of J. Trier, *Anzeiger für deutsches Altertum,* L (1035), 178-181; R. Brodführer, *Untersuchungen über die Entwicklung des Begriffes 'guot' im Minnesang* (Diss.; Leipzig, 1917) and the earlier study by Franz Schmidt, *Zur Geschichte des Wortes 'gut'; ein Beitrag zur Wortgeschichte der sittlichen Begriffe im Deutschen* (Berlin, 1898); O. Gaupp, *Zur Geschichte des Wortes 'rein'* (Diss.; Tübingen, 1920); K. Korn, *Studien über 'freude' und 'truren' bei mittelhochdeutschen Dichtern; Beiträge zu einer Problemgeschichte* ("Von deutscher Poeterey," XII; Leipzig, 1932); H. Kunisch, *Das Wort 'grund' in der Sprache der deutschen Mystik des 14. und 15. Jahrhunderts* (Münster diss.; Osnabrück, 1929); W. Schrader, *Studien über das Wort 'höfisch' in der mittelhochdeutschen Dichtung* (Bonn diss.; Würzburg, 1935); T. Scharman, *Studien über die 'sælde' in der ritterlichen Dichtung des 12. und 13. Jahrhunderts* (Frankfurt a.M. diss.; Würzburg, 1935); Lilli Seibold, *Studien über die 'huote'* ("Germanische Studien," CXXIII; Berlin, 1932); Regine Strümpell, *Ueber Gebrauch und Bedeutung von*

Little of this sort of investigation has been carried out in the literary history of the fifteenth and sixteenth centuries in Germany. The aims and technique of investigations vary from case to case. An old example noteworthy for its interesting illustrations is "débiter" in Diderot's *Encyclopédie*. Rudolf Hildebrand's famous article "Geist" in the *Deutsches Wörterbuch* has been reprinted separately. Friedrich Staub's *Das Brot im Spiegel schweizer Volkssprache und Sitte*,[42] which was a model for the articles in the *Schweizerisches Idiotikon* dealing with cultural history, is a notable contribution to the technique of these studies. Comparison of the various investigations in the history of medieval and modern words is instructive.

Wolfgang Stammler pointed out[43] the interesting possibilities offered

---

'sælde,' 'sælic' und *Verwandtem bei mittelhochdeutschen Dichtern* (Diss.; Leipzig, 1917); Friedrich Vogt, *Der Bedeutungswandel des Wortes 'edel'* (Rede beim Antritt des Rektorats; Marburg, 1909); Vera Vollmer, *Die Begriffe der 'triuwe' und der 'stæte' in der höfischen Minnedichtung* (Diss.; Tübingen, 1914); A. Vorkampff-Laue, *Zum Leben und Vergehen einiger mittelhochdeutschen Wörter* (Diss.; Halle, 1906).

Thus, we are easily led into the problem of the life and death of words, but this problem is too complicated for us to discuss here, and comment would lead us too far afield. See, e.g., Lis Jacobsen, "Om ordenes död," *Arkiv för nordisk filologi*, XXXI (1915), 236-284 and E. Huguet, *Mots disparus ou vieillis depuis le 16ᵉ siècle* (Paris, 1935).

[42] Berlin, 1868.

[43] *Von der Mystik zum Barock*, p. 9. See instances of *Abenteurer* in Grimm, *Deutsches Wörterbuch*, I (Leipzig, 1854), cols. 28-29; A. Götze, *Trübners Deutsches Wörterbuch*, I (Berlin, 1936), 9-10; J. Bolte, "Fahrende Leute in der Literatur des 15. und 16. Jahrhunderts," *Sitzungsberichte der preussischen Akademie der Wissenschaften, philosophisch-historische Klasse*, XXXI (1928), 634, nn. 4-6; J. Bolte (ed.), Johannes Pauli, *Schimpf und Ernst* (Berlin, 1924), II, 16, 17, 449; P. Dietz, *Wörterbuch zu Dr. Martin Luthers Deutschen Schriften*, I (Leipzig, 1870), 10; the last paragraph of Ulrich von Hutten's *Die Anschauenden;* a Meisterlied reprinted in J. Bolte (ed.), Georg Wickram, *Werke*, III ("Bibliothek des Literarischen Vereins," CCXXIX; Tübingen, 1903), p. 316; Johann Fischart, *Aller Praktik Grossmutter* (ed. J. Scheible, "Das Kloster," VIII; Stuttgart, 1847), p. 603, l. 1; K. A. Barack, *Zimmerische Chronik* (2d ed.; Freiburg i. B., 1882), IV, 350. The term is apparently not applied in the sixteenth century to such a man as Heraklid Basilikus. See, e.g., L. Gumplowicz, "Ein politischer Abenteurer des 16. Jahrhunderts," *Zeitschrift für allgemeine Geschichte, Kulture- und Literatur- und Kunstgeschichte*, I (1884), 712-729; T, Wotschke, "Johann Laski und der Abenteurer Heraklid Basilikus," *Archiv für Reformationsgeschichte*, XVII (1920), 47-61. At a much later time the word is borrowed again as *Avanturier;* see W. Rehm, "Avanturierroman" in *Reallexikon der deutschen Literaturgeschichte*, I (Berlin, 1925-26), 101-102; H. Schneider, "Avantiure," in *ibid.*, pp. 102-103; B. Miedebrath, *Die deutschen 'Avanturiers' des 18. Jahrhunderts* (Diss.; Würzburg, 1907). Consult also the treatises on the

by the meanings of *Abenteurer*. It originally meant "seeker after adventure," later "a traveling merchant dealing in jewels," and finally (in the eighteenth century), "a man who makes his way in the world in a daring fashion by his wits." Study of these various meanings would disclose a series of historical and cultural connections. Even very simple words yield interesting results, but only experience can teach which ones to select. Changing philosophical and religious ideas would appear in a study of the meanings of *fromm;* political and administrative conditions might be revealed in an analysis of the history of *Curtisan*. Luther gave a characteristic significance to *Arbeit*.[44] A discussion of the meanings which he attached to *Freund* would probably not prove to be an unduly difficult task.

The curious uses of the word *Oberland,* particularly in such phrases as "der smit von oberlande" signifying God, "prinsin van ueberlande" signifying the Virgin Mary, and "gen oberlande varn" signifying to die, have never been explained. It has not been ascertained that these Christian locutions were confined to any special place in Germany, but investigation might show this to be true and would then lead to inferences regarding the origin and meaning of the phrases. Jacob Grimm and others thought that the phrases might contain echoes of heathen myths; and a curious allusion to *oberlant,* a hammer, and to a wedding in Frauenlob's verse seems to support this theory.[45] In the first half

---

borrowings of French words in medieval and post-medieval German cited below (p. 37) and the essay "Die Aventure in den altfranzösischen Lais" in E. Eberwein, *Zur Deutung mittelalterlicher Existenz* ("Kölner romanistische Arbeiten," VII; Bonn, 1933). See also such works as P. Nolte, *Der Kaufmann in der deutschen Sprache* (Diss.; Göttingen, 1909); M. R. Kaufmann, "Der Kaufmannsstand in der deutschen Literatur bis zum Ausgang des 17. Jahrhunderts," *Grenzboten,* LXIX, Part IV (1910), 110-121; G. Schilperoot, *Le commerçant dans la littérature française du moyen âge (caractère, vie, position sociale)* (Groningen diss.; The Hague, 1933).

[44] Hildburg Geist, "Arbeit, Die Entstehung eines Wortwertes durch Luther," *Luther-Jahrbuch,* XIII (1931), 83-113. For the earlier history of the word see Gertrude Schwarz, *'Arebeit' bei mittelhochdeutschen Dichtern* ("Bonner Beiträge zur deutschen Philologie," III; Würzburg-Aumühle, 1938).

[45] It would lead us too far afield to consider here the curious problem of the associations of the smith and marriage. See R. Andree, *Ethnographische Parallelen und Vergleiche* (Stuttgart, 1878), p. 159. No one appears to have investigated the problem. In compiling a list of books to be consulted, one might begin with the references in Hanns Bächtold—[Stäubli], *Die Gebräuche bei Verlobung und Hochzeit mit besondrer Berücksichtigung der Schweiz,* I ("Schriften der Schweizerischen Gesellschaft für Volkskunde," XI; Basel, 1914), of which only the first volume was published, and with the articles "Ehe" and "Hochzeit" in the *Handwörterbuch des deutschen Aberglaubens.*

of the fourteenth century, Oswald von Wolkenstein contrasts *oberlant* (Heaven) with *niderlant* (the earth),[46] but this meaning for *niderlant* is rare. There is a possibility that *oberlant* may have something to do with an old Germanic series of words describing the cosmos and represented by the Old Norse *miðgarðr*, Old High German *mittilagart* (*Muspilli*, l. 54), and the like. A direct connection with Old Norse or heathen cosmology is hardly to be supposed. The name of the Bernese Oberland and that of a district south of Schlettstadt in Alsace as well as the frequent use of the contrast *oberlant: niderlant* show that the word *Oberland* was a familiar geographical term. In Southwestern Germany, the congregations of mystics recognized 'Der Gottesfreund im Oberland" or "aus dem Oberland"—the form varies—as one of their leaders. In this title the word *Gottesfreund* alludes to such passages as "Henceforth I call you not servants; for the servant knoweth not what his lord doeth; but I have called you friends' (Joh. 15:15) and "Abraham believed in God, and it was imputed unto him for righteousness; and he was called the Friend of God" (James 2:23), and is an idiom known to the Church Fathers and the Middle Ages.[47] A curious Flemish riddle about a fish and a hook may preserve a recollection of the phrase. It is:

"Man van daar, wat dœ-de gij hier?"
"De man van hierboven die stuurt mij hier."
"En als ik u pakte, wat had' gij deraan?"
"De man van hierboven, die zou me bijstaan."[48]

Riddles in dialogues are rare, and parallels to this riddle are known only in Flemish. An account of the connections in which *Oberland* and similar locutions occur may explain the origin and significance of a rather large group of phrases.[49] Jacob Grimm suggested the problem

---

[46] J. Schatz, *Die Gedichte Oswalds von Wolkenstein* (2d ed.; Göttingen, 1904), p. 276, no. 117.

[47] E. Peterson, "Der Gottesfreund; Beiträge zur Geschichte eines religiösen Terminus," *Zeitschrift für Kirchengeschichte,* XLII=N. F., V (1923), 161-201; R. Egenter, *Gottesfreundschaft: die Lehre von der Gottesfreundschaft in der Scholastik und Mystik des 12. und 13. Jahrhunderts* (Augsburg, 1929). See an extensive bibliography of the Gottesfreunde in C. Baeumker, *Der Anteil des Elsass an den geistlichen Bewegungen des Mittelalters* (Strassburg, 1912), pp. 55-57.

[48] Cornelissen, "Raadsels," *Ons volksleven,* I (1889), 7, no. 9, 79, no. 50; Amaat Joos, *Raadsels van het vlaamsche volk* (Ghent, 1888), p. 81 (it appears to have been omitted in the second, enlarged edition [Brussels, n. d. (*ca.* 1926)]).

[49] A complete discussion of these words would reward the effort. Compare, e.g., Edward Schröder, "Handschriftliche Funde von meinen Bibliotheksreisen," *Nachrichten von der Gesellschaft der Wissenschaften zu Göttingen, philologisch-historische Klasse,* 1927, p. 115 (citing a religious poem entitled "Das ist daz

long ago, but no one has undertaken to solve it. Such a description would lead to a discussion of Schwietering's hint that *der smit von oberlande* is connected with the figurative expression "to forge a rhyme."[50]

---

anderland") and *mieelhiem* in a Danish ballad (Grundtvig, *Danmarks gamle folkeviser,* II [Copenhagen, 1856], 468, "Modern under mulde," A, stanza 17). For comment on *mieelhiem* see F. Ohrt, " 'Englevist,' " *Danske studier,* 1936, pp. 27-34.

I have collected the following examples of *Oberland:* Philipp Strauch (ed.), *Der Marner* ("Quellen und Forschungen zur Sprach- und Culturgeschichte der germanischen Völker," XIV; Strassburg, 1876), pp. 75, 143 (the notion of God conceived as a smith is related, thinks Strauch, to *der esse gluot* as a name for Hell. Compare also *hellesmet* in W. Seelmann (ed.), *Gerhard van Minden* ("Niederdeutsche Denkmäler," II; Bremen, 1878), p. 110 (LXXIII, 22-23) and F. Bech, *Germania,* XXIX (1884), 30 (on Heinrich von Meissen); K. Burdach, *Der Ackermann aus Böhmen* ("Vom Mittelalter zur Reformation," III, i; Berlin, 1917), pp. 352-353 (note on 26, 26); J. Grimm, *Kleinere Schriften,* IV (Berlin, 1869), 346, V (1871), 17, and *Deutsche Mythologie* (4th ed.; Berlin and Gütersloh, 1875-78), p. 150 and III, 15; Ehrismann, p. 623 (general references on "Der Gottesfreund im Oberland"). The form of the name varies somewhat; J. Meier, *Balladen,* II (Leipzig, 1936), 297 (this may be Oberland in Alsace; cf. G. Stoffel, *Topographisches Wörterbuch des Ober-Elsasses, die alten und neuen Ortsnamen*); [F.J] M [one], *Anzeiger für Kunde der teutschen Vorzeit,* VII (1838), col. 373, no. 303; J. M. Müller-Blattau, *Das deutsche Volkslied* ("Max Hesses Handbücher," XXXIV; Berlin-Schöneberg, 1932), p. 67; Anselm Salzer, *Die Sinnbilder und Beiworte Mariens in der deutschen Literatur und lateinischen Hymnenpoesie des Mittelalters* (Linz, 1893), pp. 43, l. 8 and 94; K. Rieder, *Der Gottesfreund vom Oberland; eine Erfindung des Strassburger Johanniterbruders Nikolaus von Löwen* (Innsbruck, 1905); L. Pfannmüller, *Frauenlobs Marienleich* ("Quellen und Forschungen zur Sprach- und Culturgeschichte der germanischen Völker," CXX; Strassburg, 1913), pp. 58, 94-96; R. Minzloff (ed.), *Bruder Hansens Marienlieder* (Hannover, 1863), ll. 1365, 2379, 3730 (cf. J. Franck, *Zeitschrift für deutsches Altertum,* XXIV [1880], 390); F. Khull (ed.), *Der Kreuziger des Johannes von Frankenstein* ("Bibliothek des literarischen Vereins," CLX; Tübingen, 1882), l. 11381; K. Bartsch (ed.), *Die Erlösung* ("Bibliothek der gesammten deutschen National-Literatur," XXXVIII; Quedlinburg, 1858), p. 191, no. 3, "Ave Maria," l. 11; L. Koester, *Albrecht Lesch ein Münchner Meistersinger des 15. Jahrhunderts* (Munich diss.; n.p., n.d. [1938?]), pp. 86, 87, 106; W. Grimm (ed.) *Konrads von Würzburg Die goldene Schmiede* (Berlin, 1840), p. xxvii; P. Wackernagel, *Das deutsche Kirchenlied,* II (Leipzig, 1867), 270, no. 429, (4, 7); C. Walther *Jahrbuch des Vereins für niederdeutsche Sprachforschung,* III (1877), 71; I. V. Zingerle, *Germania,* VI (1861), 221 and *Sitzungsberichte der k. Akademie, philosophisch-historische Klasse* (Vienna), XXXVII (1861), 354; A. von Arnswaldt, *Vier niederdeutsche Schriften Ruysbroeks* (with a preface by C. Ullmann; Hannover, 1848), p. 52, l. 7 ff.; Wilhelm Wackernagel, *Kleine Schriften* (Leipzig, 1872-74), III (1874), 123.

[50] "Die Demutsformel mittelhochdeutscher Dichter," *Abhandlungen der k.*

6. *Formulae Describing Racial Peculiarities or Epitomizing an Age.*
—Historical studies in proverbs, conventional epithets, and phrases epitomizing an age or a characteristic judgment throw light on the development of ideas and their alterations.[51] It is not surprising, for example, that in German "hereditary enemy" (*Erbfeind*) once meant the Devil, then the Turk, and finally came to mean the French.[52] Tracing this development involves an exposition of the relations of the Germans and the French as well as the cultural background of the Middle Ages and later times.

The familiar *Deutsche Treue* is, it is said, an echo of a classical Latin phrase,[53] but a definite source appears to be lacking. At the time of the

---

Gesellschaft der Wissenschaften zu Göttingen, philosophisch-historische Klasse, N.F., XVII, no. 3 (1921), p. 57.

[51] See as an introduction my essays "An Introductory Bibliography for the Study of Proverbs," *Modern Philology*, XXX (1933), 195-210, and "Problems in the Study of Proverbs," *Journal of American Folk-Lore*, XLVII (1934), 1-21.

[52] F. Behrend, "Im Kampf mit dem Erbfeind," *Zeitschrift des Vereins für Volkskunde*, XXV (1915), 6-17. The continuation of this article in the succeeding volumes does not contain anything pertinent to our subject.

[53] The reference appears to be to a story told by Tacitus (*Ann.*, 13. 54) and Suetonius (*Claud.*, c. 25). The Frisian princes boasted at Rome that loyalty was characteristic of the Germanic peoples: "nullos mortalium armis aut fide ante Germanos esse." This is echoed by Enea Silvio; see F. Heininger (ed.), Aeneas Silvius, *Germanica* (Leipzig, 1926), p. 13. In classical times, it appears that the good faith of the Gauls rather than that of the Germans was proverbial. Tacitus tells us: "Italiae consensum, Galliarum fidem [Germanicus] extollit" (*Ann.*, 1, 34), but this may be rhetoric rather than tradition. Cf. R. Much, "Germani" in Pauly's *Real-Encyclopädie der classischen Altertumswissenschaft,* Supplementband III (Stuttgart, 1918), col. 563. For many helpful suggestions I thank my colleagues Kurt Latte, H. W. Prescott, and B. L. Ullman. The many studies and patriotic speeches in German national consciousness in the humanistic period, at the time of the Reformation, and at even later times, contain little or nothing for us regarding the history of this particular phrase. The following lengthy list of studies in the history of nationalism is given in the hope that it may suggest the re-examination and re-interpretation of nationalistic aspirations in late medieval Germany. See, e.g., K. Bartsch, "Die Treue in deutscher Sage and Poesie," *Gesammelte Vorträge und Aufsätze* (Freiburg i. Br., 1883), pp. 158-180; F. W. Behrens, *Deutsches Ehr- und Nationalgefühl in seiner Entwicklung durch Philosophen und Dichter (1600-1815)* (Diss.; Leipzig, 1891); A. Freybe, *Züge deutscher Sitte und Gesinnung: Das Leben in der Treue,* etc. (Gütersloh, 1888-89); A. Horawitz, "Nationale Geschichtsschreibung im 16, Jahrhundert," *Historische Zeitschrift*, XXV (1871), 66-101; J. Knepper, *Nationaler Gedanke und Kaiseridee bei den elsässischen Humanisten,* "Erläuterungen und Ergänzungen zu Janssens 'Geschichte des deutschen Volkes,'" I, nos. 2-3 (Freiburg, i. B., 1898); K. Monninger, *Der Begriff der Vaterlandsliebe bei Hans Sachs* (Diss.; Greifswald, 1921. Only an abstract, which I have not seen, was

downfall of the Roman Empire, "infidelitas germanica" was, I am told, proverbial, but the examples which William Hammer has generously given me do not fully bear this out.[54] To be sure, Velleius Paterculus says "At illi [Germani], . . . in summa feritate versutissimi natumque mendacio genus,"[55] which Much endeavors to explain away, and in the fourth century the Goths are frequently called perfidious, e.g., Ammianus Marcellinus (*ca.* A.D. 300-400) has "Gothos saepe fallaces et perfidos."[56] Salvianus Massiliensis (A.D. 390-484) expresses his opinions of the Germanic races with epigrammatic brevity and suggests proverbial usage; "Gens Saxonum fera est, Francorum infidelis, Gepidarum inhumana, Chunorum impudica, . . . numquid tam accusabilis Francorum perfidia quam nostra, . . . si perieret Francus, quid noui faciet, qui periurium ipsum sermonis genus putat esse non criminis?" and "Gothorum gens perfida, sed pudica est, Alanorum impudica, sed minus perfida, Franci

---

printed); H. Röhr, *Ulrich von Hutten und das Werden des deutschen Nationalbewusstseins* (Heidelberg diss.; Hamburg, 1926); G. Roethe, *Deutsche Treue in Dichtung und Sage* (Göttingen, 1923), *Von deutscher Art und Kultur* (Berlin, 1915), and *Die Hohenzollern-Bilder und die deutsche Treue* (Leipzig, [1919]); P. Thierse, *Der nationale Gedanke und die Kaiseridee bei den schlesischen Humanisten* ("Breslauer Studien zur Geschichte," II; Breslau, 1908); H. Tiedemann, *Tacitus und das Nationalbewusstsein der deutschen Humanisten am Ende des 15. und Anfang des 16. Jahrhunderts* (Diss.; Berlin, 1913), pp. 66-67; Ulrich Paul, *Studien zur Geschichte des deutschen Nationalbewusstseins im Zeitalter des Humanismus und der Reformation* ("Historiche Studien," CCXCVIII; Berlin, 1936); K. Viëtor, *Probleme der deutschen Barockliteratur* ("Von deutscher Poeterey," III; (Leipzig, 1928), p. 90 (note 2 on p. 69); J. Wagner, "Aeusserungen deutschen Nationalgefühls am Ausgang des Mittelalters," *Deultsche Vierteljahrsschrift für Literaturwissenschaft,* IX (1931), 389-424; and his *Nationale Strömungen in Deutschland am Ausgange des Mittelalters* (Leipzig diss.; Weida i. Th., 1929); K. Wels, *Die patriotischen Strömungen in der deutschen Literatur des Dreissigjährigen Krieges* (Diss.; Greifswald, 1913). The most recent work that I have seen is H. Holborn, *Ulrich von Hutten* ("Das wissenschaftliche Weltbild"; Leipzig, 1929; revised and translated into English, New Haven, 1937). The climax of German panegyrics on "deutsche Treue" are K. Lamprecht, *Deutsche Geschichte* (5th ed.; Berlin, 1912), I, 165-166; Houston Stewart Chamberlain, *Die Grundlagen des neunzehnten Jahrhunderts* (Munich, 1922), pp. 473 ff. (=ungekürzte Volksausgabe, 1937, pp. 561 ff.), especially pp. 504-10 (=pp. 598-605); Alfred Rosenberg, *Der Mythus des 20. Jahrhunderts* (Munich, 1936), p. 155. Compare *passim* H.-G. Fernis, "Die Klage um den toten Herrn," *Germanisch-romanische Monatsschrift,* XXV (1937), 161-178.

[54] In the classical period, faithlessness was an accusation directed against many peoples, but not the Germans; see R. Heinze, *Virgils epische Technik*[3] (Leipzig, 1915), p. 10. The passage in Velleius Paterculus which Heinze cites appears to be the only exception to his rule.

[55] *Hist. rom.* II, 118. See R. Much, "Germani," in *Pauly's Real-Encyclopädie der classischen Altertumswissenschaft,* Supplementband III (Stuttgart, 1918), col. 563.

[56] *Res gestae,* XXII, 7, 8.

mendaces, sed hospitales, Saxones crudelitate efferi, sed castitate mir-
andi : omnes denique gentes habent, sicut peculiaria mala, ita etiam quae-
dam bona."[57] The allusions in Rutilius Namatianus' *De reditu suo* (A.D.
416) :

> "Ergo age, sacrilegae tandem cadat hostia gentis
> Summitant trepidi perfida colla Getae"[58]

and Sidonius Apollinaris's letter to Pope Eutropius: "Postquam foedi-
fragam gentem [Gothos] redisse in sedes suas"[59] do not sound proverbial to me. In the sixth century, Cassiodorus seems to imply that faith-
fulness was traditionally associated with the Goths,[60] but his attiude
may perhaps be explained by his political connections. Investigation
of Gregory of Tours in this direction is likely to be profitable, but I
shall not follow the matter further at the present time. I do not attach much importance to a possible parallel in the anonymous *Descriptio
Theutoniae* (written before 1290), where we read: "Dicuntur etiam hii
homines fideles hominesque laboribus et in barbaris nacionibus aliis
hominibus cariores";[61] these seem to be no more than conventional
eulogies.

The German humanists of the fifteenth and sixteenth centuries are
supposed to have taken up the phrase in Tacitus and to have added
its present application and nationalistic coloring. In other words, the
phrase may be a derivative of "Der Deutschen Treue" used by the
nationalist Ulrich von Hutten and credited to Tacitus by Johann Agricola, the collector of proverbs.[62] I am not certain of the correctness of

[57] *De gubernatione Dei,* IV, c. 14 and VII, c. 15. See C. Halm (ed.), "Monumenta
Germaniae Historica, Auctores Antiquissimi," I, Part I (Berlin, 1877), p. 49, ll.
20-21 and p. 95, ll. 24-27; F. Pauly (ed.), "Corpus Scriptorum Ecclesiasticorum,"
VIII (Vienna, 1883), pp. 89, 176.

[58] I, 141-142. Itasius Lemniacus, i.e. Alfred Reumont *(Cl. Rutilius Namatianus
Heimkehr* [Berlin, 1872], p. 85) calls this proverbial.

[59] Epist. VI, 6 in C. Lütjohann (ed.), "Monumenta Germaniae Historica, Auctores
Anitiquissimi," VII (Berlin, 1887), p. 98, 11.

[60] See *Variae,* VIII, Epist. IX at end. This passage deals with Gesemundus.

[61] *Monumenta Germaniae Historica, Scriptores,* XVII (Hanover, 1861), 238.

[62] E. Böcking (ed.), Ulrich von Hutten *Opera,* I (Leipzig, 1859), 399 § 49: "Ich
wolle erst . . . der Teutschen trew vnd glauben anrüffen"; Johann Agricola, *Drei
hundert gemeyner Sprichwörter* (1529), p. B 1ʳᵒ: "Sinte mal gemeynklich mit der
sprache auch die sittē/ist zubesorgē/der Deutschē trew vñ glauben bestand/
wahrheit/welche tugent den Deutschē auch die Walen als Cornelius Tacitus
zugeschribē vñ gerhumet/werdē auch fallen/ . . ."

I find nothing pertinent in Vera Vollmer, *Die Begriffe der 'triuwe' und der 'staete'
in der höfischen Minnedichtung* (Diss.; Tübingen, 1914). Since this dissertation
surveys rather amply the medieval notions of loyalty and duty, we must infer
that *Deutsche Treue* is post-medieval in origin. See also *Deutsches Wörterbuch,*
XI, Abt. I, Teil 2, cols. 320-321, "Treue," III, c, § 8.

this explanation, and the matter needs more study than it has yet received before any explanation can be accepted. In the first place, the phrase meant something entirely different to Tacitus and his age; it was a boasting remark of Frisian princes at Rome. In the second place, a reference to Fazio degli Uberti's visionary journey *Il Dittamondo* which I owe to William Hammer may be evidence for the proverbial loyalty of the Germans at a time (*ca.* 1360) when Tacitus was still buried in unread manuscripts. The following passage alludes to the Bavarians:

> Molto mi parve quella gente tratta
> D'amar e portar fede al suo signore
> E nelle armi accorta e bene adatta.[63]

To be sure, the nationalistic values of Tacitus were quickly seized upon in sixteenth-century Germany, and possibly the commentaries on *Germania,* Ch. XIV will give additional material for the history of *Deutsche Treue.*[64]

According to the *Deutsches Wörterbuch,* the phrase *Deutsche Treue* is first used in Johann Fischart's *Glückhafft Schiff von Zürich* in 1577. The idea seems to have been familiar to Fischart, for I note "Alt Teutsch Standhafftigkeit" and similar phrases in his *Eikones* (1573), particularly the "Erklärung beyder hie fürgemalter Teutscher Tugenden":

> Standthafft vnd Treu, vnd Treu vnd Standschafft,
> Die machen eyn Recht Teutsch verwandtschafft.[65]

Although this fact is not an argument against the origin of the phrase in the nationalistic enthusiasm of German humanists at the beginning of the century, it is at the same time no very strong support of such an origin. It is obvious that one of the first problems in studying *Deutsche*

[63] Book IV, ch. xiv; ed. V. Monti, "Biblioteca scelta di opere Italiane," CLXXVI (Milan, 1826), p. 321.

[64] See Tiedemann's dissertation and the related studies cited above (pp. 19-20). Compare as examples of annotations to Tacitus: Hans Philipp, *Tacitus, Germania; ein Ausschnitt aus der Entdeckungsgeschichte der Germanenländer durch Griechen und Römer* (Leipzig, 1926), pp. 105 ff.; W. Reeb (ed.), Tacitus, *Germania.* Mit Beiträgen von A. Dopsch, H. Reis, K. Schumacher (Leipzig, 1930), pp. 34, 100; and the standard annotated editions.

We might also seek the history of the phrase in investigations dealing with the word "deutsch," e.g. K. Vogtherr, *Die Geschichte des Wortes 'deutsch' von Luther bis zur Aufklärung* (Berlin diss.; extract publ., Weimar, 1937). This I have not seen.

[65] Ed. A. Hauffen ("Deutsche National-Literatur," XVIII, i; Stuttgart, n.d.), I, 387-389.

Treue is establishing when and where it was first used. The interest and importance of any contribution to our understanding of the German nationalistic spirit are obvious.

The later history of *Deutsche Treue* calls for only brief mention here. Although it is naturally associated with the rise of nationalistic sentiments in the first half of the nineteenth century, I note a possible allusion in

> Der alten Barden Vaterland, dem Vaterland der Treue,
> dir, freies, unbezwung'nes Land, dir weihn wir uns aufs neue

in Matthias Claudius' "Deutsches Weihelied" (1772), which was set to music by Albert Methfessel in 1811, and a definite one in Schiller's "Deutsche Treue," first published in *Die Horen*, III (1795), 130-131.[66]

Before leaving the subject of traditional phrases descriptive of personal, national or racial qualities—a subject sadly in need of comprehensive and dispassionate study[67]—I mention a phrase with much less pleasant associations than *Deutsche Treue*. In the preface and in a sidenote to Casper Scheit's translation (1551) of Friedrich Dedekind's *Grobianus,* we find the traditional insult "porco tedesco."[68] It is not in Scheit's source. Is this insult an Italian invention and given here in

---

[66] For other examples see, e.g., "O deutsche Lieb' und Treue!" in the third stanza of E. M. Arndt's "Der Gott, der Eisen wachsen liess" (1812), "Bleibe, treu, o Vaterland!" in the second stanza of Karl Göttling's "Stehe fest, o Vaterland!" (1815), an allusion in the passage dealing with Ludwig Uhland near the end of § 4 of Heine's *Die romantische Schule* (1833), "Deutsche Frauen, deutsche Treue" in the second stanza of Hoffmann von Fallersleben's "Deutschland über alles" (1841), and "Du heil'ges Land der Treu" in Ludwig Bauer's "O Deutschland hoch in Ehren" (1859).

[67] For collections and studies of local, national, and racial epithets see G. Hesekiel, *Land und Stadt im Volksmunde* (Berlin, 1867); Archer Taylor, *The Proverb* (Cambridge, Mass., 1931), p. 97. n. 11, and the addenda in *An Index to the 'Proverb'* ("FF Communications," CXIII; Helsinki, 1934), p. 7.

[68] G. Milchsack (ed.), "Neudrucke deutscher Literaturwerke des 16. und 17. Jahrhunderts," XXXIX-XXXV (Halle, 1882), p. 4 and 31, l. 759. For parallels see G. Strafforello, *La sapienza del mondo* (Turin, [1883]), III, 290, *s.v.* "porco"; Hugo Cohn, *Tiernamen als Schimpfwörter* (Programm; Berlin, 1910), p. 8. Contrary to what one might expect, Otto von Reinsberg-Düringsfeld, *Internationale Titulaturen* (Leipzig, 1863) and G. M. Küffner, *Die Deutschen im Sprichwort* (Heidelberg, 1899) throw no light on the phrase. Although the insult is at least as old as Pindar, *Olymp.,* VI, 90, the name of the pig is used in old tribal names and therefore has a favorable connotation (see R. v. Kienle, "Tier- Völkernamen bei indogermanischen Stämmen," *Wörter und Sachen,* XIV [1932], 52-55). An otherwise interesting article on the estimate of the Germans by their neighbors brings nothing pertinent; see G. Steinhausen, "Die Deutschen im Urteile des Auslandes," *Deutsche Rundschau,* CXLI (1909), 434-452, CXLII (1910), 55-71.

Italian because it was still unfamiliar to German ears? Dante's "lurchi tedeschi" (*Inf.* xvii, 21) may belong to the background of these ideas.

The investigation of the attitudes of nations or groups toward one another may be conducted on a scale transcending the history of proverbial phrases.[69] The phrase is only a convenient unit and easily grasped. What can we learn about the judgments passed by South Germans on North Germans or vice versa?[70] What are the changing attitudes toward the peasant, the nobility, or the bourgeoisie?

Whatever their nature, be it philosophical, political, religious, or whatnot, characteristic phrases are worth studying, but we must not take them out of context.[71] Friedrich Lepp wisely indicates whether the catchwords of the Reformation in his collection were used by adherents of Luther, Melanchthon, or the Catholic church and tells when and where they were current.[72] Erich König examines "studia humanitatis," a catchword of the humanists, and in doing so illuminates the history of the movement.[73] The critical ideas involved in Horace' "Ut pictura

[69] See an excellent chapter, "The Sentiment of Europe toward the Germans in the Middle Ages," in J. W. Thompson, *Feudal Germany* (Chicago, 1928), pp. 360-384. Compare also K. L. Zimmermann, *Die Beurteilung der Deutschen in der französischen Literatur des Mittelalters mit besonderer Berücksichtigung der Volksepen* (Diss.; Münster i.W., 1910) *Romanische Forschungen*, XXIX (1911), 222-316, and, specifically, for our period, C. Dejob, "Le type de l'Allemand chez les classiques italiens," *Bulletin italien*, I (1901), 173-186 and *Zeitschrift für Kulturgeschichte*, IV (1859), 656-657.

[70] The contrast of Swabian and Bavarian was, for example, traditional. The allusion in the Cassel Glosses of the ninth century is familiar to everyone who has studied Old High German; see W. Braune, *Althochdeutsches Lesebuch* (8th ed.; Halle, 1921), p. 30, ll. 40-43. See further Philipp Strauch (ed.), *Der Marner* ("Quellen und Forschungen zur Sprach- und Culturgeschichte der germanischen Völker," XIV; Strassburg, 1876), p. 3, n. 2; W. Wackernagel, *Geschichte der deutschen Literatur* (2d ed. by Ernst Martin; Basel, 1879), I, 158 (§ 46, n. 7); R. M. Meyer, "Alte deutsche Volksliedchen," *Zeitschrift für deutsches Altertum*, XXIX (1885), 163; K. Burdach, *Reinmar der Alte und Walther von der Vogelweide* (2d ed.; Halle, 1928), p. 138.

An interesting example of an investigation by a psychologist rather than a linguist or a historian of culture is Christian Rogge's study of the changes in the meaning of "deutsch"; see his "Gedankenwandel, Sprachwandel," *Archiv für die gesamte Psychologie*, LXIV (1928), 347-64. See also the elaborate philological discussion of W. Krogmann, *Deutsch; eine wortgeschichtliche Untersuchung* ("Deutsche Wortforschung," I; Berlin, 1936).

[71] Richard McKeon, *Modern Philology*, XXXIV (1936), 3, 25.

[72] *Schlagwörter des Reformationszeitalters* ("Quellen und Darstellungen aus der Geschichte des Reformationsjahrhunderts," VIII; Leipzig, 1908).

[73] "'Studia humanitatis' und verwandte Ausdrücke bei den deutschen Frühhumanisten," *Beiträge zur Geschichte der Renaissance und Reformation; Joseph Schlecht . . . als Festgabe dargebracht* (Munich, 1917), pp. 202-207.

poesis" and in the interpretation of these words before and during the eighteenth century are well described by W. G. Howard,[74] Several scholars have traced the idea of "good taste" in French and Spanish literature and literary criticism during the Renaissance,[75] but no one appears to have done as much for possible German equivalents.

Very interesting, for example, would be an account of the changes which a Biblical passage has undergone in tradition. The advice "He that spareth his rod hateth his son: but he that loveth him chasteneth him betimes" (Prov. 13:24) has become the proverbial "Spare the rod and spoil the child."[76] The idea expressed in the Bible has been vulgarized. In the history of such a proverb, cultural changes and developments are revealed. The connection with pedagogical principles is, in this particular instance, obvious. Jacob Burckhardt's suggestion that the subject be investigated seems to have passed unnoticed. He says: "A thorough history of 'flogging' among the Germanic and Latin races, treated with some psychological power, would be worth volumes of dispatches and negotiations. When, and through what influence, did flogging become a daily practice in the German household? Not till after Walther sang, 'Nieman kan mit gerten kindes zuht beherten.' "[77] Der Marner, on the contrary, maintains

> "liebem kinde ist guot ein ris,
> swer ane vorhte wahset, der muoz sunder ere werden gris."[78]

[74] "Ut pictura poesis," PMLA, XXIV (1909), 40-123.

[75] Milton A. Buchanan, *Hispanic Review*, IV (1936), 286-287. Elias Levita's ספר טוב טעם (Liber boni gustus), published at Venice (1538) and, with a Latin translation, at Basel (1539), which is cited in J. G. T. Grässe, *Lehrbuch einer allgemeinen Literärgeschichte*, II, iii (Dresden, 1842), 985, has nothing to do with the matters discussed here; see D. W. Amram, *The Makers of Hebrew Books in Italy* (Philadelphia, 1909), pp. 193-194.

[76] See F. Zarncke (ed.), *Sebastian Brants Narrenschiff* (Leipzig, 1854), p. 312 (Note on ch. VI, ll. 21-22). Compare P. Strauch, *Der Marner* ("Quellen und Forschungen zur Sprach- und Culturgeschichte der germanischen Völker," XVI; Strassburg, 1876), pp. 124, 179 (note on XV, 238); E. L. Rochholz, *Alemannisches Kinderlied und Kinderspiel* (Leipzig, 1857), pp. 521 ff.; K. Stejskal, *Hadamars von Laber Jagd* (Vienna, 1880), p. 199 (note on st. 253); A. Wallner, *Zeitschrift für deutsches Altertum*, LXXII (1935), 266. For collections of proverbs of Biblical origin see Archer Taylor, *The Proverb* (Cambridge, Mass., 1931), p. 52.

[77] *The Civilization of the Renaissance in Italy* (Vienna: Phaidon Press, n.d.), p. 331, n. 785. See Lachmann's edition of Walther, 87, 1.

[78] Philipp Strauch (ed.), *Der Marner* ("Quellen und Forschungen zur Sprach- und Culturgeschichte der germanischen Völker," XIV; Strassburg, 1876), XV, 12, 238-239 and XV, 254 ff. See also *Hadamars von Laber Jagd* (ed. K. Stejskal; Vienna, 1880), p. 66, st. 253.

Sebastian Brant's stern reprimand of human weaknesses might lead us to expect him to approve the proverb, but he rejects it. As an indication of a change in principles compare Luther's "Der Apfel muss bei der Rute liegen."[79] An excellent example of how much we can learn about the cultural significance of a simple phrase is Eliza G. Watkins' *The Delphic Maxims in Literature*.[80]

Problems Involving an Aspect of the Whole Period

7. *The History of International Literary Relations.*—In some ways, an account of the literary relations of Germany and another country is less complicated than the literary history of a period in German literature.[81] Such an account necessarily deals with the somewhat limited mass of material derived directly or indirectly from foreign sources and not with the entire literary production of an age. Typical or illustrative documents to show the nature and course of literary influence are usually more easily found than documents which reveal the cultural and artistic growth of a period. On the other hand, an account of the literary relations of two countries presupposes an extensive and accurate knowledge of two literatures and two cultures.

A good introduction to the field would consist in reading a selection of studies. The student could then choose the type best suited to his tastes and preparation. All good studies of literary history exhibit more or less of the comparative point of view. German literature often stands apart from the line of descent—the lyric love-poetry of the Middle Ages, for example, is in a sense a branch of Provençal song, a cul-de-sac, and not the beginning of a further European development. German literature is consequently often neglected in tracing the historical development of literature. This neglect should encourage rather than discourage the student of German literature. Such a work as C. S. Lewis' *The Allegory of Love; A Study in Medieval Tradition*[82] gives little space to German allegories of love, and Ruth Mohl does not deal adequately with the German references in *The Three Estates in Medi-*

[79] Erlangen ed., LXI, 274.

[80] Chicago, 1929.

[81] For an introduction to the bibliography of comparative literature see Arnold, pp. 66-68. The most important tool is L. P. Betz, *La Littérature comparée* (2d ed. by F. Baldensperger; Strassburg, 1904). Compare the annual bibliographies by Arthur L. Jellinek in *Studien zur vergleichenden Literaturgeschichte*, I (1901)-IX (1909), of which the first two were reissued in a single volume as *Bibliographie der vergleichenden Literaturgeschichte* (Berlin, 1903), and the lists in *Revue de littérature comparée*, I (1921) ff.

[82] Oxford, 1936.

eval and Renaissance Literature.[83] German aspects of these themes may have been properly omitted in these works, but the omission leaves to students of German literature the opportunity of building on these foundations.

An account of the literary relations of two countries may take the form of a collection of essays or of a synthesis. C. H. Herford's *Studies in the Literary Relations of England and Germany in the Sixteenth Century,*[84] a collection of essays on characteristic or important literary monuments, is a model of the first type. Such accounts run the danger of falling between two stools—of failing to give a clear and well-organized impression of either culture or of generalizing superficially and prejudicially.

Perhaps the most important problem in the literary relations of Germany in the period between 1500 and 1700 is the influence of Italy.[85] This influence varies greatly from period to period during these two centuries, affects various literary genres in different ways, and colors the life and literature of the various regions of Germany in different fashions. We have no adequate survey of this influence. Much attention has been given to the extent and nature of Italian influence in the period before 1500. As is only natural, the study of Italian influence has been implied in the study of German humanism. In the century of the Reformation, interest has been greatest in the religious aspects of the Reformation. A different aspect appears in Georg Ellinger's description of Italian influence on German-Latin lyric poetry of this period.

We should differentiate periods in which the nature and the extent of Italian influence as well as the regions and the groups affected vary. These periods have not been adequately established or sufficiently characterized. Although a good deal has been written on matters essential to the study of this subject, it has not been written from the narrower

[83] New York, 1933. The literature is very abundant, and I shall cite only the latest study that has come to my attention: L. Manz, *Der Ordo-Gedanke, Ein Beitrag zur Frage der mittelalterlichen Ständegedanken* ("Vierteljahrsschrift für Sozial- und Wirtschaftsgeschichte," Beiheft XXXIII; Stuttgart, 1937).

[84] Cambridge, Eng., 1886.

[85] For this section I give no references. An interesting problem which belongs to a time just before our period is the comparison of Wittenweiler's *Ring* with its Italian analogues; see *Anzeiger für deutsches Altertum,* LIV (1935), 59. For a later period see Josefine Rumpf Fleck, *Italienische Einflüsse auf Frankfort am Main im 18. Jahrhundert* (Cologne, 1936). Methods and suggestions for the investigation of these problems may also be found in the bibliographies on French and Spanish influences on our period in Stammler, p. 522 (notes on pp. 432, 436); Dahlmann-Waitz, pp. 119-120, nos. 2170-71.

point of view of the historian of Italian-German relations. Such a historian will have to pick and choose his materials from what has been written. On the whole, enough has been said for his purposes about the period before 1500 and even for the period ending, let us say, in 1517. Then follows a transitional period of conflict. For this period, which we may close with 1530, and for the succeeding period, when the issues of the Reformation had been clearly formulated, the problem of Italian influence has never been satisfactorily stated. Note, for example, the fact that anti-Roman sentiment was weak in Southeast Germany. What consequences did this have for the literary and cultural relations? For the period after 1600, when Italian influence on German literature reaches a climax, we have no better guides than Carl Lemcke's *Von Opitz bis Klopstock*[86] and Paul Hankamer's *Deutsche Gegenreformation und deutsches Barock,*[87] both sadly deficient in bibliographical information. During the seventeenth century, Italian influence upon German literature and life appears in every conceivable form. It moulds the literary genres, alters the standards of language and style, and guides the manner of life.

In studying the influence of Italy on Germany during the sixteenth and seventeenth centuries, one could begin by collecting the evidence found in the biographical accounts in the *Allgemeine deutsche Biographie*. A collection from this source would be an arsenal of permanently useful information for further investigation of any particular aspect. One might study Italian influences on particular genres of literature—epic, dramatic, or lyric—or at particular periods of time, or on particular regions of Germany. When the evidence was once assembled, classification and interpretation would follow almost of themselves.

A general statement of a few problems in the influence of Italian ideas on German culture, the interchange of ideas between the two countries, and the development of similar trends will illustrate how these studies may be carried on. German printers issued Italian works from their presses. For example, Andreas Camutius' *De amore atque felicitate* (1574) was published by S. Kreuzer at Vienna. In this instance the explanation is obvious and easy. Andreas Camutius, an Italian doctor from Lugano in Switzerland and professor of medicine and physics at Pavia, became physician to Emperor Maximilian II in 1564 and dedicated this treatise on love to him. A striking and significant example of the literary relations of Italy and Germany is Andreas Alciati's *Emblematum liber,* the first of the long line of emblem-books.

---

[86] Leipzig, 1882.
[87] "Epochen der deutschen Literatur," II, ii; Stuttgart, 1935.

It was finished in Italy in 1521, printed at Augsburg in 1531, and dedicated to the patrician and humanist, Conrad Peutinger. A better illustration of the intimate relations of the two countries would be hard to find. The first publication of Italian in Germany is said to be the text accompanying Aldus Manutius' *Rudimenta grammatices latine lingue* (1510).

German jestbooks of the sixteenth century drew freely on Italian sources. Many conventional literary types—the sly and clever woman, the cuckold, the go-between—probably descend at least in part from Italian models. Italian influence is easily seen in details of dramatic style and technique, e.g., in the use of dialect and in introduction of a new stagecraft (the *Verwandlungsbühne*).[88] Various literary genres exhibit Italian influences or even owe their currency in Germany to the imitation of Italian models. The pastoral drama, the interlude, the drama composed for special occasions in honor of a particular person or family, and above all the opera, owe much to Italy. Italian song influenced greatly both hymns and secular song. Latin epics written in Germany followed the fashions prevailing in Italy. To be sure, epics celebrating the greatness of a noble family were composed only in Latin and left little or no trace in German literature. Particularly in the seventeenth century, the German novel took much from Italy. At this time, when the creation of societies for the purification of the German language followed in the wake of the Accademia della Crusca, Italian influence is perhaps strongest. In estimating the influence of Italy on Germany, we must consider religious currents—notably the counter-reformation and the Jesuits—and political events. Our knowledge of German translations of Italian reformers is inadequate. Ochino's *Apologe* as well as sermons and theological treatises were translated into German.

So brief a sketch of Italian and German literary relations must leave much unsaid. It can only suggest problems and hint at ways to attack them. Let it also serve, *mutatis mutandis,* as an outline for the study of German and French or of German and Dutch literary relations. In the sixteenth century, the Netherlands took much from Germany. The borrowings in the fields of folksong and hymn can be easily surveyed, but a comparison and interpretation have not yet been undertaken. In the seventeenth century, the Netherlands enjoyed great economic prosperity, and literary influence seems to have been largely upon rather than from

---

[88] Like many details mentioned in this section, the use of this device in Germany belongs to a time somewhat later than our period. First used at Florence in 1580, this bit of stagecraft is found at Torgau in 1622, at Salzburg in 1630, at Vienna after 1640, and at Ulm in 1650.

Germany. Opitz, Gryphius, Zesen, and many others visited the Netherlands and returned with new ideas and new ways of expression.

A particularly interesting problem involving the literary relations of two countries is the comparison of their traditional songs.[89] Although the problem is readily formulated and although the materials are rather easily available, studies of this sort are few. John R. Broderius reviewed the German folksongs found in Sweden, but drew no inferences.[90] Arthur Kopp studied the relations of German and Dutch song, but did not print his results.[91] G. L. Matuschka's master's thesis dealing with the same subject limited itself to a comparison of the two standard collections and also remains unpublished.[92] The investigations of Paul Alpers in the relations of Dutch and Low German song have been very instructive and are probably the best work of this sort.

Comparisons of the materials of folksongs in two countries can usually be carried out with comparative ease. The questions which arise are obvious and readily answered. How many French songs entered into the German traditional stock? To what periods do they belong? Do they exhibit any striking characteristics? The comparison of English and German balladry proves to be surprisingly difficult. It involves two aspects—stylistic differences and differences in subject-matter. Although German ballads have often been considered to be similar to English ballads, the stylistic differences, as W. P. Ker points out, are numerous and significant.[93] They require fuller discussion than they have yet received. Comparison of the subject-matter of English and German ballads discloses some very interesting problems. Although only a dozen ballads are common to English and German tradition, these represent almost every variety of English folksong (except of course the border ballad) and exemplify every conceivable type of relationship. In one case the German ballad is a close translation of a late eighteenth-cen-

[89] See as examples: Paul Alpers, *Die alten niederdeutschen Volkslieder* (Hamburg, 1924), pp. 22-28, and "Niederdeutsche und niederländische Volksdichtung und ihre Beziehungen zueinander," *Niederdeutsche Zeitschrift für Volkskunde,* V (1927), 15-41. For an admirably concise formulation of the problem see S. P. Kyriakides, "Die Herkunft der neugriechischen Balladen und ihre Beziehungen zu den deutschen," *Forschungen und Fortschritte,* XII (1936), 132-133.

[90] "German Folksongs in Sweden," *Philological Quarterly,* VIII (1929), 157-164.

[91] *Verslagen en mededeelingen der koninklijke Vlaamsche academie,* 1924, pp. 197, 611.

[92] *Interrelations of Dutch and German Folksong* (Diss.; University of Chicago, 1931).

[93] "On the History of Ballads, 1100-1500," *Proceedings of the British Academy,* 1909-10, IV (1911), 179-205.

tury English street-song, another ballad appears to have reached Germany from Scandinavia through the mediation of the Poles or the Wends, another is apparently a late medieval invention current in France and England, still another is current in England, Scandinavia, Germany, and Italy but not in France, and so on. The riddle-ballad on which I comment later is a type known only in England and Germany. In sum, the complications are very surprising, and no two folksongs common to English and German tradition appear to have the same history. I have examined this problem only superficially and hope to learn more about it in the future.

8. *Literary Influences Shown by Translations.*—A survey of the translations from foreign languages is a basis for a variety of studies in literary history. What works are translated? When do the translations of a particular author begin to appear? Can we, for example, fix the beginning of the vogue of translations of Greek drama? Where are the translations made? What cultural influences led to making them? Progress has been made in answering many of these questions.

Essential for a satisfactory estimate of the influence of Greek and Latin literature on German humanism is a list of the contemporary translations of the classics. In such a list, furthermore, one should consider the translations of Greek authors into Latin, for knowledge of Greek classics was largely transmitted in this way. For example, the Latin version of the New Testament accompanying Erasmus' edition of the Greek original was an extremely important foundation for theological exegesis, and he was compelled to defend himself against the charge that it was an attack on the authority of the Vulgate. In making a list of the translations of Latin and Greek classics, one should not content oneself with merely compiling a bibliography but should seek to interpret the facts.[94]

[94] Goedeke, I, 443-447, 492, II, 317-321. He selects titles from J. F. Degen, *Literatur der deutschen Uebersetzungen der Römer* (Altenburg, 1794-99), and *Literatur der deutschen Uebersetzungen der Griechen* (Altenburg, 1797-98) with a *Nachtrag* (Erlangen, 1801). See additions by various hands in *Allgemeiner literarischer Anzeiger,* IV (1799), coll. 1185-91, 1195-97, 1528, 1902-3. Further collectanea may be found in F. L. A. Schweiger, *Handbuch der classischen Bibliographie* (Leipzig, 1830-34) ; A. Horawitz, *Griechische Studien; Beiträge zur Geschichte des Griechischen in Deutschland* (Berlin, 1884). K. Hartfelder, *Ungedruckte deutsche Uebersetzungen klassischer Schriftsteller aus dem Heidelberger Humanistenkreis* (Program; Berlin, 1884) describes a small number of translations, many of them unpublished. Consult further the bibliographies of printed works for this period. The histories of classical scholarship, e.g., C. Bursian, *Geschichte der classischen Philologie in Deutschland von den Anfängen bis zur Gegenwart* ("Geschichte der Wissenschaften in Deutschland. Neuere Zeit," XIX;

Analogous to lists of translation of Greek and Latin literature are lists of translations from Italian, French, Spanish, or Dutch. In the field of post-medieval German studies, we have yet to learn the lesson taught by Mary Augusta Scott in her *Elizabethan Translations from the Italian.*[95] Her bibliography has been an indispensable tool for the student of the English Renaissance for more than a generation. The literary historian of the eighteenth and nineteenth centuries in Germany can refer to such standard works as those of Lawrence M. Price and B. Q. Morgan. Comparison of these with the needs of the student of the fifteenth and sixteenth centuries is instructive.

The problems raised by translation touch large questions of international literary relations. It is not unimportant, for example, that modern Russian literature reached England and America largely through translations from French rather than through translations made directly from the original. We may ask, therefore: How did an author of the fifteenth or sixteenth centuries learn to know materials in Latin or Greek?[96] On occasion, Johann Fischart drew upon Latin translations

---

Munich, 1883), do not give as much information as one might expect. R. Leppla gives a brief introduction to the subject and a short bibliography; see "Uebersetzungsliteratur" in *Reallexikon der deutschen Literaturgeschichte,* III, 400-402, § 13. Lawrence S. Thompson attacked the problem in his unpublished master's thesis, *German Translations of the Classics between 1460 and 1550* (University of Chicago, 1935). A. Geerebaert, S. J., has compiled a list of translations into Dutch; see "Lijst van de gedruckte Nederlandsche vertalingen der oude Griekse en Latijnsche schrijvers," *Verslagen en mededeelingen der koninklijke Vlaamsche academie* (Ghent), 1924, pp. 173-194, 311-399, 749-859. This is a bibliography without critical comment. Contrast it with the interpretative criticism of English translations and their backgrounds in H. B. Lathrop, *Translations from the Classics into English from Caxton to Chapman, 1477-1620* ("University of Wisconsin Studies in Language and Literature," XXXV; Madison, Wis., 1933); C. H. Conley, *The First English Translators of the Classics* (New Haven, Conn., 1927); F. O. Matthiessen, *Translating: An Elizabethan Art* (Cambridge, Mass., 1931). The bibliographical foundation is Henrietta R. Palmer, *List of English Editions and Translations of Greek and Latin Classics Printed before 1641* (London, 1911). F. S. Smith, *The Classics in Translation* (London, 1930), is a useful handbook.

[95] "Vassar Centennial Series" (Boston, 1916). Compare N. C. Shields, *Italian Translations in America* ("Comparative Literature Series; Institute of French Studies"; New York, [1931]), a list of books owned by the compiler and certain large American libraries.

[96] See in general G. Voigt, *Die Wiederbelebung des classischen Altertums* (Berlin, 1859; 3d ed., 1893); J. E. Sandys, *A History of Classical Scholarship* (Cambridge, 1903-8; 3d ed. of vol. I, 1921). For the particular problem here discussed compare the methods and results in W. F. Schirmer, *Der englische Frühhumanismus; ein Beitrag zur englischen Literaturgeschichte des 15. Jahrhunderts* (Leipzig, 1931).

of Greek texts rather than the originals. Authors of the fifteenth and sixteenth centuries often referred to florilegia instead of to the texts of classical authors.[97] For the most part, Greek literature filtered in through Latin and Italian translations. In the early editions of Greek classics, Latin translations were often printed alongside the text, and several generations elapsed before Greek works were issued in German versions. Homer was not completely translated until the middle of the eighteenth century, and the dramatic writers were even slower in appearing in German dress. The details of this slow infiltration remain to be worked out.[98]

In studying the results of classical influences on German literature we may ask: What stylistic details and what subjects did post-medieval German literature borrow? When and where were they taken up? How did it adapt these materials to its needs? What, for example, was the extent and nature of the influence of Aristophanes, Plautus, Terence, or Seneca? How did Latin historians influence German chroniclers? To most of these questions we have more or less satisfactory answers.[99]

[97] See as an introduction to the florilegia: B. L. Ullman, "Classical Authors in Mediæval Florilegia," *Classical Philology,* XXII (1928) to XXVII (1932), *passim.* He is primarily concerned with the value of quotations in the florilegia in establishing the correct text of classical authors. A valuable introduction to the early medieval anthologies is Eva M. Sanford, "The Use of Classical Latin Authors in the 'Libri Manuales,'" *Transactions and Proceedings of the American Philological Association,* LV (1924), 190-248. This will suggest problems and ways of solving them. See also A. Gagnér, *Florilegium Gallicum. Untersuchungen und Texte zur Geschichte der mittellateinischen Florilegienliteratur* ("Skrifter utgivna av Vetenskaps-Societeten i Lund," XVIII; Lund, 1936). A survey of the later florilegia with a characterization of their varieties would be useful. F. L. Schoell discusses the use of florilegia by humanists; see *Études zur l'humanisme continental en Angleterre à la fin de la Renaissance* ("Bibliothèque de la 'Revue de littérature comparée,'" XXIX; Paris, 1926). His discussion, although instructive, is limited largely to George Chapman.

[98] See, e.g., A. Horawitz, *Griechische Studien; Beiträge zur Geschichte des Griechischen in Deutschland* (Berlin, 1884); G. Bauch, "Die Anfänge des Studiums der griechischen Sprache und Literatur in Norddeutschland," *Mitteilungen der Gesellschaft für deutsche Erziehungs- und Schulgeschichte,* VI (1896), 47-98, 163-193. Compare such special studies as R. Pfeiffer, "Zu Uebersetzungen der Theophrastischen Charaktere," *Bayer. Blätter für das Gymnasial-Schulwesen,* LIV (1918), 122-125; R. Newald, "Die deutschen Homerübersetzungen des 16. Jahrhunderts," *Das humanistische Gymnasium,* XLIII (1932), 47-52; M. Radlkofer, "Die älteste Verdeutschung der Germania des Tacitus durch Johann Eberlin," *Blätter für das bayerische Gymnasial-Schulwesen,* XXIII (1887), 1-16.

[99] Stammler, pp. 37-38 (notes on p. 465), 48 (notes on p. 467), 105 (notes on p. 479), 158 (notes on p. 481), 161 (notes on p. 482), 174 (notes on p. 483). On the beginnings of German historical writing see Paul Joachimsohn (or Joachim-

Stammler suggests (p. 439) the problem of determining when the influence of Seneca on German drama yielded to that of Euripides. Concerning Lucian's influence we are well informed.[100] He was Ulrich von Hutten's model, was translated by Erasmus, and was a favorite author of humanists generally, but was later condemned as a mocker. Caspar Faber, a moralist of the end of the sixteenth century, used "Epicurische ewig verdampte Säwe, heilloser Unflat, Lucianischer Spötter und Epicurische Saw" as terms of abuse.[101] When and how did the regard for Lucian fall so low? What did Latin satire bring to German controversial writing during and after the Reformation? For such studies we have excellent guides and investigations of the relations between Latin and English satire. What, for example, can we learn about the attitudes toward Epicurean ideas? If we pass to more general subjects, we may ask: How did Homer and Virgil become known to sixteenth-century Germany? It is interesting to recall that Jörg Wickram adapted to his own age—the middle of the sixteenth century—a medieval translation of Ovid's *Metamorphoses*. Why could this happen more easily in Germany than in England or France?

In studying humanism and the influence of classical writers, one notices the lack of a convenient tabulation of the "discoveries" of classical works. When, where, and by whom were the manuscripts of clas-

sen), *Die humanistische Geschichtschreibung in Deutschland,* I (Bonn, 1895) and *Geschichtsauffassung und Geschichtschreibung in Deutschland unter dem Einflusse des Humanismus* ("Beiträge zur Kulturgeschichte des Mittelalters und der Renaissance," VI; Leipzig, 1910) ; Franz X. von Wegele, *Geschichte der deutschen Historiographie seit dem Auftreten des Humanismus* ("Geschichte der Wissenschaften in Deutschland, neuere Zeit," XX; Munich, 1885).

[100] R. Förster, "Lucian in der Renaissance," *Archiv für Literaturgeschichte,* XIV (1886), 337-63; P. Schulze, *Lucian in der Literatur und Kunst der Renaissance* (Programm; Dessau, 1906) ; Natale Caccia, *Note su la fortuna di Luciano nel rinascimento* (Milan, 1914). For references more particularly concerned with Germany see Stammler, pp. 107, 466 (notes on pp. 37-38), 479 (note on p. 105) ; A. Bauer, "Der Einfluss Lukians von Samosata auf Ulrich von Hutten," *Philologus,* LXXV (1918), 437-462, LXXVI (1920), 192-207; K. Hedicke, *Caspar Scheits 'Frölich Heimfart' nach ihren geschichtlichen und litterarischen Elementen untersucht* (Diss.; Halle, 1903), p. 30; K. Sang, *Die appellative Verwendung von Eigennamen bei Luther* ("Giessener Beiträge zur deutschen Philologie," II; Giessen, 1921), pp. 11, 24, 67; M. Heep, *Die 'Colloquia familiaria' des Erasmus und Lucian* ("Hermaea," XVIII; Halle, 1927).

[101] "Epicurische Saw," which is a similar term of abuse, occurs again in the *Faustbuch.* The phrase is an echo of "Cum ridere voles, Epicuri de grege porcum" (Horace, *Epist.,* I 14) or a similar allusion. For additional references see J. Burckhardt, *The Civilization of the Renaissance in Italy* (Vienna: Phaidon Press, n.d.), pp. 262-263; A. Hauffen, *Vierteljahrschrift für Litteraturgeschichte,* VI (1893), 169.

sical authors found and made known in Germany? The letters of the humanists contain information about these matters, and much can be learned from the editions of classical authors. A convenient tabulation, which might cover the period from 1450 to the publication of the *Epistolæ obscurorm virorum* or a later date such as 1517 or 1519, would be a useful tool in writing the history of humanism.[102]

An excellent beginning has been made in the study of the technique of translating Latin texts. Latinate translations, which use constructions so unnatural to German as the accusative for the subject of an infinitive, slowly gave way to idiomatic versions, but the change was resisted as a matter of principle. Some opportunities remain for the examination and critical comparison of the techniques of individual translators, but probably such subjects are almost worked out.[103] There is, however, room for a brief interpretation and appreciation of the various theories of translation. Such a history of the theories of translation might be treated as a review of the background of Martin Luther's *Sendbrief vom Dolmetschen* (1530) and *Summarien über die Psalmen und Ursachen des Dolmetschens* (1531-33).[104] This review might interpret

---

[102] A brief essay pertinent to this subject is E. Tièche, *Die Wiederentdeckung der antiken Bücher im Zeitalter der Renaissance* ("Bibliothek der schweizer Bibliophilen," II, 7; Berne, 1936). The standard work in this field is R. Sabbadini, *Le scoperte dei codici latini e greci ne' secoli XIV e XV; nuove ricerche* (Biblioteca storica del rinascimento"; Florence, 1914).

[103] *Sabbathsteufel* (1572) in the *Theatrum diabolorum* (1575), as cited in P. Strauch (ed.), Kaspar Scheit, *Die fröhliche Heimfahrt* ("Schriften des wissenschaftlichen Instituts der Elsass-Lothringer im Reich"; Berlin, 1926), p. 113.

See, e.g., the discussion of Nikolaus von Wyle (Stammler, pp. 463-464 [note on p. 24]) and Heinrich Steinhöwel (ibid., p. 465 [note on p. 31]). Stammler deals with the style of translations in "Zur Sprachgeschichte des 15. und 16. Jahrhunderts," *Vom Werden des deutschen Geistes; Festgabe Gustav Ehrismann . . . dargebracht* (Berlin, 1925), pp. 171-189.

Compare the studies in English translations cited in L. B. Wright, *Middle-Class Culture in Elizabethan England* (Chapel Hill, N.C., 1935), p. 340, n. 2, and P. H. Larwill, *La théorie de la traduction au début de la renaissance (d'après les traductions imprimées en France entre 1477 et 1527)* (Diss.; Munich, 1934).

[104] It must be remembered that these works defend Luther's procedure rather than establish principles of translation, but from them and from the translation of the Bible in its various forms one can bring together the essential features of Luther's theory.

On the German Bible before Luther see F. Maurer, *Studien zur mitteldeutschen Bibelübersetzung vor Luther* ("Germanische Bibliothek, II, 26; Heidelberg, 1929); W. Walther, *Die deutsche Bibelübersetzung des Mittelalters* (Brunswick, 1889-92); W. Ziesemer, *Studien zur mittelalterlichen Bibelübersetzung* ("Schriften der Königsberger gelehrten Gesellschaft, geisteswissenschaftliche Klasse," V, 5; Halle, 1928). Compare further the works reviewed by W. Kurrelmeyer, *Modern*

the sources and significance of these famous discussions of a translator's problems and indicate the extent to which Luther drew his principles from previous theorizing on the subject as well as the place which his principles occupy in the age. Scholars have made accessible the details on which such a review must rest, and an interpretation of the details in the light of cultural and political history, literary standards, and social and ethical aims is an opportunity. Did Luther, for example, find support for his theory in Nikolaus de Lyra? Paul Bretscher calls my attention to the striking similarity between Luther's theory of translation and that of John Purvey in the "General Prologue" to the revision (1388) of Wycliffe's Bible, and observes—probably with justice—that no connection is to be supposed.

Language Notes, L (1935), 471-474. G. W. Hopf, *Würdigung der Lutherischen Uebersetzung mit Rücksicht auf ältere und neuere Uebersetzungen* (Nuremberg, 1847) is still useful and is a counterpart to the effective presentation of Catholic views in Joseph Kehrein, *Zur Geschichte der deutschen Bibelübersetzung vor Luther* (Stuttgart, 1851). See further E. Hirsch, *Luthers deutsche Bibel* (Munich, 1928); Theodor Pahl, *Quellenstudien zu Luthers Psalmenübersetzung* (Weimar, 1931) with a good bibliography; and such American investigations as W. W. Florer, *Luther's Use of the Pre-Lutheran Versions of the Bible* (Ann Arbor, 1912), which is of comparatively little value, and E. H. Lauer, "Luther's Translation of the Psalms in 1523-24," *Journal of English and Germanic Philology,* XIV (1915), 1-34.

An interesting illustration of these problems is W. Kurrelmeyer's "Wes das Herz voll ist, des gehet der Mund über," *Modern Language Notes,* L. (1935), 380-382. He shows that this famous translation of Mt. 12:34, which is so often cited as an example of Luther's idiomatic use of German, descends from an earlier translation and is not Luther's invention. The translation was evidently in current use, for Johannes Geiler von Kaisersberg employs it in his sermons (1498; publ. 1520) on the *Narrenschiff* (fol. cxciii, col. a) and Nicolaus Höniger's edition (1574) of the *Narrenschiff*, which reprints portions of Geiler's sermons as commentary, contains this passage (see J. Scheible, *Das Kloster,* I, 615). In the light of Schiller's reference to this Biblical passage, viz., "Und was der Zorn und was der frohe Mut/Mich sprechen liess im Ueberfluss des Herzens" (*Wallensteins Tod,* I, 173-174), one hesitates to term the "literal" translation unidiomatic. For phrases which have been carelessly thought to be Luther's, although they are found in the Zainer Bible (1475), see Freitag, "Die Zainerbibel als Quelle der Lutherbibel," *Theologische Studien und Kritiken,* C (1927-28), 444-454. For comparisons with earlier versions see G. Buchmann, "Luthers Bibelverdeutschung auf der Wartburg in ihrem Verhältnis zu den mittelalterlichen Uebersetzungen," *Luther-Jahrbuch,* XVIII (1936), 47-82.

My colleague John G. Kunstmann has aided me greatly in understanding and formulating this problem. Incidentally useful for background is Flora Ross Amos, *Early Theories of Translation* ("Columbia University Studies in English," New York, 1920). See J. Forshall and F. Madden, *The Holy Bible* (Oxford, 1850), I, Prologue, Ch. XV, pp. 56-60; B. F. Westcott, *A General View of the History of the English Bible* (New York, 1917), pp. 13-14.

9. *Foreign and Technical Words in German.*—In studying the stylistic details of translations, one faces questions falling midway between linguistic and literary history. What words were used to translate Latin terms for institutions unknown in Germany? Wolfgang Stammler points out[105] that certain habits established themselves in translating such terms. What can we learn about the rise and currency of these habits? For example, *Helfer* was used to translate *diaconus*. When did this translation begin to be used? In what circles was it current? The religious and geographical limitations on the use of these translations will throw light on their origin.

At all periods in the history of the German language, foreign words have had a place apart. They have been taken into the language, but have retained in one way or another the stigma of foreign origin. Much has been done to illuminate the history of these borrowings, but the subject is by no means exhausted.[106] What is the attitude of humanistic translators toward foreign words?[107] What is the status of words borrowed from French, Italian, or Spanish during the sixteenth century, and does it change in the seventeenth? Little or nothing has been done in studies of this sort. Lutz Mackensen remarks that the influx of French words began after 1550, the first dictionary of foreign words appeared in 1571, and the first warnings against the use of foreign words

---

[105] *Von der Mystik zum Barock,* p. 36.

[106] An interesting essay containing some suggestions about the history of loan-words in German is H. L. Stoltenberg, *Deutsche Weisheitssprache* (Lahr i.B., 1933). To be sure, it is not the work of a professed linguist and has, moreover, its own special aim of purifying the German language. In a review (*Germanic Review,* X [1935], 52, n. 1), I have collected titles of books describing the vocabulary of the post-medieval German mystics. This list is given in expanded form in my *Literary History of Meistergesang* (New York, 1937), p. 90. These books make possible a very complete survey of foreign words used by German mystics. Incidentally, they suggest methods to be used in studying the vocabulary of German humanism.

As an introduction to the bibliography of foreign words in German, I cite the following: Arnold, pp. 232-233; Friedrich Seiler, *Die Entwicklung der deutschen Kultur im Spiegel des deutschen Lehnworts* (Halle, 1921-25. The latest editions of the various volumes are: I in 4th ed., II in 3d, III and IV in 2d); Karl von Bahder, *Die deutsche Philologie* (Paderborn, 1883), pp. 132-133, nos. 1527 ff.; Fritz Loewenthal, *Bibliographisches Handbuch zur deutschen Philologie* (Halle, 1932), pp. 66-67, nos. 763-769. Pertinent studies are D. F. Malherbe, *Das Fremdwort im Reformationszeitalter* (Diss.; Freiburg i.Br., 1906) and F. Helbling, "Das militärische Fremdwort des 16. Jahrhunderts," *Zeitschrift für deutsche Wortforschung,* XIV (1912-3), 20-70. In a later note (p. 162) on the language used by German hunters, I cite titles of works on borrowings from French.

[107] A pertinent investigation is Paul Möller, *Fremdwörter aus dem Lateinischen im späteren Mittelhochdeutschen und Mittelniederdeutschen* (Diss.; Giessen, 1915).

were issued about 1580.[108] Inasmuch as Simon Roth's *Ein teutscher Dictionarius, daz ist ein Aussleger schwerer unbekanter teutscher, griechischer, lateinischer, hebräischer, welscher und französischer Wörter* (1571), to which Mackensen is no doubt referring, appears to be a revision of an earlier work, these remarks call for further investigation. In this discussion of Roth's dictionary, the need of a survey and appraisal of dictionaries compiled in the sixteenth century is once more apparent.[109]

We can consider the problem of technical words in German in several ways. Many technical words are of foreign origin, others are German words made in imitation of foreign models or altered in meaning to include the same meanings as did the foreign word, and still others are entirely German in their origins and developments of meanings. These facts appear only in the process of compiling a historical dictionary of the special vocabulary and are best presented in such a dictionary. Too many of the Germany dictionaries of technical vocabularies are limited to modern usage. The person who undertakes to make such a dictionary must have some familiarity with the special field; for example, he must know business practices and the history of trade. Reading in the theory of lexicography is also helpful.[110] An excellent illustration here is the collection of words for weapons. William Kurrelmeyer has assembled

---

[108] *Die deutschen Volksbücher* ("Forschungen zur deutschen Geistesgeschichte des Mittelalters und der Neuzeit," II; Leipzig, 1927), pp. 99. William Kurrelmeyer calls my attention to Emil Öhmann, "Simon Roths Fremdwörterbuch," *Mémoires de la Société néophilologique de Helsingfors,* XI (1936), 225-370. See also E. Öhmann, "Nachlese zu Simon Roths 'Fremdwörterbuch,'" *Neuphilologische Mitteilungen,* XXXVIII (1937), 269-272, which was suggested by Kurrelmeyer's review in *Modern Language Notes,* LII (1937), 372-374. A. Reifferscheid did not exhaust his subject in the essay "Der Schulkomödiendichter Simon Roth als Lexikograph," *Mitteilungen der Gesellschaft für deutsche Erziehungs- und Schulgeschichte,* V (1895), 245-53. Mackensen is reporting an opinion found in W. Wackernagel, *Gechichte der deutschen Literatur* (2d ed. by Ernst Martin; Basel, 1894), II, 33, n. 36.

[109] I have commented on this above, pp. 9-10.

[110] See, e.g., A. Schirmer, "Die Erforschung der deutschen Sondersprachen," *Germanisch-romanische Monatsschrift,* V (1913), 1-22.

As examples of recent studies in the vocabulary of a special field compare Wilhelm Busch, *Die deutsche Fachsprache der Mathematik* ("Giessener Beiträge zur deutschen Philologie," XXX; Giessen, 1933) and K. Glaser, *Die deutsche astronomische Fachsprache Keplers* ("Giessener Beiträge zur deutschen Philologie," XXXVIII; Giessen, 1935). Busch does not even list the words cited. Studies of this sort are likely to devote an undue amount of space to "philosophizing" and to give too little attention to collecting and arranging materials.

valuable materials supplementing the *Deutsches Wörterbuch,* and there is now an article dealing specially with these words in Emperor Maxmilian's *Teuerdank* and *Weisskunig.*[111] Notwithstanding this excellent work, we do not have a good historical dictionary of these terms or an interpretation of the significance of the linguistic materials which have been collected. Such tools as these could be put to immediate use. For example, Paul Scherrer[112] observes that the military aspects of Thomas Murner's *Von dem grossen lutherischen Narren,* particularly ll. 1710-1815 and 3240-99, have not been adequately discussed.

A marked growth in mercantile and industrial life characterized the period in which we are particularly interested. The cities and guilds flourished. Presumably, therefore, the vocabulary of business terms was altered and enlarged. Florence Edler's *Glossary of Medieval Terms of Business,*[113] which is limited to Italian, provides a model and sets up

[111] W. Kurrelmeyer, "German Lexicography," *Modern Language Notes,* XXXIV (1919), 257-266, 411-417; XXXV (1920), 405-413; XXXVII (1922), 390-398; XXXVIII (1923), 400-410; XLIV (1929), 137-147; C. Biener, "Waffennamen zur Zeit Kaiser Maximilians I.," *Wörter und Sachen,* XVI (1934), 37-80. Kurrelmeyer cites the first important article on the subject: F. Helbling, "Das militärische Fremdwort des 16. Jahrhunderts," *Zeitschrift für deutsche Wortforschung,* XIV (1912-13), 20-70.

[112] "Zum Kampfmotiv bei Thomas Murner," *Festschrift Gustav Binz* (Basel), 1935), p. 222, n. 52.

[113] Cambridge, Mass., 1934. Richard Heinzel, *Geschichte der niederfränkischen Geschäftssprache* (Paderborn, 1874), is a description of phonological peculiarities, not vocabulary. Alfred Schirmer's *Zur Geschichte der deutschen Kaufmannssprache* (Leipzig diss.; Strassburg, 1911), an excellent introduction to the subject, is reprinted in part in his *Wörterbuch der deutschen Kaufmannssprache auf geschichtlichen Grundlagen mit einer systematischen Einleitung* (Strassburg, 1911). See the helpful remarks in Hermann Hirt, *Etymologie der neuhochdeutschen Sprache* (2d ed.; "Handbuch des deutschen Unterrichts," IV, ii; Munich, 1921), pp. 321-324; A. Schirmer, *Vom Werden der deutschen Kaufmannssprache; sprach- und handelsgeschichtliche Betrachtungen* ("Glöckners Handelsbücherei," CIX; Leipzig, 1925). T. Krejči, *Einfluss des Handels auf die Entwicklung und Gestaltung der deutschen Sprache. Versuch einer wirtschaftslinguistischen Studie* (Prague, 1932) containing only a few bibliographical indications and emphasizing chiefly the vocabulary and usage of modern business. So, too, L. Wendelstein, *Die Sprache des Kaufmanns und seiner Korrespondenz* (Leipzig, 1912) and D. H. von Beseler, *An English-German and German-English Dictionary of Law and Business Terminology* (Berlin, 1929) deal primarily with matters of present interest and offer us comparatively little for the fifteenth and sixteenth centuries. Altogether the best indication of what can be gleaned in the older field is the linguistic chapter (pp. 35-79) of K. Krieger, *Die Sprache der Ravensburger Kaufleute um die Wende des 15. und 16. Jahrhunderts bearbeitet auf Grund der Obser-Schulte'schen Akten aus Schloss Salem* (Heidelberg diss., 1933; Friedrichshafen, [1935]). Sibylla Konz's admirable dissertation, *Die Ent-*

suitable restrictions on the choice. The need of an Italian-German mercantile dictionary was felt as early as 1498, when one was issued at Milan.[114]

The admirable dictionaries of trades sponsored by the Koninklijke Vlaamsche Akademie are models to be emulated and extended by the inclusion of historical materials. Special studies in thieves' jargon[115] and

---

wicklung der kaufmännischen Fachliteratur bis zum Ende des 17. Jahrhunderts (Cologne diss.; Bergisch Gladbach, 1926) surveys much of the material which needs to be consulted. A characteristic document combining juristic and theological ideas with information for the merchant is J. Nider, *Tractatus de contractibus marcatorum* [*sic*] (Cologne, *ca.* 1468) ; it was reissued as late as the middle of the sixteenth century. For a study of a related group of words see H. Heidel, *Die Terminologie der Finanzverwaltung Frankreichs im 15. Jahrhundert* ("Leipziger romanistische Studien," XV; Leipzig, 1936). An old study by a man familiar with many aspects of the age is C. Nisard, *Étude sur le langage populaire sur le patois de Paris et sa banlieue; précédée d'un coup d'oeil sur le commerce de la France au Moyen-Age, . . . et l'influence qu'il a dû avoir sur le langage* (Paris, 1872). Although Nisard is not a specialist in the study of language, he brings a freshness of view to the subject.

[114] The identification of the Italian-German dictionary to which I refer seems to offer some difficulties. Dr. Konz (p. 19) cites it at secondhand and remarks that it had a second edition in 1501.

[115] See an introductory bibliography in Hermann Hirt, *Etymologie der neuhochdeutschen Sprache* (2d ed.; "Handbuch des deutschen Unterrichts," IV, ii; Munich, 1921), pp. 331-333, § 197. Comparison of the books essential for a study of jargon is interesting and instructive. Friedrich Kluge, *Rotwelsch*, I, *Rotwelsches Quellenbuch* (Strassburg, 1901. No more pub.), collects and reprints the materials for a dictionary, but lacks an index of words. F. C. B. Avé-Lallemant, *Das deutsche Gaunertum* (Leipzig, 1858-62; available in a modern reprint), surveys jargon and speakers of jargon from the point of view of the historian of culture (No index of words). L. Günther, *Die deutsche Gaunersprache und verwandte Geheim- und Berufssprachen* (Leipzig, 1919), is an informative, well-organized handbook. Compare also his *Das Rotwelsch des deutschen Gauners* (Leipzig, 1905) ; Soldatensprache, Rotwelsch und 'Kunden'-deutsch in ihrem Verhältnis zueinander," *Zeitschrift für den deutschen Unterricht*, XXXIII (1919), 129-150; "Die Geographie in der deutschen Gauner- und Kundensprache," *Beilage der Allgemeinen Zeitung* (Munich), 1905, no. 257. Friedrich Kluge's extensive materials are in the library of the University of California at Los Angeles; an edition of the *Liber vagatorum* entitled *Die Rotwelsch Grammatic* (1520) is in the Newberry Library. On the *Liber vagatorum* (1509) see Kluge, pp. 35-80. Compare also the edition by J. C. Hotten which has been reissued with some improvements by D. B. Thomas, *The Book of Vagabonds and Beggars* (London, 1932). Thomas' preface shows that no one has taken the trouble to describe the various editions with the necessary bibliographical care.

A curious pamphlet in eight leaves—the last is blank—contains a list of criminals wanted in Merseburg for various offences and 19 symbols used by criminals to give information to their kind. This pamphlet—[Ambrosius Trota], *Der Mordtbrenner Zeichen und Losunge* (1540)—which was issued to 340 magis-

the vocabularies of cooking, brewing, sewing, agriculture, mining,[116] music, or hunting would be profitable. Such undertakings are not to be begun lightly. Friedrich Kluge has printed a volume of materials for the study of thieves' jargon, but it lacks an index of words cited. J. M. Wagner spent years in preparing an edition of the *Liber vagatorum* (1509), a pamphlet in fourteen sheets, but never finished the task. Possibly studies in this field are too difficult for the beginner, but the attentive reader will have noticed in my brief remarks the suggestion of undertakings within the powers of any careful worker. Indices to the words cited in the two standard works—Avé-Lallemant and Kluge—on German jargon are desiderata which mere clerical compilation could satisfy. A comprehensive edition of the *Liber vagatorum* with all of the editorial paraphernalia would not be so helpful as editions or facsimiles of unpublished texts. Such undertakings will introduce the student to the field of jargon and will suggest further investigation to him. A knowledge of Hebrew and Gypsy will be of great value in prosecuting studies in jargon.

Dictionaries in other fields are feasible undertakings, but should be started only by a student possessing competence and interest in both the special field and in linguistic studies. If such dictionaries are limited and do not extend beyond our period, they will not prove too long for a diligent worker. Ordinarily, a literary monument of our period provides a convenient terminus. For example, the oldest German cookbook is in print, good bibliographies guide us to the literature of gastronomy, a readable introduction gives us the background, and in our period, M. Rumpolt's *Ein new Kochbuch* (1587) ornamented with Jost Amman's woodcuts is the standard compendium of cookery.[117] Several useful

---

trates throughout Germany, is a very early example of an official bulletin describing a criminal. For similar symbols see L. Bechstein, "Die Mordbrenner und ihre Zeichen," *Deutsches Museum,* I (1842), 307-320 and II (1843), 309-316; A. Tille, "Gauner, Brenner und ihre Zinken in Thüringen 1540," *Mitteldeutsche Blätter für Volkskunde,* VIII (1933), 129-131; and the very useful collectanea in E. A. Stückelberg, "Gaunerzeichen," *Schweizer Volkskunde,* III (1889), 151-152; H. F. Friedrichs, "Geheimzeichen des fahrenden Volkes," *Hessische Blätter für Volkskunde,* XXIV (1925), 106-108 with a bibliographical note (pp. 108-109) by L. Günther.

[116] This has already been studied in E. Göpfert, *Die Bergmannssprache in der 'Sarepta' des Johann Mathesius* ("Beiheft" III [Strassburg, 1902] to *Zeitschrift für deutsche Wortforschung*). There is a copy of *Sarepta* in the University of Chicago Library. No one seems to have consulted Johann von Paltz, *Das Buchlein wird genannt dye Hymelisch Funtgrub* (1492), a mystical treatise comparing the Passion to a gold mine. It might contain early examples of technical words.

[117] [Der König vom Odenwalde], *Ein Buch von guter Speise* ("Bibliothek des

works preliminary to a study of musical vocabulary are available.[118]

Literarischen Vereins," IX, b; Stuttgart, 1844); Georges Vicaire, *Bibliographie gastronomique* (Paris, 1866). Compare C. H. Handschin, "Die Küche des 16. Jahrhunderts nach Johann Fischart; eine kulturgeschichtliche Studie," *Journal of English and Germanic Philology,* V (1903-5), 65-76. Examine the methods and aims of William Edward Mead, *The English Medieval Feast* (London, 1931), and compare such a popular book as C. Cooper, *The English Table in History and Literature* (London, [1929]) or such a collection of miscellaneous materials as M. S. Serjeantson, "The Vocabulary of Cookery in the Fifteenth Century," *Essays and Studies by Members of the English Association,* XXIII (1938), 25-37. The first modern treatise on gastronomy, Bartholomaeus de Platina's *De honesta voluptate et valetudine* (Cividale, 1480), falls within our period. A copy is in the Newberry Library. Carl Georg, *Verzeichnis der Literatur über Speise und Trank bis zum Jahre 1887* (Hannover, 1888), is a bibliographical guide. See the useful materials and the suggestions of unpublished texts in Ehrismann, p. 650.

Incidentally useful as a later example of bibliographical collections in the field are A. W. Oxford, *Notes from a Collector's Catalogue with a Bibliography of English Cookery Books* (Edinburgh, 1909), and *English Cookery Books to 1850* (Oxford, 1913). See an attractively presented survey of medieval cookery in F. E. J. M. Baudet, *De maaltijd en de keuken in de middeleeuwen* (Diss.; Leiden, 1904). As an example of a text reprinted in consequence of these studies compare *Het eerste Nederlandsche gedrukte Kookboek* (the Hague, 1925), a facsimile of a book printed by Thomas van der Noot at Brussels about 1510. See also A. J. J. Van de Velde, "Bromatologicon of Bibliographie der geschriften over de levensmiddelen tot 1800 in het licht gezonden," *Verslagen en mededeelingen der koninklijke Vlaamsche academie voor taal- en letterkunde,* 1933, pp. 247-277, and supplements in subsequent years.

[118] See in general Hugo Riemann, *Geschichte der Musiktheorie im 9.-19. Jahrhundert* (Leipzig, 1889). Compare such studies as D. Treder, *Die Musikinstrumente in dem höfischen Epos der Blütezeit* (Greifswald diss.; Bamberg, 1933); D. Fryklund, *Vergleichende Studien über deutsche Ausdrücke mit der Bedeutung 'Musikinstrument'* (Diss.; Upsala, 1910); C. Jacobsthal, "Ueber die musikalische Bildung der Meistersänger," *Zeitschrift für deutsches Altertum,* XX (1876), 69-91. As an example of a parallel study compare J. Bücker, *Der Einfluss der Musik auf den englischen Wortschatz im 16. und 17. Jahrhundert* (Diss.; Cologne, 1926). Since the vocabulary is borrowed at least in part from Latin, such a work as M. Appel, *Terminologie in den mittelalterlichen Musiktraktaten* (Berlin diss.; Bottrop, 1935), is useful. The histories of music—notably H. J. Moser, *Geschichte der deutschen Musik bis zum Ausgang des 30-jährigen* Kriegs, I (5th ed.; Stuttgart, 1930)—and dissertations—Sr. Maria Carmelita (Clothilde Pfleger), *Untersuchungen am deutschen geistlichen Lied des 13. bis 16. Jahrhunderts* (Diss.; Berlin, 1937) is typical—indicate sources to be consulted. Reliable and inexpensive guides to medieval music are T. Gérold, *La musique au moyen âge* ("Les classiques français du moyen âge," LXXIII; Paris, 1932), and his more popular work, *Historie de la musique des origines à la fin du XIV° siècle* ("Manuels d'histoire d'art"; Paris, 1936). Moser's *Tönende Volksaltertümer* (Berlin-Schöneberg, 1935) illustrates many minor musical forms and, although it does not contribute much directly to the understanding of our period, it is useful.

The very peculiar vocabulary of hunting offers attractive problems.[119] Special words associated with hunting are known from very early times. We might, for example, consider the replacement of the Indo-European word for *bear* which was akin to *ursus* by new formations in Germanic and Slavic languages as examples of hunters' languages. In the later development, the tabu is less obvious than in these examples. The description of the hunt in *Nibelungenlied* and the breaking of the deer in Gottfried von Strassburg's *Tristan* contain technical words. Not all of the puzzles in Sebastian Brant's "Von unnützem Jagen" (ch. LXXIV) and "Von bösen Schützen (ch. CXXXIX) have been solved. The native vocabulary was later altered greatly by the introduction of new fashions from France. Various allegories—some of them still unpublished—of the fourteenth and fifteenth centuries deal with hunting as a symbol for love and thus contribute to our knowledge of the German technical vocabulary.[120] They do not contain so many technical words as we might expect. This is perhaps explained by the fact that the allegories were ultimately suggested by Christian symbolism rather than by an immediate association with hunting.[121] A convenient terminus for the study of the technical vocabulary of hunting is the introduction of books of venery from France about the middle of the fifteenth century, or the compilation of the first vocabulary at the end of the same century, or the appearance of *Das geheime Jagdbuch* of Maxmilian I.

Akin to these studies is the investigation of the *Waidmannsfragen,* a group of conventional questions which an experienced hunter puts to a

---

Typical Renaissance works to be consulted are Luscinius (i.e., Othmar Nachtigall), *Musurgia, seu Praxis Musicae. Illius primo quae Instrumentis agitur certa ratio duobus libris absoluta. De Concentus Polyphoni, id est, ex plurifariis vocibus compositi, canonibus, libri totidem* (Strassburg, 1536), which was republished in Italy, and Andreas Ornithoparchus, *Musicae activae Micologus* (Leipzig, 1519), which was translated into English by John Dowland. In Germany, the first music printed from type is found in P. Tritonius, *Melapoiae, sive harmoniae tetracenticae super XXII. genera carminum . . . ductu Chunradi Celtis foeiciter impresse* (Augsburg, 1507). This rare and instructive work in ten folio leaves can be photographed for a small expenditure.

[119] See the bibliographical material in Appendix III, pp. 275-278. On the vocabulary of hunters in various languages see some general remarks by Paul Trost, "Zur Sondersprache der Jäger," *Wörter und Sachen,* XVI (1934), 61-67.

[120] The old printed text at Giessen cited by Ehrismann (p. 501) has been republished. See Hans Hofmann, *Ein Nachahmer Hermanns von Sachsenheim* (Diss.; Marburg, 1893). E. E. Hefe, *Die Jagd Hadamars von Laber* ("Deutschkundliche Arbeiten, Allgemeine Reihe," III; Breslau, 1936), is evidence of interest in this neglected genre.

[121] K. Burdach, *Vorspiel* ("Deutsche Vierteljahrsschrift für Literaturwissenschaft, Buchreihe," I; Halle, 1925), I, 78-79.

beginner.[122] Although a considerable mass of pertinent material has been printed, it has not been studied.

The task of compiling a dictionary in a special field is an important one, and the information in such a dictionary can be converted to the uses of the historian of literature and culture. For example, Gustav Bihlmeyer asks us to investigate the share which the preaching friars had in transferring words from the courtly sphere to theological and secular uses.[123] His question is a difficult one, but an answer to it will illuminate the influences which created the vocabulary of the fifteenth century.

10. *Acquaintance with Medieval German Literature in the Fifteenth and Sixteenth Centuries.*—Instead of considering the influence of a foreign language or literature upon German writers of our period, we may ask ourselves what earlier German writings were read in the fifteenth and sixteenth centuries and why. A comprehensive survey is a large but not insuperable task. Bibliographies and literary histories do not show readily the older works which were circulated during the fifteenth and sixteenth centuries. I shall limit myself to suggesting a few problems in the field. One might examine the vogue of medieval chivalric romance in bourgeois circles.[124] Similar problems involving the reputation and currency of the more important medieval and post-medieval authors are easily formulated and can be undertaken with the

---

[122] See Andreas Sutor, *Chaos latinum* (Augsburg, 1740), pp. 774-780; J. and W. Grimm, *Altdeutsche Wälder,* III (Cassel, 1813), 97-148; J. B. Friedreich, *Geschichte des Räthsels* (Dresden, 1860), pp. 5-6; L. Uhland, *Schriften zur Geschichte der Dichtung und Sage,* III (Stuttgart, 1866), 200-202, 302; J. M. Wagner, "Weidsprüche und Jägerschreie," *Archiv für die Geschichte deutscher Sprache,* I (1874), 133-160; K. Müllenhoff and W. Scherer, *Denkmäler deutscher Poesie und Prosa vom 9. bis zum 12. Jahrhundert* (3d ed.; Berlin, 1892), II, 308 (note on "Das Traugemundslied," 9, 3); W. Uhl, *Die deutsche Priamel* (Leipzig, 1897), pp. 277-279; Paul Lembke, *Studien zur deutschen Weidmannssprache* (Rostock diss.; Dresden, 1898), p. 12; Reinhold Köhler, *Kleinere Schriften,* III Berlin, 1900), 452-494 (reprinted with additions from *Weimarisches Jahrbuch,* III [1856], 329-358); C. Clewing, *Musik und Jägerei* ("Denkmäler deutscher Jagdkultur," I; Kassel, 1938).

[123] *Heinrich Seuses Schriften* (Stuttgart, 1907), p. 146*, n. 3.

[124] Compare as an example of method: R. S. Crane, *The Vogue of Medieval Chivalric Romance during the English Renaissance* (University of Pennsylvania diss.; Menasha, Wisconsin, 1919). See also L. B. Wright, *Middle-Class Culture in Elizabethan England* (Chapel Hill, N.C., 1935), pp. 375 ff. Friedrich Schneider's painstaking dissertation, *Die höfische Epik im frühneuhochdeutschen Prosaroman* (Bonn, 1915), deals with a few monuments representing the survival of medieval literature, but does not provide the necessary survey or give an interpretation of the significance of the survivals. As an example of the history of an author's reputation, compare G. Gerstmeyer, *Walther von der Vogelweide im Wandel der Jahrhunderte* ("Germanistische Abhandlungen," LXVIII; Breslau, 1934).

aid of a comprehensive bibliography of editions and investigations.[125]

We perceive almost immediately that several important medieval poems exist only in copies of the fifteenth or sixteenth centuries. A manuscript of *Orendel*, the early minstrel epic, written in 1477, at a time when interest in the seamless coat of Christ (now kept at Trèves) has been reawakened, was burned in 1870. The epic survives today in two versions of about 1512, one in prose and one in verse. *Gudrun* and Hartmann von Aue's *Erec* are found only in the famous Ambras manuscript of the early sixteenth century. Konrad von Würzburg's *Engelhard*, written in the middle of the thirteenth century, now exists only in a version of the late sixteenth century. All of these poems are accessible to us only in reconstructions written in standardized Middle High German. Opinions will differ about the need or even the desirability of having at our disposal an accurate reproduction of the original instead of a reconstruction.

In some instances the post-medieval text is known to be important for a knowledge of the original, but has not been made available for scholarly use. The incunabulum edition of *Der jüngere Titurel* (1477) contains many readings superior to those of the manuscript used by K. A. Hahn for his edition,[126] but these readings are accessible only to those who can consult this rare and costly volume. A generation ago, Rudolf Biedermann discussed the value of the fifteenth-century variants in the Colmar manuscript of Meistergesang *(Cod. germ. mon. 4997)* for the reconstruction of the text of Heinrich von Meissen (Frauenlob) and more recently, Johannes Siebert has used similar materials for Der Tannhäuser.[127] We may hope to learn much by consulting such sources.

Contrary to the general impression that medieval German literature was edited primarily by scholars in the period of Romanticism, the printing of such materials had been going on long before the beginning of the nineteenth century.[128] Fragments of the *Nibelungenlied* were in

---

[125] See the remarks below (pp. 53-54) on the problem of a critical bibliography of an author.

[126] "Bibliothek der gesammten deutschen Nationalliteratur," I, 24 (Quedlinburg, 1842).

[127] *Die Einwirkung der Kolmarer Meisterliederhandschrift (t) auf die Textgestaltung der Gedichte Heinrichs von Meissen* (Diss.; Berlin, 1897); *Der Dichter Tannhäuser* (Halle, 1934).

[128] See Gustave Otto Arlt, *Acquaintance with Older German Literature in the Eighteenth Century* (University of Chicago diss.; Crawfordsville, Ind., 1931); F. Gotthelf, *Das deutsche Altertum in den Anschauungen des 16. und 17. Jahrhunderts* ("Forschungen zur neueren Literaturgeschichte," XIII; Berlin, 1900); Karl Wagner, *Das deutsche Mittelalter in den Vorstellungen der gebildeten Kreise des 17. Jahrhunderts bis zum Beginn der romantischen Bewegung* (Programm; Stendal, 1914); R. Sokolovsky, *Das Aufleben des altdeutschen Min-*

print about the middle of the sixteenth century. As early as 1695, Johann Schilter published an anthology of Old and Middle High German literature, and J. G. Scherz enlarged it in 1726-28 to include almost all of Old High German literature. The history of such editions offers a problem associated with the literary history of the older periods.[129] What authors are reprinted at particular times? In what ways does the choice of authors to be reprinted disclose the character of the later age? Shortly after 1800, for example, we notice a special interest in the writings of Friedrich Spee. This probably reflects the Romantic turn toward Catholicism. Stimulated by the adaptations of Friedrich Schlegel (1805), the interest in Spee bore fruit in Clemens Brentano's edition (1808) and continued in full force until the fourth decade of the nineteenth century.[130] The history of the discovery of the medieval German mystics has been written.[131] Can we not perceive more clearly the characteristic qualities of a modern literary period by considering its attitude toward such typical figures or movements as Spee and mysticism? Interest in baroque literature, a current appearing in German literature just before 1900, is probably to be credited in part to Max Freiherr von Waldberg's treatise, *Die deutsche Renaissance-Lyrik*.[132] This older kind of literature appealed to the modern age and must have had some qualities of particular significance which will help us to understand the modern age. How and why did Arno Holz, a poet intimately associated with the literary ideas and controversies of the closing years of the nineteenth century, write *Dafnis; lyrisches Porträt aus dem 17. Jahrhundert?*[133]

---

nesangs in der neueren deutschen Literatur, I (Diss.; Jena, 1891). A painstaking study containing some suggestions in method is Dorothy Doolittle, *The Relations between Literature and Mediaeval Studies in France from 1820 to 1860* (Diss.; Bryn Mawr, Pa., 1933).

[129] See also the remarks below (p. 104 ff.) on the history of a theme.

[130] Gustave Otto Arlt, "Friedrich von Spee's 'Trutznachtigall'; the Editions and a Bibliography," *Modern Philology,* XXXIII (1935), 159-168.

[131] Gottfried Fischer, *Geschichte der Entdeckung der deutschen Mystiker Eckhart, Tauler, Seuse im neunzehnten Jahrhundert* (Diss.; Freiburg in Uechtland, 1931).

[132] Berlin, 1885.

[133] Munich, 1904.

Chapter II

PROBLEMS IN THE STUDY OF AN AUTHOR

The Biography, Bibliography, and Editing of an Author

THE biography of an author, the bibliography of his works and of investigations into them, and the editing of these works are tasks too difficult and often too extensive for our present survey. In considering the task of the biographer,[1] I pass over those writers whose works have been edited completely or almost completely,—e.g., Martin Luther, Thomas Murner, Hans Sachs, and Jörg Wickram—and who have been the centers of active discussion. Many important lesser writers have been neglected. Serious but not insuperable difficulties beset the biographer. The writings of authors in our period are often hard to come by. Articles about them are frequently printed in local periodicals difficult of access. Finally, it is always probable that additional information may be found in unsearched archives.

11. *The Biography of an Author.*—Some very important figures in the fifteenth and sixteenth centuries have not received their well-deserved biographical treatment. Sebastian Brant, Johannes Geiler von Kaisersberg, and Johann Eck are conspicuous examples of such neglect. In preparing to write a biography of one of them, the student will find so many tasks that he will have much to do before he is ready to go to Europe and search the archives there. Such lesser figures as Aesticampanius, Erhart Gross, and Bartholomäus Ringwaldt represent one or another characteristic aspect of post-medieval literature.[2] Biographical studies conceived on a large scale demand wide reading and good judgment. Although they are too difficult to begin with, they stimulate the student in his orderly progress toward scholarly maturity.

The figure which can be studied most easily and successfully in this

[1] See Morize, pp. 210-224, Ch. IX, "Treatment of Biographical Material in the History of Literature."

[2] I select names pointed out by Wolfgang Stammler. For the importance of these men, the problems connected with them, and the necessary bibliographical information see Stammler; Goedeke, *Grundriss;* Rochus Freiherr von Liliencron (ed.), *Allgemeine deutsche Biographie;* and other standard works of reference. Stammler calls particular attention (p. 484, note on p. 192) to the need of a comprehensive study of Sebastian Brant. One of his suggestions has been taken up by one of his students; see Franz Breitkopf, *Marcus von Weida, ein Prediger und theologischer Volksschriftsteller des ausgehenden Mittelalters* (Diss.; Greifswald, 1932).

country is perhaps Johannes Geiler von Kaisersberg. From about 1480 to 1510, he was a popular preacher of force and vigor in Strassburg. A representative of the best aspects of German ecclesiastical life at that time, he was in touch with the life of the common man, the universities, literature, theological and doctrinal disputes, municipal government, and the endeavors to correct social abuses both within and without the church. Closely allied in spirit to Jean Gerson, chancellor of the University of Paris and leader in the efforts of the conciliar movement to reform the church from within, Johannes Geiler spoke to the common man in simple words and homely symbols. Thirty volumes by Geiler or ascribed to him are in the University of Chicago Library. These works were printed in the first quarter of the sixteenth century and with minor exceptions have never been reprinted. In this collection only the *Evangelibuch* (1515) and the German translation of *De arbore humana* (1521) are lacking. A complete edition of Geiler's works has been recently proposed, but it seems likely to remain a pious wish. Most of the critical literature on Geiler, including J. M. B. Clauss's admirable review[3] of pertinent investigations, is also accessible in the University of Chicago Library. An interpretative and critical account of the man and his work might well become also a survey of life and thought in Southwestern Germany before the Reformation. Preparatory to so large a work as a biography of Geiler is the study of the *Lucubratiunculæ* (1498),[4] a collection of letters written by Peter Schott, Geiler's nephew and ward, while studying in Italy. Unfortunately, the letters of guidance and counsel from Geiler have been lost. The *Lucubratiunculæ* might lead one into a description of the intellectual currents passing from Italy into Germany. Another sidelight on Geiler is found in the "Scommata" appended to Adelphus Muling's *Margarita facetiarum* (1508).[5] Muling, who translated several of Geiler's works into German and was one of those who knew the great preacher intimately, added these vulgar jests to his anthology of jokes in spite of Geiler's protest. Possibly the "Scommata" are too vulgar to be reprinted. At any rate, it is an interesting commentary on the age that its greatest preacher, a man for many years officially appointed to the cathedral of Strassburg, could have such stories attached to his name. One might begin by interpreting these jests, turn them to the *Lucubratiunculæ*, and take up finally the

[3] "Kritische Uebersicht der Schriften über Geiler von Kaysersberg," *Historisches Jahrbuch*, XXXI (1910), 485-519. See also Dahlmann-Waitz, p. 572, no. 8910; Gustav Wolf, *Quellenkunde der deutschen Reformationsgeschichte* (Gotha, 1915), I, 337-342. This will be referred to as Wolf.

[4] A copy in the Newberry Library.

[5] A copy in the Newberry Library.

sermons in order to arrive at a characterization of the man. In commenting on the jests, one should not yield to the temptation to judge the man by puritanical standards.

Curiously enough, Geiler's sermons did not appear in print until some years after his death. During his lifetime, he published only admonitory and doctrinal works of no great interest—*Wie ein Mensch sterben soll* (1482), translations of Jean Gerson, and the *Oratio dominica* (1483, 1510). The sermons on Brant's *Narrenschiff* were in press at the time of his death in January, 1510. From shortly before 1520 on, when Geiler had been in his grave for a decade, thick quartos of his sermons were compiled from recollections and notes. Latin editions appeared first and were soon followed by adaptations and paraphrases in German. Two publishers, one of whom claimed to rely upon Geiler's own notes, competed for the trade. We must not deal with such texts as if we had the very words of Geiler before us, but must treat the sermons as what Geiler might have said, as typical of the preaching of his day.

I shall deal but briefly with the two other conspicuous figures which I have mentioned as deserving a biography. For neither Sebastian Brant nor Johann Eck are the circumstances so favorable as for Johannes Geiler. In America we have a good collection of original editions of Geiler and a survey of the work which has been done on him. The easiest step to be taken toward a biography of Brant or Eck is the compilation of a critical bibliography of what has been accomplished. This would disclose many things to do.

Although there is a good deal of literature on Johann Eck, it is largely from hostile pens. In recent years, some of Eck's works have been published, notably in the "Corpus Catholicorum," and some of his correspondence has been made accessible, particularly by Greving. It would be interesting to learn whether there are more letters in the archives of the Vatican. Collection and organization of the very scattered material dealing with Johann Eck is perhaps the most important enterprise in the history of the Reformation in Germany. A sympathetic interpretation of the man and his rôle will reward anyone brave enough to undertake the task.

Seductive as the comprehensive study and biography of a single characteristic figure is, the opportunities for undertaking such work in this country are comparatively rare. To be sure, distinguished investigations of our period have been written in America. I mention only Preserved Smith's *Martin Luther* and his *Erasmus,* Ephraim Emerton's *Desiderius Erasmus,* and (on a smaller scale) Robert Herndon Fife's *Young Luther*. There is a real need now for a work on Thomas Münzer.

His *Briefwechsel* and *Gesammelte Schriften* have been published; monographs on special subjects have appeared. New studies dealing with the Peasants' War give the background. The time is ripe to gather the results. To a certain extent, the same is true of Sebastian Franck, but his works are less easily accessible. As soon as the *Corpus Schwenckfeldianorum* is complete, someone should undertake a comprehensive investigation of Caspar Schwenckfeld. Inasmuch as the many volumes of the *Corpus* represent the one instance in which American scholars have reprinted the work of a sixteenth-century reformer, they should inspire further studies by Americans.

12. *The Explanation of Literary Works From the Author's Life.*— The interpretation of a man's acts is always difficult to carry through to a sound conclusion, and especially so in the sixteenth century when our materials are fragmentary. In the nineteenth century, materials sufficient in quantity and quality are occasionally within our reach. Thus, we can probably learn to understand the suicide of Charlotte Stieglitz more fully than was possible a century ago. Since Mundt's apologia of 1835, two serious efforts to interpret the suicide and an important collation of the most significant letters in the *Denkmal* have appeared.[6] A fresh study might throw light into dark corners. It would be an interesting adventure into the medico-psychological aspects of literature.

In my *Literary History of Meistergesang,* I have suggested the problem of determining precisely when Hans Sachs lost interest in Meistergesang.[7] In 1556, he wrote 155 Meisterlieder; in 1557, only 18. Since we have very good records of his literary activities, e.g. Sachs's own chronological list of his writings and his minutes of the school at Nuremberg for this period, it should be possible to fix even to the month the time when he changed his attitude. Possibly the fact that he wrote the first summary of his writings, "Suma all meiner gedicht," on September 30, 1556, indicates that he was bringing his work to a close of some kind. When we have fixed the time when he ceased actively writing Meisterlieder, we may discover some reason for the change in his attitude. If

[6] Ernst Seillière, *Études de psychologie romantique: une tragédie d'amour au temps du romantisme* (Paris, 1909) ; Eliza M. Butler, *The St. Simonian Religion in Germany* (Cambridge, Eng. 1926), pp. 331-342; H. H. Houben, *Jungdeutscher Sturm und Drang* (Leipzig, 1911), pp. 395-462. The admirable bibliography of Heinrich and Charlotte Stieglitz, which has just appeared in Goedeke, *Grundriss,* XIII, 305-312, greatly facilitates an approach to this problem.

[7] New York, 1937. See p. 29. Julius Sahr has a convenient collection of the biographical details mentioned in Hans Sachs's works; see "Zu Hans Sachs," *Zeitschrift für den deutschen Unterricht,* IX, (1895), 688-690. For additional materials see E. Goetze, (ed.), *Hans Sachs,* XXVI "(Bibliothek des Literarischen Vereins," CCL; Tübingen, 1908), 82-84.

we turn our attention to the sources on which Hans Sachs drew, we see
that his earliest borrowings from the *Decameron* are from the Fourth
Day. Should we conjecture that, inasmuch as these tales deal with un-
requited love, he was inspired by an unhappy love-affair?[8]

A much larger task is the interpretation of Catholic and Protestant
writers of the first half of the sixteenth century in the light of their
connections with particular orders. For example, Jacques Maritain finds
a partial explanation of Luther's defection in his Augustinian training.[9]
I should be interested to discover the way in which Thomas Murner's
Franciscan background influenced his writing.[10] Similar problems can
be stated for many of the important figures of the time. An effective
treatment of such problems implies a sympathetic understanding of the
characteristics of the various orders, as well as an intimate knowledge of
an author. The task is difficult, to be sure, but not impossible. Thus,
William A. Nitze brilliantly demonstrates the significance of the Cister-
cian background in the reworking of *Perlesvaus*.[11] H. Hauser[12] commends Etienne Gilson's investigation of the Franciscan antecedents of
Rabelais as "études remarquables par leur nouveauté et leur profon-
deur."

I shall not venture to suggest further enterprises in the field of psychological interpretation. Such important events as Luther's decisions
to enter a monastery or to renounce Catholicism have been the objects
of much speculation of this sort. Within limits, such speculations are

---

[8] L. Sorieri, *Boccaccio's Story of 'Tito e Gisippo' in European Literature* ("Comparative Literature Series, Institute of French Studies"; New York, 1937), p. 203,
n. 2. He cites Julius Hartmann, "Das Verhältnis von H. Sachs zur sogenannten
Decameronenübersetzung," *Acta Germanica*, N. R., Heft 2, (Berlin, 1912), p. 21.

[9] *Three Reformers: Luther—Descartes—Rousseau* (New York, 1936) p. 10.

[10] As a foundation, use T. Liebenau, *Der Franziskaner Dr. Thomas Murner*
("Erläuterungen und Ergänzungen zu Janssens 'Geschichte des deutschen
Volkes,'" IX, 4-5; Freiburg i. Br., 1913); Ernst Benz, *Ecclesia spiritualis.
Kirchenidee und Geschichtstheologie der franziskanischen Reformation* (Stutt-
gart, 1934); and P. Scherrer, "Zum Kampfmotiv bei Thomas Murner," *Fest-
schrift Gustav Binz* (Basel, 1935), pp. 226-227.

[11] *Le Haut Livre du Graal Perlesvaus* (Chicago, 1937), II, 83-89 and 181-182,
n. 17.

[12] *La modernité du XVIᵉ siècle* (Paris, 1930), p. 18. Robert Valentine Merrill
and S. F. Will have kindly supplied the necessary references: Plattard, "Etat
présent des études rabelaisiennes," *Études françaises*, XII (1927), 19 and *L'Oeuvre
de Rabelais . . .* (Paris, 1910), pp. 88-93, and more particularly E. Gilson, "Rabelais franciscain," *Revue d'histoire franciscaine*, I (1924), 257-287, "Notes médiévales au 'Tiers Livre,'" *ibid.*, II (1925), 72-88, and "A propos de Rabelais
franciscain," *ibid.*, p. 113. Gilson's second article deals with the theological background rather than the Franciscan atmosphere of Rabelais.

profitable, but they easily get out of bounds. Psychological interpretation is also a task of literature. Here Conrad Ferdinand Meyer or Alfred Neumann have shown what can be done.[13]

13. *The Influence of an Author*.—An author's influence may be studied as it operated either on an age or on an individual. In the former case, we are concerned with larger issues and must select as a starting-point an author who formulated new ideas, created a new and striking style, or enjoyed close relations to the age. J. M. Gálvez's examination of Guevara's influence in England suggests the possibility of a similar undertaking for Germany.[14] Similar is the problem of the influence of the politician and journalist Trajano Boccalini.[15] These problems demand a rather wide reading.

[13] See above, p. 3.

[14] *Guevara in England* ("Palaestra," CIX; Berlin, 1916). Although the literary relations of Germany and Spain have been surveyed bibliographically several times, there is no satisfactory interpretative account of the results. See, e.g., Adam Schneider, *Spaniens Anteil an der deutschen Literatur des 16. und 17. Jahrhunderts* (Strassburg, 1898); J. Schwering, *Literarische Beziehungen zwischen Spanien und Deutschland* ("Kritische Studien," I; Münster i.W., 1902); H. O. Lyte, *A Tentative Bibliography of Spanish-German Relations* (Privately mimeographed; Minneapolis, 1936); Georg Schreiber, "Spanische Motive in der deutschen Volksreligiosität," *Gesammelte Aufsätze zur Kulturgeschichte Spaniens* ("Spanische Forschungen der Görresgesellschaft," I, 5: Münster i.W., 1935), and *Deutschland und Spanien; Volkskundliche und kulturkundliche Beziehungen; Zusammenhänge abendländischer und ibero-amerikanischer Sakralkultur* ("Forschungen zur Volkskunde," XXII-XXIV; Düsseldorf, 1936); H. Tiemann, *Das spanische Schrifttum in Deutschland von der Renaissance bis zur Romantik* ("Ibero-amerikanische Studien," VI; Hamburg, 1936). See also P. Scheid, *Zum spanischen Sprachgut im Deutschen* ("Deutsches Werden," IV; Greifswald, 1934). It is a significant detail for the historian of culture that, for example, the business term *Risiko* is borrowed from Spanish and not, as we might have expected, from Italian. Are we to think of the loans of Charles V which proved so disastrous to German financiers? For some Spanish words which had established themselves in the German business vocabulary before 1520 see K. Krieger, *Die Sprache der Ravensburger Kaufleute um die Wende des 15. und 16. Jahrhunderts* (Heidelberg diss., 1933; Friedrichshafen, [1935]). *Risiko* is not among them. The study of the cultural relations of Germany and Spain might concern itself either with the exchange of ideas or with the geographical aspects of the reception of Spanish ideas in Germany. The latter approach to the problem seems particularly attractive to me. Contrast, for example, the choice and use of Spanish materials in Hamburg and Munich in the seventeenth century.

[15] Suggested in a review of Karl Schottenloher's *Flugblatt und Zeitung*. See, however, P. Stötzner, "Der Satiriker Trajano Boccalini und sein Einfluss auf die deutsche Literatur," Herrig's *Archiv*, CIII (1899), 107-147 and F. Behrend, "Trajano Boccalini und die deutsche Literatur," *Deutsche Studien* (Berlin, 1936), pp. 33-61. Compare R. Thomas, "Trajano Boccalini's Influence upon English Literature," *Aberystwyth Studies*, III (1922), 73-102 and C. L. Thijssen-Schoute, *Nic-*

The somewhat easier problem of describing the influence exerted by one author upon another has been somewhat looked down upon in recent years. The parallels cited to prove a relationship have often been insignificant, and the result of the whole investigation has at times turned out to be merely the proof of the obvious. Nevertheless, enterprises of this sort will often justify themselves. Gustav Bebermeyer, for example, suggests that Sebastian Brant's influence on Johann Fischart might be studied.[16] When the source is marked by striking stylistic peculiarities, problems of this sort should be especially attractive and easy to solve. The unusual style of Johann Fischart should be readily apparent in borrowings, and consequently the identification of what Johann Sommer and Aegidius Albertinus took from Fischart should not be difficult.[17] The facts would be interesting because they would throw light on Fischart's influence in a Catholic region of Germany.

14. *The Critical Bibliography of an Author.*—Bibliographical studies of individual authors are very useful; and by organizing what has been accomplished, they serve as the basis for further investigation.[18] In general, we cannot do much in this country in collecting and comparing original editions of the sixteenth century.[19] To be sure, such an admirable survey as Léon Dacheux' *Les plus anciens écrits de Geiler de Kaysersberg*[20] is indispensable for the investigator, but it utilizes the resources of many German libraries. On the other hand, a bibliographical and critical survey of an individual author can be executed fairly satisfactorily in this country. It will disclose problems for further study.[21] I shall cite an example from an earlier period in literary history. A generation ago, Friedrich Panzer issued a comprehensive critical bibliography

---

olaas *Jarichides Wieringa* ("Teksten en Studien," II; Assen, 1939), *passim.*

[16] *Reallexikon der deutschen Literaturgeschichte,* II, 447.

[17] Goedeke, *Grundriss,* II, 584, no. 12 and 579, no. 18. The borrowings are said to be rather extensive and entirely undisguised.

[18] See Morize, pp. 70-81, Ch. IV, "Establishing a Critical Bibliography."

[19] I have suggested one such problem; see below pp. 64-65.

[20] Freiburg i.Br., 1882. The German edition of the same date, which I have not seen, includes the *XXI Artikel* and letters.

[21] From the bibliographical point of view, Hans Sachs and Martin Luther have been treated most thoroughly of all German writers of the sixteenth century. See the excellent bibliography of Luther in the Weimar edition; it needs only an index. For Hans Sachs, compare F. Hintner, *Bausteine zu einer Sachs-Bibliographie* (Programm; Wels, 1914-16); K. Schottenloher, *Bibliographie zur deutschen Geschichte im Zeitalter der Glaubensspaltung,* II (Leipzig, 1935), 198-213; and the collectanea fundamental to all study of Hans Sachs in E. Goetze (ed.), *Hans Sachs,* XXV, XXVI ("Bibliothek des Literarischen Vereins," CCXXV, CCL; Tübingen, 1902, 1908).

of Wolfram von Eschenbach.[22] Much has been published since then, and a fresh bibliography with critical comment would be a praiseworthy venture—but not an easy one. Among the authors of the fifteenth and sixteenth centuries, it is difficult to select for special mention those deserving of a critical bibliography. I have already mentioned the names of Sebastian Brant and Johann Eck in connection with the writing of a biography. I might add Conrad Celtis and Ulrich von Hutten as examples of writers deserving a critical bibliography, but in their cases the need for a new biography is not quite so great as in the cases of Brant and Eck. Critical bibliographies of Celtis and Hutten should summarize scholarship and point the way to new investigations rather than prepare the way immediately for the writing of a biography.

15. *Editing the Works of an Author.*—Editions of the complete works of a post-medieval German author are comparatively rare.[23] The writings of Thomas Murner, Ulrich von Hutten, Martin Luther, Caspar Schwenckfeld, and Jörg Wickram are available. Those of Hans Sachs and Johann Fischart, not to mention many an author of less note, are accessible only in part. In the period before 1550, the lack of editions is especially striking and troublesome. It suffices to point out that the best comprehensive edition of Erasmus is still that of 1706. Only the most important writers of the fifteenth and sixteenth centuries deserve a complete edition, but literary history has not yet reached a point where it can always advise us competently on selecting them, and bibliography has not progressed so far that it can assure us of completeness and accuracy.

In contrast to the literature of medieval Germany, of which virtually all important texts have been reissued in editions of some kind, many significant works of the fifteenth and sixteenth centuries have never been reprinted. Genres so characteristic of this period as Meistergesang or Latin drama are incompletely known to us because the texts have never been published. Fortunately, editorial custom regarding the literature of this period differs from that adopted for the earlier period. In printing texts of the fifteenth and sixteenth centuries, editors ordinarily reproduce the original and do not rewrite it to conform to an artificially standardized language. The *Nibelungenlied* or the works of Hartmann von Aue

---

[22] *Bibliographie zu Wolfram von Eschenbach* (Munich, 1897). See also G. Boetticher in R. Bethge (ed.), *Ergebnisse und Fortschritte der germanistischen Wissenschaft* (Leipzig, 1902), pp. 272-280.

[23] See Morize, pp. 37-69, Ch. III, "The Preparation of an Edition"; Georg Witkowski, *Textkritik und Editionstechnik neuerer Schriftwerke* (Leipzig, 1924). These works deal with the editing of modern texts and do not answer all of the questions arising in editions of our period.

are, for example, printed in a normalized language; scribal variations are removed and only incompletely recorded in the notes. Literary monuments of the fifteenth and sixteenth centuries, however, are usually reprinted with a minimum of editorial interference. Editions for the general reader should of course give a reasonably modernized text (one as easily understood as possible) and should avoid in the main the minutiæ of literary scholarship. Editions for the scholar should reproduce all the essential features of the original.

The facilities for reprinting post-medieval German literature are by no means so numerous as one might wish, and editions are seldom printed except in such admirable series as the "Neudrucke deutscher Literaturwerke des 16. und 17. Jahrhunderts" and the "Bibliothek des Literarischen Vereins." Unfortunately, these series have not received adequate support and their continuation appears to be somewhat doubtful. Furthermore, the choice of works for reprinting has been somewhat haphazard, and it will be difficult to improve this aspect of the situation. The standards of the admirable "Corpus Catholicorum" are especially to be commended on this score. Beside it we can set the "Veröffentlichungen der Commission zur Erforschung der Geschichte der Reformation und Gegenreformation." In this series we find very welcome reprints of the correspondence of such humanists as Celtis and Cuspinianus. On the whole, such English undertakings as the editions of the Elizabethan sonnet-cycles, the Elizabethan dramatists, and the collected works of individual authors, furnish models to be emulated.

In reprinting the complete works of an author, one will therefore do well to make haste slowly. Without access to manuscript sources, it is difficult to assemble the materials for a complete edition. Gregor von Heimburg, for example, might be reissued entire. Karl Euling, an authority on Hans Rosenplüt, says—and no doubt correctly—that a new edition of Rosenplüt is greatly needed,[24] but in the absence of a satisfactory list of manuscripts of his writings, an American scholar will have trouble in deciding at long range what needs to be photographed. A new edition of the writings of Peter Suchenwirt seems worth undertaking.[25] His works are now found only in a virtually unobtainable

[24] *Reallexikon der deutschen Literaturgeschichte,* II, 724.

[25] Ed. Alois Primisser (Vienna, 1827). See the useful collectanea of H. Niewöhner, "Suchenwirt-Handschriften," *Zeitschrift für deutsches Altertum,* LXVIII (1931), 273-274; F. Kratochwil, "Ueber den gegenwärtigen Stand der Suchenwirt-Handschriften," *Germania,* XXXIV (1889), 203-244, 303-345, 431-487; the critical notes of A. Leitzmann, "Suchenwirtiana," *Beiträge zur Geschichte der deutschen Sprache,* XLIV (1920), 312-315; and the bibliographical introduction in Ehrismann, pp. 490-491. A few poems have been edited after Primisser's edition: Joseph

edition of 1827. Suchenwirt was a poet at the Viennese court, in the critical days after chivalry had definitely lost its supremacy and when the middle class was establishing itself in a position of power. Although attached to the court in spirit, he reflects the changing social conditions of the age. His verse, if considered as literature, has perhaps deserved the neglect into which it has fallen. As a mirror of contemporary life, his works must be examined with greater care than has hitherto been the case. Even more inaccessible than Suchenwirt's works are the writings of Der Teichner.[26]

Editions of Single Works.

When choosing separate works for new editions, one will naturally be guided by their relative importance and the light which fresh knowledge will throw upon the field. In contrast to medieval literature, where practically all of the important monuments are easily accessible in satisfactory or relatively satisfactory versions, German literature of the fifteenth and sixteenth centuries is not always easily come by. Even the "greater" writers,—Hans Sachs, Fischart, and the more important humanists,—are not fully known to us. Editions of their works are more urgently needed than republications of the works of the "small fry."[27] A judicious reading of the list of Hans Sachs's works will readily disclose texts which ought to be printed. The second edition of Fischart's *Aller Praktik Grossmutter* is still buried in Scheible's *Kloster*. Much of Conrad Celtis is beyond the reach of the ordinary American scholar. And so it goes.

Perhaps nothing will make my point clearer than the citation of Stammler's interesting list of the significant events—literary, political, and artistic—in our period.[28] This "Zeittafel" extends from the death of Meister Eckhart in 1327 to the publication of *Liebeskampf oder 2. Teil der englischen Komödien vnd Tragödien* in 1630. The number of literary monuments in this list which have never been reprinted is amazing and gives the thoughtful reader some notion of the inadequacy

Chmel, "Der Würfel: Gedicht von Suchenwirt," *Blätter für Literatur, Kunst, und Kritik,* (1835), pp. 61-63; G. E. Friess, "Fünf unedierte Ehrenreden Suchenwirts," *Sitzungsberichte der Wiener Akademie,* LXXXVIII (1877), 99-126. A recent summary of information about Suchenwirt is Otfried Weber, *Peter Suchenwirt. Studien über sein Wesen und Werk* ("Deutsches Werden," XI: Greifswald, 1937).

[26] On Der Teichner see Ehrismann, p. 489; Niewöhner in *Verfasserlexikon,* II, cols. 234-252.

[27] See, e.g., a very helpful note in R. H. Fife's stimulating essay, "Humanistic Currents in the Reformation Era," *Germanic Review,* XII (1937), 79, n. 11.

[28] *Von der Mystik zum Barock,* pp. 526-541.

of his knowledge of the period. I can suggest no better guide for those disposed to occupy themselves with the making of new editions.[29]

I shall add a few remarks on texts which have been pointed out for one reason or another and shall conclude with suggestions for the methodical discovery of texts deserving of a new edition. Wolfgang Stammler calls for editions of Eberhard Windeck's vividly-written chronicle of the years from 1362 to about 1445 and Ambrosius Lobwasser's translation (1573) of the Psalms in iambic rhythms with French tunes. Inasmuch as Lobwasser's hymns were often reprinted even as late as the middle of the eighteenth century,[30] a new edition is perhaps less urgently needed than is the case with other works. Probably the most attractive of all such opportunities that I have noted in casual reading is the unpublished manuscript of the first imitation of an Italian commedia: Enea Silvio's *Chrysis* in the National Library at Prague.[31] Wolfgang Stammler calls attention to some interesting manuscript comment on the Seven Liberal Arts in *Cod. lat. mon. 3941.*[32] He ran into it when investigating the origins of the Dance of Death. Few books have had the title "first" applied to them in so many ways as Conrad Celtis' *Ludus Diane, in modum Comedie coram Maximiliano Rhomanorum Rege Kalende Martiiss et ludis saturnalibus Danubii actus* (1501). It is one of the earliest plays by a living author to appear in print and is "quite certainly the first to contain the music performed on this occasion." It has been called the first German opera and the first German comedy, and the text has been described as the first libretto to be printed. These descriptions raise questions—we need not stop to answer them here—which make it imperative to know the book at first hand.[33] A modern edition—prefer-

---

[29] Compare also Paul van Tieghem, *Répertoire chronologique de littérature moderne* (Paris, 1935-37). The reviews have not been altogether favorable. As an example of a list for a single country, compare [J. C. Ghosh], *Annals of English Literature, 1475-1925* (Oxford, 1935), which Brandl commends highly ([Herrig's] *Archiv,* CLXXI [1937], 226).

[30] The University of Chicago has the editions of 1700 and 1736. For a discussion of the author see E. Trunz, "Ambrosius Lobwasser, Humanistische Wissenschaft, kirchliche Dichtung und bürgerliches Weltbild im 16. Jahrhundert," *Altpreussiche Forschungen,* IX, (1932), 29-97.

[31] Beutler, pp. 13-14. See also Georg Voigt, *Die Wiederbelebung des classischen Altertums* (3d ed.; Berlin, 1893), II, 409. Voigt describes the *Chrysis* as a Terentian comedy marred by obscenity.

[32] *Die Totentänze des Mittelalters* ("Einzelschriften zur Bücher- und Handschriftenkunde des Mittelalters," IV; Munich, 1922), p. 34.

[33] I should call *Ludus Diane* a pageant. No one has undertaken to discuss the authenticity of the ascription of the *Ludus Diane* to Celtis, and probably the doubts raised more than a century ago (*Allgemeiner literarischer Anzeiger,* IV [1799],

ably a facsimile—will serve many scholars. Upon such an edition, there will follow as a matter of course the correct appraisal of the *Ludus Diane.*

I could go on listing works which various historians have said ought to be printed, but I should not succeed in making clear how one ought to discover them. The reprinting of texts suggested by casual and random reading will not advance our knowledge as rapidly as the systematic study of a person, genre, or movement. Systematic study will almost immediately disclose texts which ought to be printed. For example, anyone who studies Meistergesang sees at once that the art was bound by rules. This is an essential characteristic of Meistergesang and if we are to understand Meistergesang, our knowledge of the rules must be more than superficial.[34] The student sees, furthermore, that Adam Puschman's *Gründlicher Bericht des deutschen Meistergesangs* (1571), the first code of rules to be printed, occupies an important position. He learns that the author revised the *Bericht* several times. Finally, he sees that these revisions, of which one was actually printed in 1596, have never been reprinted or even compared with the first edition.[35] So, too, one might reprint the four pages of Hans Winter's *Ein kurtzgefasster Bericht von der alten löblichen Kunst des teutschen Meister-Gesangs.*[36] This was written at Nuremberg in 1625, just after the bitter dispute over

---

311-312) do not need to be laid. Since this was written, Virginia Gingerich has prepared an edition of the *Ludus Diane* for the *Germanic Review.*

An account of German pageantry is greatly to be desired. It will naturally find much to imitate in Robert Withington's *English Pageantry; an historical outline* (Cambridge, Mass., 1918-20). The brief study of S. Sieber, *Volksbelustigungen bei deutschen Kaiserkrönungen* (Leipzig diss.; Frankfurt a.M., 1911), may serve as a starting-point. A sixteenth-century compendium is Franciscus Modius, *Pandecta triumphales, sive pomparum, et festorum ac solennium apparatuum, conviviorum spectaculorum, simulacrorum bellicorum equestrium et pedestrium* (Frankfurt am Main, 1586), issued in two volumes and adorned with woodcuts by Jost Amman. Maximilian I will occupy a conspicuous place in the survey of German pageantry, and discussion of the pageants inspired by him will supply useful materials.

[34] Since I am here concerned with the problem of publishing wisely chosen texts and not with the problem of this history of the rules of Meistergesang, I have passed immediately to the printed texts of the rules. I have elsewhere called attention to the problem of defining the rules of Meistergesang by the study of allusions to the rules in the writings of the early Meistersinger; see my *Literary History of Meistergesang* (New York, 1937), pp. 49-50.

[35] Several versions have been printed. See Archer Taylor and F. H. Ellis, *A Bibliography of Meistergesang* ("Indiana University Studies," XXIII; Bloomington, Ind., 1936), p. 62.

[36] August Hartmann, *Deutsche Meisterlieder-Handschriften in Ungarn* (Munich, 1894), p. 60, no. 15. Thanks to the kindness of the Hungarian National Museum

the acceptance or rejection of new metrical principles had ended in rejecting the principles of Martin Opitz. Perhaps even more interesting would be a study of the rules printed at Memmingen in 1660.[37] In them, Meistergesang sought to adjust itself to the current fashions in verse and to recognized French models. Or, to state another group of problems, consider how little we know of characteristic periods in the poetic activity of Hans Sachs. The quantity of verse which he wrote before 1520 is inconsiderable, but it is scarcely known to us. An edition of this verse would give a firm foundation for the understanding of his ideas before he met and accepted the Reformation. Continuing the same manner of thinking, the student of Hans Sachs learns not without surprise that "Die wittenbergisch Nachtigall," the Meisterlied in which Hans Sachs celebrated his acceptance of the new ideas, has never been printed. Finally, the student learns that Hans Sachs lost interest in Meistergesang about 1556 and that, although materials for the interpretation of his change of heart are within reach, no one has endeavored to interpret them.[38] Such logical and natural procedures as these lead us to the discovery of texts worthy of special study or new editions.

MINOR PROBLEMS IN STUDYING AN AUTHOR'S LIFE AND WORKS

In the critical study of an author preparatory to a comprehensive account of his life and works, many minor problems call for solution. Obviously these minor problems vary in character. The author's life, friends, and circumstances, or his source, language, style, editions, and influence—all may raise questions as yet unanswered. Adolf Hauffen's exhaustive biography of Johann Fischart exemplifies a synthesis of a myriad of special studies. With it as a model, the student perceives how the results of a minor investigation fit into a larger scheme. After all, the ultimate aim of the literary historian is synthesis and interpretation, and the investigation of such minor problems as I shall name in the following pages is but threshing dry straw unless its use and value are clearly seen.

16. *Authenticity and Ascriptions.*—Perhaps first in importance among the problems concerning an author's life and works is establishing what he wrote.[39] Writings of the late fifteenth and sixteenth centuries

---

and Dr. John A. Honti, I have a photostat of these pages. Dr. Carl P. Klitzke has undertaken to edit them.

[37] Archer Taylor, *The Literary History of Meistergesang* (New York, 1937), p. 51.

[38] See above, pp. 50-51.

[39] See the discussion in Morize, pp. 157-193, Ch. VII, "Problems of Authenticity and Attribution."

were frequently circulated under false names or pseudonyms, and authors did not always claim or acknowledge their compositions. Max Herrmann calls attention to an interesting and important problem in the authorship of the anonymous eulogy of Nuremberg (*Sag von Nürnberg, ca.* 1424).[40] According to Herrmann, the concluding rhyme *gut : mut* suggests that the name of Hans Rosenplut has been eliminated. A comparison of the language of the eulogy with Rosenplüt's linguistic habits might either confirm or deny his authorship. To be sure, the matter is by no means as simple as it seems, for the name "Rosenplüt" or "Rosenplut" is said to be occasionally attached to unauthentic verses. Furthermore, the examples of Rosenplüt's signature collected by Michels indicate that the name was Rosenplüt, not Rosenplut. The matter should be discussed and, if possible, settled, because the eulogy appears to have been written by one who was not a native of Nuremberg. Demme draws the pertinent inference for the life of Rosenplüt from this fact, but seems not to have looked sharply enough at the foundations. Establishing authenticity or non-authenticity of the poem would, moreover, illuminate the history of the genre as well as the life of Rosenplüt. The *Sag von Nürnberg* is the oldest German example of a poem eulogizing a city.[41] The question of its authorship is important in the history of the genre.

Almost at the end of the sixteenth century, we find a poem accompanying a picture of Rostock which raises the question of the correctness of an ascription.[42] Although the poem bears the signature of Hans Sachs, it was published several years after his death. Furthermore, it does not appear in the various lists of his works compiled by the poet. Its authenticity has been denied, but a recent writer has again claimed it for Sachs. Comparison of this poem on Rostock with the undisputed poems on cities which we know that Sachs wrote might establish or refute its authenticity. The use of such stylistic comparisons is pertinent in the case of Hans Sachs, who wrote a number of undisputed poems of this sort, but it does not promise to be equally valuable in the discussion of the

[40] *Die Reception des Humanismus in Nürnberg* (Berlin, 1898), p. 18, n. 3. See also A. von Keller, Fastnachtspiele aus dem 15. Jahrhundert ("Bibliothek des Literarischen Vereins," XXX; Stuttgart, 1853), III, 1168-1171; V. Michels, *Studien über die ältesten deutschen Fastnachtspiele* ("Quellen und Forschungen zur Sprach- und Kulturgeschichte der germanischen Völker," LXXVII; Strassburg, 1896), pp. 123-126; J. Demme, *Studien über Hans Rosenblüt* (Diss.; Münster, 1906), pp. 15, 25-27. On poems eulogizing a city see below pp. 117-123 and Appendix IV.

[41] The two Latin poems celebrating Iglau appear to have no connection with the later development of the genre. See below pp. 121-122.

[42] See H. Giske, "Ueber den Hans Sachs zugeschriebenen Lobspruch auf die Stadt Rostock," *Archiv für Literaturgeschichte*, X (1881), 13-34.

ascription to Hans Rosenplüt. Such choice and adaptation of the means to the case in hand must be made in every study of this sort.

Only writers and works significant in cultural or literary history deserve the attention necessary to establish or refute an ascription. The authenticity of five Meisterlieder usually ascribed to Hans Folz is a case in point. The five Meisterlieder are the basis of the story which makes him the innovator of a new fashion in the art of Meistergesang;[43] consequently ascertaining the authorship of these verses or at least the place where they were written is a matter of importance to the literary historian. The problem is much more difficult than it seems at first sight, for it involves studying the dialect of Hans Folz in his authentic poems. Now, for this task we must have both a grammar of the dialect of Worms—and there is none—and some knowledge of the conventional rhymes of Meistergesang. Only when these matters have been cleared up, can we apply the methods of Zwierzina and Schauerhammer.

The *Bockspiel M. Luthers* (1531) has been assigned to Cochlæus and to Emser and, probably wrongly, to Murner.[44] Although the authorship has been the subject of some dispute and is therefore a confused question, it probably merits further study in view of the importance of the claimants. In this case, a minute knowledge of the historical aspects of the controversies associated with Luther would be pertinent to the discussion.

As a last example of discussions of ascriptions, I mention the hotly-disputed figure of Arigo, translator of Boccaccio's *Decameron*.[45] No one has satisfactorily identified him. Suffice it to say that one candidate is Heinrich Steinhöwel, a prolific translator in the second half of the fifteenth century. The tests used to prove or disprove his identity with Arigo might be used again in discussing Lutz Mackensen's suggestion that Steinhöwel was the anonymous translator of *Apollonius* (1471).[46]

[43] Archer Taylor, *The Literary History of Meistergesang* (New York, 1937), pp. 46-47, 65-66. I have overstated the case against the possibility of the verses being in the dialect of Nuremberg. Our ignorance of the conventional rhymes used by the Meistersinger should prevent us from making dogmatic assertions regarding the language of a particular Meisterlied.

[44] Wolf, I, 330-331, n. 1; Schottenloher, I, 507, nos. 11894-98.

[45] Stammler, p. 464 (note on p. 27), which mentions the fundamental study of Karl Drescher, *Arigo, der Uebersetzer des 'Decamerone' und der 'Fiore di Virtù'* ("Quellen und Forschungen zur Sprach- und Kulturgeschichte der germanischen Völker," LXXXVII; Strassburg, 1900). See also H. Kars, *Arigo* (Halle diss.; Osterwick-Harz, 1932).

[46] *Die deutschen Volksbücher* ("Forschungen zur deutschen Geistesgeschichte des Mittelalters und der Neuzeit," II; Leipzig, 1927), p. 45. For references to Steinhöwel's abilities as a translator see J. Nadler, *Literaturgeschichte der deutschen Stämme*, I (3d ed.; Regensburg, 1929), 558.

Roderich von Stintzing's casual suggestion[47] that Nikolaus von Wyle or Albrecht von Eyb translated the so-called *Belial* of Jacobus Palladini de Teramo might be examined. This work narrating a hypothetical suit brought by the Devil to obtain his "rights" enjoyed an enormous popularity throughout Europe from the end of the fourteenth to the beginning of the seventeenth century. Examination of this problem will involve largely stylistic matters rather than such linguistic, historical, or dogmatic matters as are pertinent in the other examples here mentioned.

The methods used in investigating and establishing the authorship of an anonymous or pseudonymous work will vary from case to case. Such distinguished studies in the ascription of texts of uncertain authorship as Paul Merker's assignment of *Eccius dedolatus* to Nicolaus Gerbel, Walther Brecht's summary of the theories about the writing of the *Epistolae obscurorum virorum,* and—belonging to a period somewhat later than ours,—Albert Köster's investigation of Kaspar Stieler and *Die geharnschte Venus* provide indications of the methods to be used.[48]

17. *Dedications of Books as Evidence of Personal Relationships.*— Much can be learned about the connections existing between writers of the sixteenth century from the often effusive dedications prefixed to their works.[49] The value of these dedications varies greatly from case to case,

---

[47] *Geschichte der populären Literatur des römisch-kanonischen Rechts in Deutschland am Ende des 15. und im Anfang des 16. Jahrhunderts* (Leipsig, 1867), p. 278. On the *Belial* see J. W. Spargo, *Virgil the Necromancer* ("Harvard Studies in Comparative Literature," X; Cambridge, Mass., 1934), p. 336, n. 46. J. Fey, *Albrecht von Eyb als Uebersetzer* (Diss.; Halle, 1888), does not mention Stintzing's suggestion.

[48] Paul Merker, *Der Verfasser des 'Eccius dedolatus' und anderer Reformationsdialoge; mit einem Beitrage zur Verfasserfrage der 'Epistolae obscurorum virorum'* ("Sächsische Forschungsinstitute in Leipzig, Forschungsinstitut für neuere Philologie," II, "Neugermanistisches Institut," I, i; Halle, 1923); see also the summary in J. H. Scholte, *Neophilologus,* XI (1926), 108-115; H. Rupprich, *Der 'Eckius dedolatus' und sein Verfasser* (Vienna, 1931); Otto Clemen, "Wer ist der Verfasser des 'Eccius dedolatus,' " *Archiv für Reformationsgeschichte,* XXIX (1932), 249-253; On the *Epistolæ* see Stammler, p. 471 (note on p. 63); Walther Brecht, *Die Verfasser der 'Epistolæ obscurorum virorum'* ("Quellen und Forschungen zur Sprach- und Culturgeschichte der germanischen Völker," XCIII; Strassburg, 1904); A. Bömer, "H. v. d. Busches Anteil an den 'Epistolæ obscurorum virorum,' " *Aus Vergangenheit und Gegenwart, Festgabe F. Philippi . . . gewidmet* (Münster i.W., 1923), pp. 86-99. For other examples of ascription see F. Behrend, *Ueber den Verfasser des 'Eselkönig'* (Diss.; Berlin, 1905), which assigns this work to W. Spangenberg; the discussion of Sebastian Frank's share in *Die Gelehrten, die Verkehrten* (see Wolf, II, 277); and Albert Köster, *Der Dichter der 'Geharnschten Venus'* (Marburg, 1897).

[49] Heinrich Meyer of the Rice Institute has kindly suggested this enterprise. The literature on dedications includes general works, e.g. E. M. Brown, *Dedications,*

but something can almost always be learned from them. A survey of this material is an enterprise implying a long stay in Germany. More modest tasks can contribute to our knowledge. For example, Paul Merker draws inferences of great significance to his argument for the existence of close relations between Vienna and Strassburg from dedicatory and eulogistic verses in Viennese publications in the years between 1512 and 1514.[50] Accordingly, we can say that studies in the dedications of books published at a particular time or written by a particular author are likely to disclose information of value. It is or should be obvious that such studies cannot be undertaken without some knowledge of the social and literary background and of the relations of the significant figures on the contemporary scene. To whom for example, are Sebastian Brant's works dedicated and what authors accompany these works with encomiastic verses? The answers to these questions might throw new light on Sebastian Brant, but it is clear that adequate answers imply interpretation of the facts. Dedications and encomiastic verses may reveal the connections of an author with one university or another and may thus enable us to understand and describe his intellectual back-

---

an *Anthology of the Forms Used From the Earliest Days of Bookmaking to the Present Time* (New York, 1913) ; studies in the theory and practice of dedications written in the eighteenth century (I have not noticed any from an earlier time), e.g., D. F. Ianus, *Dissertatio historica et litteraria de fatis dedicationum librorum* (Wittenberg, 1714) ; N. H. Gundlingius, "Praefatio de abusu dedicationum," *Observationes Halenses*, III, 1-48; J. C. Nemeiz, "Anmerckung von Dedicationen oder Zueignungs-Schriften," *Vernünfftige Gedancken über allerhand Materien*, II (Frankfurt a. M., 1739), 95-110; E. Silberradius, *Disputatio de dedicationum litterariarum moralitate* (Strassburg, 1714) ; F. P. Tackius, *Commentatio historica et litteraria de dedicationibus librorum, qua earum antiquitas, moralitas, varia genera, aliaque ad eas pertinentia, ob oculos ponuntur* (Wolfenbüttel, 1733) ; and, finally, studies in the dedications of classical works, e.g. J. G. Walch, "Diatribe de dedicationibus librorum veterum latinorum" in C. Cellarius, *Epistolae et Praefationes* (ed. J. G. Walch; Leipzig, 1715), pp. 1-112; J. Ruppert, *Quaestiones ad historiam dedicationis librorum pertinentes* (Diss.; Leipzig, 1911). These references I owe to John W. Spargo; I have not seen the books themselves. We can see what a collection of dedications might look like in W. C. Hazlitt (ed.), Henry Huth, *Prefaces, Dedications, and Epistles, Selected From Early English Books, 1540-1701. With Indexes of Names and Subjects*, which was privately printed in 1874 in 50 copies. Leicester Bradner gives me a good example of a study dealing with dedications, viz., W. D. Macray, "Early Dedications to Englishmen by Foreign Authors and Editors," *Bibliographica*, I (London, 1895), 324-347, 455-473.

[50] *Der Verfasser des 'Eccius dedolatus' und anderer Reformationsdialoge* ("Sächsische Forschungsinstitute in Leipzig, Forschungsinstitut für neuere Philologie, II, Neugermanistische Abteilung," 1; Halle, 1923), pp. 247-249. Much of Merker's argument is based on references in contemporary letters, but enough evidence is found in dedications to illustrate the point which is made in the text.

ground. The atmosphere of Erfurt, for example, was altogether different from that of Heidelberg, and if we can use the names occurring in dedications to show that an author has maintained active relations with say Erfurt, we have gained a useful bit of information.

18. *The Characterization and History of a Book.*—The bibliographical description, and the characterization in the light of cultural history of a rare or significant book is often a useful contribution to the stock-in-trade of the literary historian. Thus, for example, Friedrich Zarncke[51] sought vainly for the edition of the *Narrenschiff* published at Zürich in 1563, for it is said that it varies curiously from the other editions. With the so-called *Adagia* (Paris, 1500), Erasmus began a new epoch in the use of proverbial and sententious material.[52] The first edition—a very rare book indeed—should be analyzed and compared with later editions. Its influence on the purposes, methods, and ideals of similar work in the sixteenth century should be estimated. The study might begin with a discussion of the contents and sources of the first edition, proceed through the many enlargements issued during the author's life, and conclude with analyses of the revisions made in consequence of the criticisms of the Council of Trent (1545) and the greatly enlarged redaction of Paulus Manutius (1578). These and other changes modified considerably the nature of the *Adagia*. As to the difficult question of the sources, is it significant that Erasmus edited the moralizing verses of the *Disticha Catonis* in 1514, during the time when the *Adagia* were undergoing alteration and enlargement? The importance of the *Adagia* in interpreting the culture of the sixteenth century can scarcely be overrated. It was the most popular book of the age, reaching perhaps one hundred and twenty editions. It was at one and the same time a guide for writers, a manual of style, a dictionary of synonyms, a storehouse of illustrative tales, a florilegium of classical Greek and Latin literature, and an encyclopedia of sententious moralizing. A detailed

---

[51] (Ed.), *Sebastian Brants Narrenschiff* (Leipzig, 1854), pp. xci-ii.

[52] For the present, the best appraisal of the *Adagia* and the various editions is W. H. D. Suringar, *Erasmus over Nederlandsche spreekwoorden* (Utrecht, 1873), pp. iii, n. 1, viii, n. 1. For criticism of the first edition see W. Stirling-Maxwell, *Miscellaneous Essays* (London, 1891), pp. 51-53. Compare the general comment on the *Adagia* in Wolf, I, 353-355. For the bibliography and circulation of the *Adagia* see *Bibliotheca Erasmiana* (Ghent, 1897-1908), a reprint from the *Bibliotheca Belgica,* especially F. van der Haeghen, *Bibliographie des oeuvres d'Erasme: Adagia, Apophthegmata* (Ghent, 1897-1901), and L. Enthoven, "Ueber Druck und Vertrieb Erasmischer Werke," *Neue Jahrbücher für das klassische Altertum,* XXVIII (1911), 33-59. I have a photostat of the first edition (1500) ; the University of Chicago Library has various early editions, e.g., Strassburg, 1515; Basel, 1518; Venice, 1520; Basel, 1520; Basel, 1533, and several later editions.

account of so influential a work is greatly to be desired and might lead to an estimate and interpretation of the value of the *Adagia* to its age. Luther uses images from the *Adagia* again and again. It may be possible to identify them in writings of Nicodemus Frischlin or Johann Fischart, and such popular writers as Burkhard Waldis and Erasmus Alberus may have drawn on the *Adagia*. Except for the earliest editions, copies of the *Adagia* may be purchased at surprisingly low prices.[53]

Johann Neander of Bremen wrote, as I have read, the most serious and most informative of early books on tobacco (1622). What, then, was the background of this book? On what sources did Neander draw? What effect, if any, did his book have? In England, a king condemned the use of tobacco and the subject of tobacco has ever since interested everyone. What is the nature of the lesser interest in tobacco in Germany?[54] Questions of this sort are easily asked. Although drinking is a traditional fault of the Germans, I cannot point to a satisfactory study of the history of the tradition about it or a good account of the attitudes toward drinking in the century of the Reformation.[55] In this place, where I am dealing with the characterization of a book, I cannot examine these questions more closely.

Two works by Abbot Johannes Trithemius, a patriotic German humanist, review the current literature of the late fifteenth century and survey the older periods.[56] They are at the same time biographical dictionaries, bibliographies, and literary histories. A critical estimate of their value and significance need not go far beyond the covers of the books. Problems in the sources of Trithemius are more difficult. Particularly interesting are his remarks on Otfrid von Weissenburg, for he may have known a

---

[53] Compare, e.g., F. Sánchez y Escribano, "Algunos aspectos de la elaboración de la 'Philosophía vulgar,'" *Revista de filología española*, XXII (1935), 274-284. A careful comparison of the various editions of the *Adagia* with the Spanish texts would probably clarify the relationships. See M. Bataillon, *Erasme et l'Espagne, Recherches sur l'histoire spirituelle du XVIᵉ siècle* (Paris, 1937).

[54] See, e.g., H[offmann] v[on] F[allersleben], "Der Tabak in der deutschen Literatur," *Weimarisches Jahrbuch für deutsche Sprache*, II (1855), 243-260; V. Wendel, *Pegasus in Tabakwolken. Deutsche Räuchergedichte vom 30-jährigen Krieg bis zur Gegenwart* (Leipzig, 1934). I have not seen P. Ssymank, "Der deutsche Student und das Tabakrauchen," *Der Tabak*, II (1938), 1-18.

[55] A starting-point for this study might be the tracts "De ebrietate" and "Ad virgines de ebrietate et sobrietate" in the pseudo-Augustinian *De anima et spiritu*, for which see, e.g., *Gesamtkatalog der Wiegendrucke*, III, 130-131, no. 2936. See the references collected in A. Hauffen, *Vierteljahrschrift für Litteraturgeschichte*, VI (1893), 174-175, n.21.

[56] *Catalogus illustrium virorum* (Mainz, 1495) in the University of Chicago Library; *De scriptoribus ecclesiaticis* (Basel, 1494) in the Newberry Library.

manuscript now lost. Discussion of the sources and comparison of his methods and purposes with those of later works are problems too difficult to recommend here.[57] In the choice of his titles Trithemius is continuing an old tradition.[58] The *De illustribus viris* by St. Jerome should, the author said, have been called *De scriptoribus ecclesiasticis,* and Trithemius uses both of these titles. The existence of a tradition appears in the use of *De scriptoribus ecclesiasticis* by Isidor of Seville, Ildefonsus, Archbishop of Toledo, Sigebert of Gembloux, and Henricus Gandavensis (Henricus Goethals of Ghent). The incipit, moreover, of Trithemius' *De illustribus viris* contains the variant title *De luminaribus,* which echoes the *De luminaribus ecclesiae* of Honorius Augustodunensis. Such details as these contribute to our appreciation of the background of Trithemius' works.

19. *Comparison of the Adaptations of a Book.*—When preparing a full account of an author's life and works, one will start wisely by comparing the varying editions of his more important writings. If the editions were issued during the author's lifetime and under his supervision, the comparison will throw light on him and his way of thinking. If the editions appeared without his knowledge or cooperation, the comparison may disclose how his book was received or understood. Obviously, we need consider, in cases of posthumous or unauthorized publication, only the variants of passages offering difficulties in interpretation. Since Sebastian Brant's *Narrenschiff* (1494) was one of the most significant and widely-read books of its age, Hans van Ghetelen's Low German adaptation (1497) and an anonymous revision (1519) ought to be examined for evidences of the way in which the original was received.[59] Burkhard Waldis' edition (1553) of Emperor Maximilian's *Teuerdanck* (1517) informs us about the reviser and the attitude of his age toward chivalry.[60] It is curious that an outspoken Hessian Protestant

---

[57] As an introduction see F. W. E. Roth, "Studien zum Johann Trithemius—Jubeljahr (1516) 1916," *Studien und Mitteilungen zur Geschichte des Benediktinerordens,* XXXVII (1916), 265-301. This excellent summary is the basis for further investigation and supersedes I. Silbernagl, *Johannes Trithemius* (2d ed.; Ratisbon, 1885). For the special problem discussed here see F. Falk, "Kommentar zu des Trithemius 'Catalogus scriptorum ecclesiasticorum,'" *Zentralblatt für Bibliothekswesen,* XV (1898), 112-124.

[58] For the following see T. Bestermann, *The Beginnings of Systematic Bibliography,* (2d ed.; Oxford, 1936), p. 4.

[59] Stammler, p. 196. Revised editions and translations are often invaluable aids in interpreting difficult passages. They tell us what contemporaries thought the text meant.

[60] C. Breuer, "Die Fassungen des Teuerdanck," *Zeitschrift für deutsches Altertum,* LXVII (1930), 177-196. A study by K. Ries—*Die Bearbeitung des 'Teuer-*

of bourgeois origin should choose to reissue the work of an Austrian Catholic emperor inspired by medieval chivalry. Comparing the early editions of Dedekind's *Grobianus* (1549) or, still better, Caspar Scheit's translation (1552) with the condensation published in the *Renovierte Hobelbank* (1660) would perhaps throw light on the changes in morals during a much troubled century.[61] In *Nebulo nebulonum*,[62] Johannes Flittner greatly alters the intent of his source, Murner's *Schelmenzunft*, by adopting the style and appearance of an emblem-book and the technique of the collections of adagia. A comparison of the two versions would be instructive and might be extended to include the German translation of Flittner's Latin text.

20. *The Sequence of an Author's Works.*—The sequence of an author's works often reveals his intellectual development or discloses his relations and reactions to his age.[63] In medieval and post-medieval literature, we find many works which bear no immediately apparent date, and thus arises the problem of establishing their chronology. A critical understanding of a writer is possible only if we know when and under what circumstances a work was composed and what writings preceded and followed it. Much of the study of Shakespeare, for example, has dealt with the order in which he wrote his plays. Problems of this sort naturally arise in studying authors of major importance. For the most part, the writings of Martin Luther are sufficiently well dated. The circumstances, however, in which he wrote "Ein feste Burg," the triumphant summary of Protestant faith, have long been a subject of

---

danck' durch B. Waldis (Diss.; Heidelberg, 1921)—was never printed. Entirely linguistic is T. Heppner, *Die Laut- und Flexionsverhältnisse in B. Waldis' Bearbeitung des Teuerdanck im Verhältnis zu denen des Originals* (Munich diss.; Erlangen, 1907).

[61] Compare also Hans Sachs's use of Grobianus: E. F. Clark, "The 'Grobianus' of Sachs and its predecessors," *Journal of English and Germanic Philology*, XVI (1917), 390-96. *Grobianus* had a rebirth in the eighteenth century: *Ludwig Tölpels ganz funkel nagel neue Bauern Moral, mit einem lächerlichen Wörterbuch vermehret* ([Stettin in Ulm], 1752).

[62] See Goedeke, *Grundriss*, II, 117, no. 241 for mention of editions of 1610 and 1663. My copy is dated 1620. For the German translation of Flittner see Goedeke, II, 117, no. 20 and III, 239, no. 19. The University of Chicago Library has a German translation of Flittner dated 1665 which does not seem to be known to Goedeke.

The sub-title of Flittner's book, viz. "Iocoseria modernae nequitiae censura carmine iambico," suggests to A. Hauffen (*Vierteljahrschrift für Litteraturgeschichte*, VI [1893], 167, n. 9) the existence of a minor variety of humorous and satiricial writings defined by the name "Iocoseria." He does not comment on the similarity of this name to *Schimpf und Ernst*, on which see below, pp. 100-101.

[63] For a description of the problem see Morize, pp. 132-156.

dispute.[64] Some put it in 1521, others in 1523 or 1524, others in 1527, and still others in 1528. G. Wolfram[65] even puts it in 1529 and finds in it a reference to the dangers threatened by the Turks. A fresh study of the problem is too difficult to undertake, for it was not solved in a book of six hundred pages! In a period a little earlier than that dealt with in this essay falls the unsolved problem of the sequence of Der Pleier's three long Arthurian romances. Scholars agree in putting *Garel von dem blühenden Tal* first, but disagree about the order of *Tandareis* and *Meleranz.* The studies which dealt with the order of Hartmann von Aue's works will suggest methods for investigating Der Pleier.[66]

In a rather long work, we can often perceive stages in its composition. Morize describes how to learn from Montaigne's essays their approximate dates.[67] Zarncke has discovered the two chief stages in the writing of Brant's *Narrenschiff.*[68] At first, Brant had no idea of writing a book. He issued a number of broadsides, each describing individual fools, illustrated with a woodcut. When these met with approval, he collected them, relating them by the notion of a ship bearing fools to Narragonia. A more detailed analysis of the *Narrenschiff* is conceivable, but is too difficult and uncertain to recommend here. Comparable is Gustav Roethe's analysis of the *Urfaust.*[69] We know that Goethe wrote down at various times the ideas which he intended to use. Roethe undertakes to identify the separate passages, to date them, and to show what verses were composed to tie the earlier passages together. Although specialists in Goethe have not accepted Roethe's results, his methods are instructive —all the more so since they are applied by a scholar of great ability to a monument within the horizon of every student of German literature.

[64] Schottenloher, I, 531-533, nos. 12413, 12417, 12425 (compare the important review in *Göttingische gelehrte Anzeigen,* CLXVIII [1906], i, 257-298), and the special bibliography of no less than fifty-seven items in Schottenloher, I, 533-535, nos. 12, 455-511; W. Maurer and H. Hermelink, *Reformation und Gegenreformation* ("Handbuch der Kirchengeschichte," III; 2d ed.; Tübingen, 1931), p. 106; Wolf, II, 215, n. 1.

[65] *Eine feste Burg ist unser Gott. Die Entstehungszeit und der ursprüngliche Sinn des Lutherliedes* (Berlin, 1936).

[66] See G. Ehrismann, *Geschichte der deutschen Literatur bis zum Ausgang des Mittelalters,* II, ii, 1 (Munich, 1926), 146, n. 1. More recent studies are E. Sievers, "Zur äusseren und inneren Chronologie der Werke Hartmanns von Aue," *Festgabe Philipp Strauch zum 80. Geburtstage* ("Hermaea," XXXI, Halle, 1932), pp. 53-66; H. Sparnaay, *Hartmann von Aue; Studien zu einer Biographie,* I (Halle, 1933).

[67] Pp. 143-156.

[68] "Zur Vorgeschichte des Narrenschiffes," *Serapeum,* XXIX (1868), 49-54, and *Zur Vorgeschichte des Narrenschiffes; 2. Mitteilung* (Leipzig, 1871).

[69] "Die Entstehung des 'Urfaust,'" *Sitzungsberichte der preussischen Akademie der Wissenschaften,* 1920, pp. 642-678.

In the study of the literary works of our period, Spanier's effort to establish the order in which Murner wrote the *Narrenbeschwörung* and the *Schelmenzunft* illustrates the problem once more.[70] His results have been disputed. As an example of the ways and means of dating a text very exactly compare Gustave Arlt's "Conclusions" regarding the composition of Johann Meier von Eck's *Schiff des Heils*.[71] Such exactness as this is rarely possible in dealing with texts of our period. Only when an author produced works related among themselves and involving illusions to political or historical events, can we successfully attain such results.

21. *Problems in Typography and Printing.*—Closely related to the bibliographical studies just described are questions which arise in the fields of printing and typography. Occasionally, these questions can be answered with the materials available to us in America. Thus, for example, Gustave Arlt has identified the section removed by the printer from the German edition of Johannes Geiler's sermons on Brant's *Narrenschiff*, and explained the curious errors in its foliation.[72] The life of Geiler which had been allowed to circulate in Latin contained passages so critical of the church that a German translation would have been dangerous. In all of the known copies of Johannes Geiler von Kaiserberg's *Sermones praestantissimi* (1514), signature B is lacking.[73] This seems to be true also of the variant form entitled *Sermones . . . fructuosissimi De arbore humana* (1519). This defect in two issues belonging to rather widely separated years, and the fact that the signature was removed after both issues had been fully printed and perhaps even circulated, raise the hope that a perfect copy may yet be found. No gap appears to exist in the German translation called *Das buoch Arbore humana* (1520), but the bibliographers do not make clear how the gap was hidden. It is not likely that we can discover what the missing signature contained or what circumstances attended its removal, but these enterprises are worth trying.

The discovery of problems in printing and typography is more or less a matter of chance for the student of literature, and solving them

---

[70] "Ueber Murner's 'Narrenbeschwörung' und 'Schelmenzunft,' " *Beiträge zur Geschichte der deutschen Sprache,* XVIII (1894), 1-71. For contradictory opinions see Wolf, I, 334, n. 3.

[71] "Indiana University Studies," XIX-XX (Bloomington, Indiana, 1932-33), pp. 19-22.

[72] "The Foliation of Geiler von Kaisersberg's 'Narrenschiff,' " *Modern Philology,* XXVIII (1931), 271-279.

[73] L. Dacheux, *Les plus anciens écrits de Geiler de Kaysersberg* (Colmar, 1882), pp. cxxiv-cxxv.

depends upon accurate knowledge of the methods of printers. To be sure, one can acquire the necessary special information readily enough, but the student of German literary history has no such satisfactory guide as R. B. McKerrow, *An Introduction to Bibliography for Literary Students*.[74] A pamphlet by the Alsatian teacher and humanist Jakob Wimpfeling entitled *De arte impressoria* (1507) appears to have been lost in very recent times;[75] it would tell us much about these matters. As an example of a problem in the methods of printers, consider the four editions of Dedekind's *Grobianus* issued in 1549. Although they have already been examined with some care, the order in which they appeared has not been settled.[76] The claims of the edition issued by Egenolph in 1549 appear to be superior to those of any other edition, and the modern editors have accepted Hauffen's conclusions. A re-examination of the differences in the four editions might perhaps change our opinions, but the reward would be out of proportion to the labor involved. The question is typical nonetheless of problems in typography and the chronology of editions.

22. *The Interpretation of the Text.*—We must understand the mean-

[74] Oxford, 1927. Compare K. Schottenloher, *Das alte Buch* ("Bibliothek für Kunst- und Antiquitätensammler," XIV; 2d ed.; Berlin, 1921); H. Bohatta, *Einführung in die Buchkunde* (2d ed.; Vienna, 1928).

As an example of a minute examination of an old book compare E. E. Willoughby, *The Printing of the First Folio of Shakespeare* ("Supplement to the Bibliographical Society's Transactions," VIII; Oxford, 1932). German studies of a similar nature may be found in the Weimar edition of Luther. A Götze, "Die 12 Artikel der Bauern 1525," *Historische Vierteljahrsschrift*, V (1902), 1-33, is linguistic rather than bibliographical. A better example is G. Bauch, "Die Urdrucke der 'Epistolae obscurorum virorum,'" *Zentralblatt für Bibliothekswesen,* XV (1898), 297-327, and compare Stammler, p. 471 (note on p. 63).

A. Götze, *Hochdeutsche Drucker der Reformationszeit* (Leipzig, 1905), and specialized studies like K. Schottenloher, *Philipp Ulhart, ein Augsburger Winkeldrucker und Helfershelber der "Schwärmer" und "Wiedertäufer"* ("Historische Forschungen und Quellen," IV, Munich, 1921), contain useful information.

[75] See J. Knepper, *Jakob Wimpfeling* ("Erläuterungen und Ergänzungen zu Janssens 'Geschichte des deutschen Volkes,'" III, 2-4; Freiburg i.Br., 1902), p. 236; K. Hartfelder, *Ungedruckte deutsche Uebersetzungen klassischer Schriftsteller aus dem Heidelberger Humanistenkreis* (Programm; Heidelberg, 1884), p. 4. Hans Rupprich seems to imply that the *De arte impressoria* is extant; see *Humanismus und Renaissance in den deutschen Städten* ("Deutsche Literatur"; Leipzig, 1935), p. 13.

[76] See Gustav Milchsack's preface to the German translation in "Neudrucke deutscher Literaturwerke des 16. und 17. Jahrhunderts," XXXIV-XXXV (Halle, 1882), pp. xiv-xv; Aloys Bömer's preface to the Latin original in "Lateinische Litteraturdenkmäler des 15. und 16. Jahrhunderts," XVI (Berlin, 1903), pp. lxxvii-lxxviii. There are two copies of Egenolph's edition of 1549 in the University of Chicago Library.

ing of the text. It might seem unnecessary to make so obvious a remark, but a brief examination of Sebastian Brant's *Narrenschiff*, probably the most fully annotated text of the fifteenth or sixteenth centuries, discloses many obscurities. Take, for example, the allusion in

> Eyn krut das hat solch krafft, vnd gwalt
> Glych wie die salb ym Alabaster
> Dar vsz die scherer all jr plaster
> Machent.[77]

It puzzled Friedrich Zarncke and Karl Goedeke. They left it unexplained, and no one has since commented on the passage. More troublesome is the phrase "Hye zwischen Ach," which seems to mean "nowhere."[78] Brant's allusion to Hercules is far from clear, and an explanation of it might throw light on his sources.[79] The *Narrenschiff* offers many examples of confusion regarding the names and details of Biblical and classical story; diligent search in contemporary writings might disclose how Brant fell into these errors. Friedrich Zarncke often calls attention to these difficulties[80] and tells where he has looked in vain for an explanation. The interpretation of Brant's comments on hunting —a problem which has already been noted above[81]—occupied Zarncke and Goedeke, but they left some puzzling words without adequate explanations. Single phrases often present interesting and unsolved difficulties. What, for example, does the phase "Uf sant Zilorgentag" in a Swiss historical song of 1335 mean?[82]

Failure to understand the meaning of a word or phrase can easily

[77] Ch. lv, ll. 16 ff. The salve in alabaster is probably the salve with which the unnamed woman annoints the feet of Jesus in the house of Simon the leper at Bethania (Mt. 26:6; Mk. 14:3. St. John, 12:3, calls her Mary, but does not mention the box of alabaster). Brant seems to have a specific allusion in mind.

[78] *Narrenschiff*, Ch. lxxx, 1. 24. I have commented on the phrase in *Journal of American Folk-Lore*, XLVII (1934), 11.

[79] *Narrenschiff*, Ch. lxxv, 54. Friedrich von Bezold's interesting book, *Das Fortleben der antiken Götter im mittelalterlichen Humanismus* (Bonn, 1922) does not comment on this point. Douglas Bush has written similar studies on English literature. Comparison of methods will suggest new problems to the attentive reader.

[80] See, e.g., Demades and Phythias (X, 13), Dalide (XIII, 68), Holofernes (XVI, 55), and Achor (XX, 23). I have selected these examples from the notes to the first twenty chapters.

[81] P. 43.

[82] Rochus Freiherr von Liliencron *Die historischen Volkslieder der Deutschen*, I (Leipzig, 1865), 44, 1. 10; Archer Taylor, "'Niemals' in einem historischen Schweizer Volkslied," *Volkskundliche Gaben John Meier zum 70. Geburtstage dargebracht* (Berlin, 1934), p. 281. Fritz Frauchiger has found what seems to be the correct explanation of the phrase; see *Modern Language Notes*, LIII (1938), 508.

lead to serious errors. It might seem unnecessary to point out that even the best of scholars have erred, but I do so in order to encourage the beginner to form his own opinions and to avoid the unquestioning acceptance of those of others. A distinguished scholar's inferences from the phrase "den armen Judas singen" are a case in point. Since the phrase means "to be humiliated" or "to suffer disgrace" as in the description of Faust's death in the *Faustbuch,* it can scarcely be used to prove that ecclesiastical songs were widely sung. The annotations in one of the most easily accessible editions of Hans Sachs contain elementary mistakes, and there is a bad slip in one of the most highly esteemed editions of a classical work in our period. "Quandoque bonus dormitat Homerus" is a venerable proverb, and it would be ungracious to call attention to flaws which the careful reader will perceive.

Johann Fischart took over and greatly expanded the list of games recited by Rabelais. This German list has been interpreted,[83] but the corresponding passage in Urquhart and Motteux's English translation offers many a hard nut which no one has attempted to crack. Although the problem is readily perceived, its solution is not easy. Possibly comparison with the picture of children's games painted by Pieter Breughel the Elder might throw light on the games.[84] His similar picture composed of scenes representing proverbs has been studied several times, but still contains unsolved puzzles.[85]

[83] H. A. Rausch, "Die Spiele der Jugend aus Fischarts Gargantua. cap. XXV," *Jahrbuch für Geschichte, Sprache und Literatur Elsass-Lothringens,* XXIV (1908), 53-145. This article is also a doctoral dissertation and was reviewed a number of times.

[84] Perhaps the most conveniently accessible reproduction is that in J. W. P. Drost, *Het Nederlandsch kinderspel vóór de zeventiende eeuw* (The Hague, 1914). Compare Charles de Tolnay, *Pierre Breugel l'ancien* (Brussels, 1935). The promised article in the *Jahrbuch für Spiel- und Sportforschung,* I (1935), has not yet appeared, and the journal appears to be uncertain of existence. See K. Haiding, "Das Spielbild Pieter Bruegels," *Bausteine zur Geschichte, Völkerkunde und Mythologie,* VI (1937), 58-74. On the genre see the preface by F. Winkler on the "Sittenbild" in Anon., *Der Leipziger Valerius Maximus* (Leipzig, 1921). Particularly valuable is J. Bolte, "Zeugnisse zur Geschichte unserer Kinderspiele," *Zeitschrift des Vereins für Volkskunde,* XIX (1909), 381-414, which contains (p. 395) a list of paintings similar to that of Breughel.

[85] Archer Taylor, *The Proverb* (Cambridge, Mass., 1931), p. 182. A. Götze reviews W. Fraenger, *Der Bauern-Breughel und das deutsche Sprichwort* (Erlenbach-Zürich, n.d. [1923]) in *Anzeiger für deutsches Altertum,* XLIII (1924), 144-145 and calls attention to some of the unexplained scenes. See also L. Maeterlinck, "Nederlandsche spreekwoorden handelnd voorgesteld door Pieter Breughel den Oude," *Verslagen en mededeelingen der Koninklijke Vlaamsche academie voor taal- en letterkunde,* 1903, pp. 109-129. Jan Graul wrote a pamphlet of 11 pages to accompany a photographic reproduction of Breughel's picture issued in 1937 by Gevart, Oude God, Amsterdam; this I have not yet seen.

CHAPTER III

PROBLEMS IN THE LITERARY HISTORY
OF A GENRE

THE genres and types of post-medieval German literature have not been adequately discussed by literary historians. Although a literary history of a genre or type might seem to be quite as difficult a problem as a thorough biographical study, it is really simpler.

In studying the history of a genre or type, one can ordinarily assemble a fairly satisfactory series of representative texts in modern editions. The gaps in such a series can then be filled by obtaining photographs of the necessary texts. Fortunately, the notable examples of certain genres are already available in good reprints. For example, the existing editions of fifteenth- and sixteenth-century folk-song and lyric verse are almost adequate for the needs of the literary historian. A large part of medieval drama, particularly in the oldest period, has been reissued; the same is true of the jest-books of the late fourteenth and early fifteenth centuries. Later I shall deal with these matters at greater length. It is sufficient to indicate here that a good deal of spade-work has already been accomplished for certain genres. The accessibility of the materials should encourage the student to undertake a review and estimate.

In the following illustrations of problems in the literary history of a genre or type, I shall not attempt to give or even to suggest all the questions which one may ask. Stated in general terms, these questions are in the main the same for every genre. What conventions in form and matter characterize the genre? What are its beginnings? What are its relations to contemporary culture? What periods can we distinguish in its history? What writers are typical representatives of the various periods or of the transitions from one period to another? Can we trace the rise and decline of the genre or of certain aspects and conventions within it? Some undertakings may have a particular importance in the literary history of one genre and only a minor significance in that of another. Ordinarily, to be sure, the reprinting of texts is a matter of prime importance. In many instances, the compilation of satisfactory bibliographical tools is essential to rapid and efficient progress in the study of a genre. The following survey examines briefly problems in the literary history of various genres, and selects as illustrations the genres which exemplify a particular problem. My endeavor has been to illustrate the problems and not to supply a statement of all the problems in a single genre.

Such movements, genres, or types as mysticism, humanism, or Meistergesang, translations from Latin and Greek literatures, collections of proverbs and apophthegms, travel-books, chapbooks, and the like are easily defined and bounded by readily perceived limits. Although the master of German studies long ago blazed the trail, such subjects have been largely neglected by investigators in literary history. Jacob Grimm wrote *Ueber den altdeutschen Meistergesang*[1] and Joseph Görres *Die teutschen Volksbücher: nähere Würdigung der schönen Historien-, Wetter- und Arzneybüchlein, welche theils innerer Werth, theils Zufall, Jahrhunderte hindurch bis auf unsere Zeit erhalten hat.*[2] Ludwig Uhland left unfinished an essay on German folk-song.[3] Few have followed in the paths thus marked out, and these few belong to the generation which immediately followed upon Grimm, Görres, and Uhland. As examples, I name Leo Cholevius' *Die bedeutendsten deutschen Romane des siebzehnten Jahrhunderts*[4] and Felix Bobertag's *Geschichte des Romans und der ihm verwandten Dichtungsgattungen.*[5] For the most part, historians of German literature in the fifteenth and sixteenth centuries have avoided writing treatises on genres or types. They might profitably return to the models set by the founders of Germanic philology.

In the following pages, I select and describe problems in the more important genres of post-medieval German literature with the aim of illustrating the tasks of the literary historian. I shall not attempt to discuss any genre fully,[6] but pass from one genre to another, selecting apposite illustrations. After exemplifying the need for bibliographies and new editions, I call attention to such matters only casually. I begin with the history of the jest-book as representative of a variety of problems, e.g., identification and description of literary types, bibliographical and editorial desiderata, sources, style, and influence. The history of the drama provides examples in the literary history of a theme (*Stoffgeschichte*). The history of mysticism illustrates problems in tracing influences. The history of folk-song exemplifies problems in the use and

---

[1] Göttingen, 1811.

[2] Heidelberg, 1807.

[3] "Abhandlung über die deutschen Volkslieder," *Uhlands Schriften zur Geschichte der Dichtung und Sage,* III (Stuttgart, 1866), and also published as the second volume of his *Alte hoch- und niederdeutsche Volkslieder.*

[4] Leipzig, 1866.

[5] Three volumes, Berlin, 1881-84.

[6] See my discussion of problems in *The Literary History of Meistergesang.* In a sense, this discussion is complementary to the present essay.

survival of literary conventions. The histories of the city-poem and of Devil-literature illustrate problems in the origin of a genre. The history of handbooks on marriage illustrates the interrelations of literary and cultural history. Comparison of the various sections will readily disclose problems that I have not mentioned.

23. *The History of Various Minor Literary Genres.*—Before undertaking the study of typical problems in the history of literary genres, I shall mention several varieties of literary and semi-literary materials deserving of brief historical treatment. Although some of these materials lie on the borders of literature, they offer interesting problems to the student of literature and culture.

A survey of German (and Latin) saints' legends comparable to Gordon Hall Gerould's stimulating introduction to the English legends and Rudolf Kapp's detailed review extending to the end of the Elizabethan age is greatly to be desired.[7] To be sure, the task is huge and should be

[7] G. H. Gerould, *Saints' Legends* (Boston, 1916) ; R. Kapp, *Heilige und Heiligenlegenden in England; Studien zum 16. und 17. Jahrhundert,* I (Halle, 1934).

As an introduction to the German saints' legend, see Paul Merker, "Legende," in *Reallexikon der deutschen Literaturgeschichte,* II, 176-200; F. Wilhelm, *Deutsche Legenden und Legendare* (Leipzig, 1907). For bibliography see Arnold, p. 241; Dahlmann-Waitz, p. 204, nos. 3465-75.

The German dictionaries of saints are full and accurate. See, e.g., J. E. Stadler and F. J. Heim, *Vollständiges Heiligen-Lexikon* (Augsburg, 1858-82) ; F. von Sales Doyé, *Heilige und Selige der römisch-katholischen Kirche* (Leipzig, 1929).

Much of the early history of the saints' legend in Germany has been written and is thus a foundation for studies in the later periods. See Paul Ernst Lucius, *Die Anfänge des Heiligenkults in der christlichen Kirche* (ed. G. Anrich; Tübingen, 1904). For the materials of which legends are made, see, e.g., Otto Weinrich, *Antike Heilungswunder* ("Religionsgeschichtliche Versuche und Vorarbeiten," VIII, 1; Giessen, 1909) ; F. Pfister, *Der Reliquienkult im Altertum* ("Religionsgeschichtliche Versuche," V; Giessen, 1909-12; P. Saintyves (= E. Nourry), *Les Saints successeurs des dieux* (Paris, 1907) ; H. Günter, *Die christliche Legende des Abendlandes* ("Religionswissenschaftliche Bibliothek," II; Heidelberg, 1910). For the history of early medieval legends in Germany see L. Zoepf, *Das Heiligenleben im 10. Jahrhundert* ("Beiträge zur Kulturgeschichte des Mittelalters und der Renaissance," I; Leipzig, 1908) ; G. Eis, *Beiträge zur mittelhochdeutschen Legende und Mystik* ("Germanische Studien," CLXI; Berlin, 1935).

For the period with which we are concerned see, e.g., W. Crecelius, "Die Heiligenverehrung in der Schweiz im 16. Jahrhundert," *Alemannia,* III (1875), 53-61; Anselm Schmidt, *Die deutsche Heiligenlegende von Martin von Cochem bis Alban Stolz* (Diss.; Freiburg i.Br., 1932) ; W. Schmitz, "Verehrung der Heiligen beim Ausgange des Mittelalters," *Pastor bonus,* XVIII (1905-06), 529-541; H. Siebert, *Beiträge zur vorreformatorischen Heiligen- und Reliquienverehrung* ("Erläuterungen und Ergänzungen zu Janssens 'Geschichte des deutschen Volkes,'" VI, i; Freiburg i.Br., 1907) ; Eleanore Hamm, *Rheinische Legenden des 12. Jahrhunderts* (Cologne diss.; Würzburg, 1937), which has a good bibliography and a list of

undertaken only by a brave spirit after full consideration of ways and means. The problem is extremely attractive to one interested in the details of medieval religious thought. Medieval hagiology is, as Heinrich Siebert says,[8] a fantastic edifice: the oldest part belongs to the post-apostolic age, its heathen elements are derived from an even older period, and each succeeding century has added a chapel in its own style. An adequate survey of German saints' lives would aid us in gaining a view of this edifice and a sympathetic understanding of its origins and history.

More limited in some regards than a comprehensive survey of German saints' legends is a review and interpretation of the varying attitudes towards legends in the sixteenth century. Neither Catholics nor Protestants maintained a consistent stand. We might perhaps begin with a simple statement of the orthodox position. The *Dialogus de veneratione et invocatione sanctorum, contra perfidiam Lutheranam* (1524)[9] by Jacob Hochstraten, inquisitor at Cologne, opponent of Reuchlin and champion of orthodoxy, may be taken to represent the official view of Catholic theologians at that time. More interesting than the Catholic views would be an analysis of the attitude of Protestants. Martin Luther did not at all times hold to the low estimate of saints' legends exemplified by his pamphlet *Die Lügend von St. Joanne Chrysostomo* (1537).[10] In this instance, Luther may have been moved by resentment at the fantastic and unhistorical elements in the story of St. John Chrysostom.

A study similar to Jost Trier's admirable account of St. Jodocus[11] is

---

saints' lives; and the references in Schottenloher, IV, 258, s.v. "Hagiographie" and 269, s.v. "Heiligenverehrung." For comment on the interesting change in the Catholic attitude toward legends in the sixteenth century see Georg Schreiber, *Wallfahrt und Volkstum* ("Forschungen zur Volkskunde," XVI-XVII; Düsseldorf, 1934), p. 34.

[8] Siebert (as cited in the preceding note), p. 42.

[9] A copy in the University of Chicago Library. See also the edition in S. Cramer and F. Pijper, *Bibliotheca reformatoria neerlandica,* III (The Hague, 1905), 375-498. I have not seen K. Schatzger, *Von der lieben heiligen Eerung vnnd Anrueffung* (1523).

[10] See R. H. Fife, *Young Luther* (New York, 1928), pp. 33-34. The many satirical comments on saints' relics form a chapter which I have not discussed here; Erasmus, Valdés, Calvin, and Ochino deal with the subject, each in his own way. Some pertinent materials may also be found in the Protestant satire on the Confraternities of St. Francis.

[11] *Der heilige Jodocus; sein Leben und seine Verehrung, zugleich ein Beitrag zur Geschichte der deutschen Namengebung* ("Germanistische Abhandlungen," LVI; Breslau, 1924). See also his "Patrozinienforschung und Kulturgeographie," *Historische Zeitschrift,* CXXXIV (1926; also under the title *Festgabe für K. Wenck*), 320-349, and "Volksreligiosität im deutschen Lebensraum," *Volk und Volkstum,* I (1936), 40-45, § 3, "Das Kultdynamische."

perhaps too difficult to suggest here. Trier examines the sources of the legend, the history of the name, the center from which the veneration of the saint spread, and the dissemination of the saint's name and cult. His monograph is an important example of the study of the geography of a saint's cult. The spread of the legend and cult of St. Oswald has been competently investigated. E. A. Stückelberg, an authority in this field, has long called for studies of this sort. As an introduction to the subject of saints' lives, one might obtain a photograph of the important unpublished life of St. Jodocus by Isembard, make an edition of it, and indicate its relation to the results obtained by Trier.[12]

The need of an interpretative account of German love-poetry, particularly of the allegorical species, written in the fourteenth century is apparent even to a hasty observer.[13] Although German has contributed the word *Frauendienst* to the vocabulary of the discussion of love-service, our knowledge of German writings and more particularly of the relation of German writings to the development of the species is superficial. Our knowledge consists of summaries of the texts and bibliographies of investigations into them.

Wolfgang Stammler suggests[14] that a discussion of the survival of the medieval rhymed chronicle offers interesting problems.

The heraldic verse (*Wappendichtung*) of the fourteenth and later centuries attained no high poetic levels: Peter Suchenwirt of Vienna and Hans Rosenplüt of Nuremberg, whom we have already noted as writers deserving of a new and complete edition, are the masters of the genre. According to the fourteenth-century author of the *Karlmeinet*, the ability to compose verse suggested by a coat of arms was expected of a minstrel: "Ouch quamen dar me dan vere/Hundert mynistrere,/

---

[12] Trier, p. 16. Millett Henshaw has undertaken this task.

[13] On German love-poetry see Ehrismann, pp. 495, 501. On German allegorical verse see Ehrismann, pp. 495-510, 586, 680. Ehrismann serves admirably as a basis for further study and interpretation. Perhaps the best essay on these subjects is Friedrich Ranke, "Zur Rolle der Minneallegorie in der deutschen Dichtung des ausgehenden Mittelalters," *Festschrift Theodor Siebs zum 70. Geburtstag 26. August 1932* ("Germanistische Abhandlungen," LXVII; Breslau, 1933), pp. 199-212.

For suggestions of methods in the investigation of allegorical verse dealing with love see C. R. Post, *Medieval Spanish Allegory* ("Harvard Studies in Comparative Literature," IV; Cambridge, Mass., 1915); C. S. Lewis, *The Allegory of Love; a Study in Medieval Tradition* (Oxford, 1936). Lewis' introductory remarks (pp. 1-111) are instructive. The remainder of the book deals with the *Roman de la rose* and English writers to, and including, Spenser.

[14] Pp. 209-210. Compare F. J. Starke, *Populäre englische Chroniken des 15. Jahrhunderts, eine Untersuchung über ihre literarische Form* ("Neue deutsche Forschungen, Abteilung Englische Philologie," III; Berlin, 1935).

De wir nennen speleman,/Ind van wapen sprechen kan" (A 287, 11-14). These verses are often allegorical eulogies ending in a description of a coat of arms. Sebastian Brant described the heraldic friezes on the city-hall at Strassburg, Caspar Scheit composed heraldic verse in the middle of the sixteenth century, and Gabriel Rollenhagen has some echoes at the end of the seventeenth. The examples of heraldic verse are ordinarily brief enough to be easily photographed. The literary historian will ask what the origins of the genre are, what conventions it employed, what literary and cultural significance it had, what works of artistic value it produced, and how it disappeared.[15] The growing interest of the bourgeoise in heraldry during the fourteenth and fifteenth centuries deserves more investigation than it has received. Heraldic verse is but one aspect of this interest.

A minor poetic genre which has had no survey of its literary history for three generations is the New Year's greeting or *Klopfan*.[16] Although

[15] See some brief indications of the literary history of the genre in W. von Wickede, *Die geistlichen Gedichte des Cgm. 714* (Rostock diss.; Hamburg, 1909), pp. 65-67. Compare A. Galle, "Wappenwesen und Heraldik bei Konrad von Würzburg," *Zeitschrift für deutsches Altertum*, LIII (1912), 209-259; K. Hedicke, *Casper Scheits 'Frölich Heimfart' nach ihren geschichtlichen und literarischen Elementen untersucht* (Diss.; Halle, 1903), pp. 57-58; H. F. Rosenfeld, *Das deutsche Bildgedicht* ("Palaestra," CXCIX; Leipzig, 1935), pp. 87-89, and "Nordische Schilddichtung und mittelalterliche Waffendichtung," *Zeitschrift für deutsche Philologie*, LXI (1936), pp. 232-269; W. Wackernagel, *Geschichte der deutschen Literatur* (2d ed. by E. Martin; Basel, 1879), I, 287-288, n. 18. Otfried Weber, *Peter Suchenwirt, Studien über sein Wesen und Werk* ("Deutsches Werden," XI; Greifswald, 1937), pp. 21, 114, 167-170. Weber's remarks are of fundamental importance to the historian of the genre. For the rich development of heraldic motives in contemporary French literature see R. E. Pike, "The 'Blasons' in French Literature of the Sixteenth Century," *Romanic Review*, XXVII (1936), 223-242.

A rather late example of heraldic verse is found in Karl Aue, " 'Gedicht auf das sächsische Wappen' verfasst von dem Landzeugmeister Jacob Preuss, 1532," *Zeitschrift des Vereins für thüringische Geschichte und Altertumskunde*, III (1859), 354-360.

For references to the literature on heraldry see Arnold, p. 281; Dahlmann-Waitz, pp. 42-44, nos. 771-799; L. J. Paetow, *A Guide to the Study of Mediaeval History* (Rev. ed.; New York, 1931), p. 43; K. F. Bauer, *Das Bürgerwappen* (Frankfurt a.M., 1935).

[16] See Oscar Schade, "Klopfan. Ein Beitrag zur Geschichte der Neujahrsfeier," *Weimarisches Jahrbuch*, II (1855), 75-147; L. Uhland, *Alte hoch- und niederdeutsche Volkslieder*, II: Abhandlung (Stuttgart, 1866), 257, 351, n. 355; P. Heitz, *Neujahrswünsche des 15. Jahrhunderts²* ("Drucke und Holzschnitte des 15. und 16. Jahrhunderts," III; Strassburg, 1900); P. Sartori, *Sitte und Brauch* ("Handbücher zur Volkskunde," VII-VIII; Leipzig, 1914), III, 58, n. 21; Schottenloher, IV, 465, *s.v.* "Neujahr"; E. Speyer, "Die Klöpfle-Lieder und ihre Bedeutung," *Zeitschrift für Volkskunde*, XLIII (1935), 273-277.

this literary type, which was conventional in the fifteenth century, produced no composition of aesthetic value, its history should be brought
up to date.

We have good accounts of German preaching, but there is probably
still room for interpretative studies, works like G. R. Owst's *Preaching
in Mediaeval England* and *Literature and Pulpit in Mediaeval England;
a neglected chapter in the history of English letters and of the English
people.*[17] Comparison should stimulate someone to undertake the appraisal of cultural values in the sermon of the sixteenth century. As we
have so often noted in the course of this survey, the medieval background has been fairly well described. The preaching of the medieval
mystics also had its characteristic methods. How did it affect the new
age? Great differences existed among the types of sermons used in
various circumstances and for various groups; the historian of literature
can endeavor to describe these types as literary phenomena. What features differentiated the preaching of Catholics from that of Protestants?
A starting-point for answering this question is the comparison by Hans
Sachs entitled *Inhalt zweier Predigt* (1529). Lutheran preaching borrowed freely from Ciceronian rhetoric and from sources made available
by humanists.[18]

A minor literary form which survives from the Middle Ages into the
fifteenth century and later is the rhymed sermon. A few examples have

[17] "Cambridge Studies in Mediaeval Life and Thought"; Cambridge, Eng., 1926
and 1933. I have collected references to books dealing with German sermons in
Modern Philology, XXXV (1937), 101-102.

[18] For the medieval period see H. Caplan, "Classical Rhetoric and the Mediaeval
Theory of Preaching," *Classical Philology,* XXVIII (1933), 76-96. We now have
excellent guides to the medieval instructions to preachers in Caplan's *Mediaeval
'Artes Praedicandi'; a hand-list* ("Cornell Studies in Classical Philology," XXIV;
Ithaca, 1934), and *Mediaeval 'Artes Praedicandi'; a supplementary hand-list*
("Cornell Studies in Classical Philology," XXV; Ithaca, 1936) ; T. M. Charland,
Les 'Artes Praedicandi'; contributions à l'histoire de la rhétorique au moyen âge
("Publications de l'institut d'études médiévales d'Ottawa," VII; Ottawa, 1936).
Many texts—short and long—are indicated as worthy of publication. The influence
of such fundamental bibliographical studies appears very quickly. See, e.g., W. C.
Ross, "A Brief 'Forma Predicandi,'" *Modern Philology,* XXXIV (1937), 337-341.
Compare further H. Denifle, "Ueber die Anfänge der Predigtweise der deutschen
Mystiker," *Archiv für Literatur- und Kulturgeschichte des Mittelalters,* I (1886),
641-652; F. Landmann, "Die spätmittelalterliche Predigt der Franziskaner-Kon-
ventualen nach den Handschriften der Konsistorial bibliothek zu Colmar," *Archiv
für elsässische Kirchengeschichte,* V (1930), 19-88; H. Mertens, *Die Form der
deutschen Predigt bei Berthold von Regensburg* (Diss.; Bonn, 1937). In *Das
Stereotype in den altdeutschen Predigten* (Diss.; Greifswald, 1903), Albert Hass
preaching at Strassburg which are cited below, pp. 152-153, and E. C. Kiessling's
excellent study, *The Early Sermons of Luther and Their Relation to the Pre-
Reformation Sermon* (Chicago diss.; Grand Rapids, 1935).

been collected,[19] but the history of the form has never been written. The closely related parodistic sermon often degenerates into obscenity.[20] Its history has been merely sketched. A distant relative of the genre is the Capuchin's sermon in *Wallensteins Lager*.

Collection and study of medieval parodistic materials in the vernacular are yet to be undertaken. Paul Lehmann's *Die Parodie im Mittelalter*[21] suggests compiling and interpreting similar German materials. Until now, reprints of parodies have been available almost solely in casual publications issued in small editions and very difficult to obtain.[22] As examples of these materials, I add my collectanea on the parodies and imitations of the Paternoster.[23] These have never been adequately discussed. For

[19] Edward Schröder, *Anzeiger für deutsches Altertum*, VII (1881), 189.

[20] F. Lehr, *Studien über den komischen Einzelvortrag in der älteren deutschen Literatur, I: Die parodistische Predigt* (Diss.; Marburg, 1907). As a study in sources and method compare M. de Meyer, "Het sermoen van Bacchus en de oorsprong van de geparodiëerde sermoenen," *Album opgedragen aan Prof. dr. J. Vercoullie* (Brussels, 1927), pp. 351-355. For examples of parodistic sermons see G. J. Boekenoogen, A. de Cock, F. W. Drijver, *Volkskunde*, XX (1909), 73-80, 117-118, 178-179, 232-234; XXI (1910), 37-40, 80-83, 150-155; XXII (1911), 80-82; Huet and others, *Revue des traditions populaires*, XXIV (1909), 65-66, XXVI (1911), 111, no. 11, etc. A sermon too vulgar to print is found in *Cod. germ. mon. 379* (see a photostat in the University of Chicago Library) ; compare Lehr, p. 6, no. 7.

[21] Munich, 1922. He prints his materials in a supplement entitled *Parodistische Texte* (Munich, 1923).

[22] See, e.g., [F. Pfeiffer], *Futilitates Germaniae medii aevi* (n.p., 1864), and T. G. Ritter von Karajan, *Svarmvs spvrca loqvens: ein kurtzweilige Fassnichtpredigt* ([Vienna, 1851]). The latter text is also accessible in *Idunna und Hermode*, II (1813), 42-44. Compare in passing P. H. Schroeder, *Parodiëen in de Nederlandsche letterkunde* (Diss.; Amsterdam, 1932). On the whole, German parodies have been neglected by historians of literature.

[23] E. Ilvonen, *Parodies des thèmes pieux dans la poésie française du moyen âge: pater, credo, ave Maria, laetabundus* (Helsingfors, 1914). The German examples seem, in general, to belong to a later period; see R. M. Werner, "Das Vaterunser als gottesdienstliche Zeitlyrik," *Vierteljahrschrift für Literaturgeschichte*, V (1892), 1-49; Mehring, "Das Vaterunser als politisches Kampfmittel," *Zeitschrift des Vereins für Volkskunde*, XIX (1909), 129-142, and compare Becker, *ibid.*, p. 186, F. B[öhm], *ibid.*, XLII (1932), 275-276; M. de Meyer, "Het sermoen van Bacchus en de oorsprong van de gepariodiëerde sermoenen," *Album opgedragen aan Prof. dr. J. Vercoullie* (Brussels, 1927), pp. 351-355; H. H[epding], *Hessische Blätter für Volkskunde*, XXVI (1927), 184-185 (a useful bibliographical note). For further examples see A. Hollaender, *Jahrbuch für Geschichte, Sprache und Litteratur Elsass-Lothringens*, V (1889), 112-14; G. Planitz, "Ein Spottvaterunser des 16. Jahrhunderts," *Neues Archiv für Sächsiche Geschichte*, XXII (1901), 181-83; F. Pfeiffer, *Altdeutsches Uebungsbuch* (Vienna, 1866), pp. 171-72, "Des Wucherers Paternoster"; J. O. Opel and A. Cohn, *Der dreissig-jährige Krieg* (Halle, 1862), p. 32; A. Becker, "Gebetsparodien," *Schweizerisches Archiv für Volkskunde*,

the history of still another variety of parodies I have already collected materials elsewhere.[24] This variety, the *Lügenlied* or *Lügenmärchen*,

XX (1916), 16-28; O. Menghin, *Kriegsvaterunser und Verwandtes* (Munich, 1916); A. Wrede, "Das Vaterunser der kurkölnischen Bauern," *Zeitschrift des Vereins für rheinische und westfälische Volkskunde,* XIII (1916), 76-78; W. Hardebeck, "Das Vaterunser der osnabrückischen Bauern," *ibid.,* XIV (1917), 125-126; A. Gittée, "Volkshumor in geestelijke zaken," *Volkskunde,* III (1890), 185-94, 209-18, IV (1891), 55-61, 71-75, 113-119, V (1892), 25-32, 46-55; J. W. Muller, *Tijdschrift voor Nederlandsche taal- en letterkunde,* XVIII (1899), 208-209, no. 20. A reviewer of Menghin's little pamphlet calls attention to the need of a good survey of the subject of parodies; see *Literarisches Zentralblatt,* 1916, col. 1058.

[24] *The Literary History of Meistergesang* (New York, 1937), p. 101, n. 45, where I have collected primarily sources in popular literature. For discussion and collections of parallels in medieval and later literature see C. Müller-Fraureuth, *Die deutschen Lügendichtungen bis auf Münchhausen* (Halle, 1881) and R. Köhler's review, *Literaturblatt für germanische und romanische Philologie,* IV (1883), cols. 412-415; Gustav Roethe, *Die Gedichte Reinmars von Zweter* (Leipsig, 1887), pp. 248-250; P. Strauch (ed.), *Der Marner* ("Quellen und Forschungen zur germanischen Sprach- und Culturgeschichte," XIV; Strassburg, 1876), p. 166 (note on XIV, 177 ff.); R. Rodenwaldt, *Die Fabel in der deutschen Spruchdichtung* (Programm; Berlin, 1885), p. 7; A. Berger, "Die volkstümlichen Grundlagen des Minnesangs," *Zeitschrift für deutsche Philologie,* XIX (1887), 456; W. Wackernagel, *Geschichte der deutschen Literatur* (2d ed. by Ernst Martin; Basel, 1879), I, 282-283, nn. 52, 53; F. Rosenberg, *Ueber eine Sammlung deutscher Volks- und Gesellschaftslieder in hebräischen Lettern* (Berlin diss.; Brunswick, [1888]. Reprinted from *Zeitschrift für die Geschichte der Juden in Deutschland,* II [1888], 232-296, III [1889], 14-28). For individual examples in literature see J. Werner, "Kalenderhumor," *Alemannia,* XVI (1888), 181-183; [F. J.] M[one], "Verkehrte Welt," *Anzeiger für Kunde der teutschen Vorzeit,* VIII (1839), col. 598 ("The World Upside-Down" is a form closely related to the Lügenlied); F. H. von der Hagen, "Alterthumskunde aus altdeutschen Handschriften, 17, Lügenmäre," [von der Hagen's] *Germania,* VIII (1848), 308-313 (The *Wachtelmære* is also printed here. The University of Chicago Library has a photostat of the very rare, privately-printed edition of the *Wachtelmære*); W. Wackernagel, "Drei Lügenmärchen," *Zeitschrift für deutsches Altertum,* II (1842), 560-569; E. Martin, "Weiggers Lügen," *ibid.,* XIII (1866-67), 578-579; J. M. Wagner, "Lügenmärchen," *ibid.,* XVI (1873), 437-466; K. Bartsch (ed.), *Die Meisterlieder der Colmarer Handschrift* ("Bibliothek des Literarischen Vereins," LXVIII; Stuttgart, 1862), pp. 394-395, no. 77; Adalbert von Keller (ed.), *Fastnachtspiele aus dem 15. Jahrhundert* ("Bibliothek des Literarischen Vereins," XXVIII; Stuttgart, 1853), I, 298-299, no. 39, ll. 17ff., III ("Bibliothek des Literarischen Vereins," XXX; Stuttgart, 1853), 1449, no. 24, 1486 (note on 93, 3), 1514 (note on 562, 1) and *Fastnachtspiele . . .; Nachlese* ("Bibliothek des Literarischen Vereins," XLVI; Stuttgart, 1858), p. 337; K. Lachmann, *Des Minnesangs Frühling* (5th ed. by F. Vogt; Leipzig, 1930), p. 430 = p. 308 (2d ed.), a note on p. 194, ll. *18-*33, containing a stanza wrongly ascribed to Reinmar von Zweter; Herzog Heinrich Julius von Braunschweig, *Von einem Wirthe,* I, iv, III, iv, V, i (ed. W. L. Holland, "Bibliothek des Literarischen Vereins," XXXVI; Stuttgart, 1855, pp. 302-304, 317-319,

occurs in both prose and verse. The history of these compositions which collect fantastic impossibilities or inversions of reality in a mad whirl of nonsense has been hastily sketched, but a serious effort to describe the various forms, to seek their origins, and to write the history of the more interesting devices, such as that of the fox preaching to geese,[25]

329-330; ed. J. Tittmann, "Deutsche Dichter des 16. Jahrhunderts," XIV; Leipzig, 1880, pp. 82-84, 95, 102-104. See also Holland's collectanea, pp. 868-870, 897-903) ; J. Bolte, "Fahrende Leute in der Literatur des 15. und 16. Jahrhunderts," *Sitzungsberichte der preussischen Akademie der Wissenschaften, philosophisch-historische Klasse,* XXXI (1928), 639-640, 653-655.

J. Poeschel, "Das Märchen vom Schlaraffenlande," *Beiträge zur Geschichte der deutschen Sprache,* V (1878), 389-427, may serve as an introduction to the related field of the Utopias, Never-Never Lands, and Lands of Coquaigne.

For additional traditional examples of the *Lügenlied* see F. Liebrecht, *Literaturblatt für germanische und romanische Philologie,* I (1880), col. 70, and *Germania,* XXVI (1881), 119-120, XXVII (1882), 232; G. Meyer, "Ostfriesische Kinder- und Volksreime," *Korrespondenzblatt des Vereins für niederdeutsche Sprachforschung,* III (1878), 58; H. Abels and B. Graupe, *ibid.,* VII (1882), 73-74; Otto Böckel, *Deutsche Volkslieder aus Oberhessen* (Marburg, 1885), pp. cvii, cli-clii (repeated with some enlargement in his *Psychologie der Volksdichtung* [2d ed.; Leipzig, 1913], pp. 306-309) ; J. W. Muller, *Tijdschrift voor Nederlandsche taal- en letterkunde,* XVIII (1899), 215-216, no. 25; A. Kopp, *Euphorion,* VIII (1901), 357; Ph. Koukoules, "To Byzantikon ainigmatodes asma," *Laographia,* II (1910), 195-198.

[25] Archer Taylor, *Index to the 'Proverb'* ("FF Communications," CXIII; Helsinki, 1934), p. 34 (the reference to Bolte and Polívka should be to vol. II) ; L. Maeterlinck, *Le genre satirique dans la peinture flamande* (Ghent, 1903), pp. 63-64 (reprinted unchanged in 2d ed., Brussels, 1907, pp. 58-59) and *Le genre satirique, fantastique et licencieux dans la sculpture flamande et wallone; les miséricordes de stalles (art et folklore)* (Paris, 1910), pp. 76, 176, 271. I have not seen some popular books which might contain pertinent materials, e.g. Richard Piper, *Das Tier in der Kunst* (2d ed.; Munich, 1910) ; L. B. Bridahan, *Gargoyles, Chimeres, and the Grotesque in French Gothic Sculpture* (New York, 1930) ; Walter Botz, *Mittelalterliche Groteskplastik* (Leipzig, 1937) ; M. D. Anderson, *Animal Carvings in British Churches* (Cambridge, Eng., 1938). German examples appear to be comparatively few. N. C. Kist, "Het humoristisch karakter der christelijke kunst in het tijdvaak, hetwelk de kerkhervorming der XVde eeuw heeft voorbereid . . . ," *Nederlandsch archief voor kerkelijke geschiedenis,* 2d Ser., IV (1844), 392-393, suggests that the idea is derived from Ezek. 13:20 and cites a few carvings. J. van Lennep and J. ter Gouw cite additional examples and tell a story connected with the theme; see *De uithangteekens* (Leiden, n.d. = 1888), pp. 126-127. See L. Uhland, *Schriften zur Geschichte der Dichtung und Sage* (Stuttgart, 1866), III, 326, n. 214; C. Müller-Fraureuth, *Die deutschen Lügendichtungen* (Halle, 1881), pp. 95-96, n. 38; Dr. Widmann, "Der Fuchs predigt den Gänsen," *Nassauische Annalen,* XIX (1885-86), 71-75; F. W. Ebeling, "Ein lehrhafter Sermon von dem Spruch, dass der Wolf den Gänsen predige," *Zerstreutes und Erneutes* (Berlin, 1890), pp. 149-169 (a reprint of the last chapter of W. Spangenberg's *Gans-König*) ; Paul Merker, *Der Verfasser des 'Eccius dedolatus' und anderer Reformationsdialoge* ("Sächs-

is still to be undertaken. The connections with tradition concern both the origin and the dissemination of the idea, and lead us to the study of plastic representations.

The history of German letter-writing begun in Georg Steinhausen's *Geschichte des deutschen Briefes*[26] must be taken up again and carried out on a larger scale. Probably enough letters are in print to make the

iche Forschungsinstitute in Leipzig, Forschungsinstitut für neuere Philologie, Neugermanistische Abteilung," I; Halle, 1923), p. 37; M. T. Bergenthal, *Elemente der Drolerie und ihre Beziehungen zur Literatur* (Bonn diss. [Berlin, 1934]), pp. 142-144; Dora Lämke, *Mittelalterliche Tierfabeln und ihre Beziehungen zur bildenden Kunst in Deutschland* ("Deutsches Werden," XIV; Greifswald, 1937), pp. 91-102; B. J. Whiting, *Proverbs in the Earlier English Drama* ("Harvard Studies in Comparative Literature," XIV; Cambridge, 1938), pp. 16, 69, 245, 272.

[26] Berlin, 1889-91. See also his *Deutsche Privatbriefe des Mittelalters*, I-II ("Denkmäler der deutschen Kulturgeschichte," I-II; Berlin, 1899-1907), and the important reviews of W. Uhl (*Zeitschrift für deutsche Philologie*, XXXIII [1901], 390-393) and G. Ehrismann (*Göttingische gelehrte Anzeigen*, 1910, pp. 231-235). The promised third volume dealing with commercial correspondence never appeared. On this type of correspondence see B. Penndorf, "Die kaufmännische Korrespondenz als Unterrichtsgegenstand im Mittelalter," *Deutsche Handelsschul-Lehrer-Zeitung*, V (1908), Heft 41-42, and "Die historische Entwicklung des kaufmännischen Briefstils," *ibid.*, VI (1909), Heft 42, 43, 45, 46, 48; A. Schirmer, *Zur Geschichte der deutschen Kaufmannsprache* (Diss.; Strassburg 1911), pp. 15, 19. Much new material, particularly in Latin, has recently been made accessible to us. See, e.g., "Humanistenbriefe" of Conrad Peutinger, Johann Cuspinian, and Conrad Celtis in the "Veröffentlichungen der Kommission für Erforschung der Geschichte der Reformation und Gegenreformation" (Munich, 1923-34). We have additional information about handbooks for letter-writing and their stylistic requirements. See, e.g., K. Burdach and G. Bebermeyer, *Schlesisch-böhmische Briefmuster aus der Wende des 14. Jahrhunderts* ("Vom Mittelalter zur Reformation," V; Berlin, 1926) and such special studies as A. Bütow, *Die Entwicklung der mittelhochdeutschen Briefsteller bis zur Mitte des 12. Jahrhunderts mit besonderer Berücksichtigung der Theorieen der 'Ars dictandi'* (Diss.; Greifswald, 1908); Paul Krüger, *Bedeutung und Entwicklung der Salutatio in den mittelalterlichen Briefstellern bis zum 14. Jahrhundert* (Diss.; Greifswald, 1912); G. Petzsch, *Ueber Technik und Stil der mittelhochdeutschen Privatbriefe des 14. und 15. Jahrhunderts* (Diss.; Greifswald, 1913).

Various literary genres make use of epistolary devices. Compare, e.g., W. Wattenbach, "Ueber erfundene Briefe in Handschriften des Mittelalters, besonders Teufelsbriefe," *Sitzungsberichte der königlich preussischen Akademie*, 1892, i, 91-123 (he suggests some texts to be edited); Albert Ritter, *Altschwäbische Liebesbriefe* ("Grazer Studien zur deutschen Philologie," V; Graz, 1897); Emil Meyer, *Die gereimten Liebesbriefe des deutschen Mittelalters* (Diss.; Marburg, 1899); E. Mayser, "Briefe im mittelhochdeutschen Epos," *Zeitschrift für deutsche Philologie*, LIX (1934-35), 136-147. Compare the interpretative accounts in C. H. Haskins, "The Life of Mediaeval Students in Their Letters," in *Studies in Mediaeval Culture* (Oxford, 1929), pp. 170-192 and E. N. S. Thompson, "Familiar Letters" in *Literary Bypaths of the Renaissance* (New Haven, 1924), pp. 91-126.

undertaking feasible. In his study of Luther's letters, Theodor Locke-
mann made a good beginning.[27] The history of German letter-writing
will deal with such matters as the formulae used in correspondence, the
influence of Latin or Italian models, the influence of official documents,
the expression of individuality, and the attitude toward the person addressed. Many varieties—letters of mystics, political letters, love-letters,
letters of scholars—are to be characterized.

The collections of proverbs made during the fifteenth and sixteenth
centuries are yet to be listed and appraised.[28] Passing over the bibliographical problem of compiling a list, I shall comment on the task of
appraisal. Except for a brief discussion in Seiler's *Deutsche Sprichwörterkunde,*[29] we have no competent treatment of the changing purposes
which guided collectors of proverbs. The minute and painstaking studies
which have revealed the history and connections of early medieval
glosses might suggest the manner of studies which would disclose and
interpret the significance of collections of proverbs. Investigators of
collections of proverbs should examine the contents of the collections,
the relations of the collections among themselves, and the aims of the
collectors. The earliest collections appear to be casual jottings, but careful study might show them to be something more. Later collections, such
as the Dutch *Proverbia communia sive seriosa* (*ca.* 1485) serve as school
books. Richard Jente's forthcoming edition of this collection will settle
many questions regarding its origin and influence. So far as we can see,
it was the most important collection of proverbs at that time, both in the
Netherlands and in Germany. Humanists found its Latinity intolerable,
and Heinrich Bebel corrected many of its errors in his *Proverbia germanica* (1508). Alongside these pedagogical tools there developed collections with more definitely literary and cultural aims. The *Traditio
morum venustatem complectens* (*ca.* 1490), containing sixty-seven Latin
distichs with renderings in German quatrains, has never been examined
for its proverbial content, nor has it been compared with a similar work
of about the same time, the *Regimen scholarium,* which contains seventy-
two Latin distichs and German quatrains.[30] I should like to know more

[27] *Technische Studien zu Luthers Briefen an Friedrich den Weisen* ("Probefahr-
ten," XXII; Leipzig, 1913).
[28] I have commented elsewhere on problems in the study of proverbs and collections of proverbs. See *Journal of American Folk-Lore,* XLVII (1934), 1-21.
[29] "Handbuch des deutschen Unterrichts," IV, 3 (Munich, 1922, pp. 98-131.
[30] For the *Traditio* see L. Hain, *Repertorium typographicum* (Stuttgart, 1831),
II, 474, no. 15, 596; Robert Proctor, *An Index to the Early Printed Books in the
British Museum* (London, 1898), I, 190; *Catalogue of Printed Books from the
Fifteenth Century in the British Museum,* III (London, 1913), 631 (the editor

than the title of Isaac Medicus, *De particularibus dictis libellus* (Padua, 1487. Per Magistro Cerdonem de Windischgraet). The Bohemian humanist Bohuslaus Lobkowitz wrote an *Oratio proverbiorum* (1500) at a time when a wider interest in proverbs was awakening[31] and at the same time Philippus Beroaldus issued an *Oratio proverbiorum qua doctrina remotior continetur* (Paris, 1500). The little-known collection of Johannes Fabri de Werdea (1505) is more than a school-book.[32] Like the others mentioned here, it should be described for its literary and cultural values, and perhaps might be reprinted. Josef Nadler gives only scanty details, about the manuscript collection of proverbs made by Georg Handsch (d. 1578),[33] and tempts us to go farther. The 'Gnomologia ex omnibus Sylvii operius collecta" is, I suspect, a collection of sententious remarks from the works of Aeneas Silvius rather than a collection of proverbs; it is appended to the edition of his works published at Basel in 1571 and perhaps to other editions. Comparable to it is Adrian Barlandus' *Proverbialium versuum ex principe poetarum Vergilio collectanea* (Basel, 1535), an annotated collection of sententious materials from the *Bucolics*. These may serve as examples of the loose use of *proverb* and its synonyms in the sixteenth century. Such difficulties will complicate somewhat the survey of proverbial literature at this time. On the unparalleled influence of Erasmus' *Adagia* I comment elsewhere. Here I shall point out only that Ludwig Volkmann[34] thinks that an investigation of the relations between the *Adagia* and emblems would be interesting. These problems are typical of the various aspects of the interest in proverbs manifested during the fifteenth and sixteenth centuries. Although Friedrich Seiler has a good critical review of these collections,[35] it is much too brief; we need a fuller one

---

asks whether this copy is the same as Hain, no. 15, 596); E. H. Vouilliéme, *Die Inkunabeln der Königlichen Bibliothek und der anderen Berliner Sammlungen* ("Beihefte zum Zentralblatt für Bibliothekswesen," XXX; Leipzig, 1906), no. 1308.

For the *Regimen* see W. A. Copinger, *Supplement to Hain's 'Repertorium typographicum,'* II, ii (London, 1902), 46, no. 5070; Vouilliéme, no. 1307.

[81] R. Wolkan, *Böhmens Anteil an der deutschen Literatur des 16. Jahrhunderts* (Prague, 1890), pp. 111, 484.

[82] For references see Taylor, *Journal of American Folk-Lore,* XLVII (1934), 5. See further S. P. Ludwig Glückert, O.S.B., "Hieronymus von Mondsee (Magister Johannes de Werdea), ein Beitrag zur Geschichte des Einflusses der Wiener Universität im 15. Jahrhunderts," *Studien und Mitteilungen zur Geschichte des Benediktinerordens und seiner Zweige,* N.F., XVII (1930), nos. 1-2.

[83] *Literaturgeschichte der deutschen Stämme* (3d ed.; Regensburg, 1929), II, 257.

[84] *Bilderschriften der Renaissance* ("Veröffentlichungen des deutschen Vereins für Buchwesen und Schrifttum"; Leipzig, 1923), p. 74.

[85] *Deutsche Sprichwörterkunde* ("Handbuch des deutschen Unterrichts," IV, 3; Munich, 1922), pp. 98-131.

with some estimate of the contents and cultural influences. As we have seen, moralists of the sixteenth century complained about the attitude toward women displayed in Sebastian Franck's collection of proverbs. Thus a collection of proverbs in the sixteenth century was something different from what it is today. A more complete review of these collections might also determine their relations. Something has been done in this field, but probably too much influence has been ascribed to the *Proverbia communia*.[36] This review might also describe the changes in the collections which finally ended by transforming them into anthologies of *bons mots* or guides to manners and morals.

The emblem-books of the sixteenth and seventeenth centuries are allied to the didactic spirit of the proverb, but only infrequently use actual proverbs. These books enjoyed an extraordinary vogue in the Italian and English Renaissance,—a vogue which must yet be traced historically and interpreted.[37] In particular, the limited field of German

---

[36] A. Wesselski, "Humanismus und Volkstum," *Zeitschrift für Volkskunde*, XLIV (1935), 1-35.

[37] See notable collections of emblem-books in Folger Shakespeare Library, Harvard College Library, the Henry E. Huntington Library, and the Newberry Library. My remarks on emblems in the *Proverb* (p. 176) are inadequate. For an introduction to the field see Harold Bayley, *A New Light on the Renaissance Displayed in Contemporary Emblems* (London, 1909); Henry Green, *Shakespeare and the Emblem Writers; an exposition of their similarities of thought and expression. Preceded by a view of emblem literature down to A.D. 1616* (London, 1870),—a useful book in spite of Max Rubensohn's well-founded objections (*Griechische Epigramme und andere kleinere Dichtungen in deutschen Uebersetzungen des 16. und 17. Jahrhunderts* ["Bibliothek älterer deutscher Uebersetzungen," II-V; Weimar, 1897]); Georges Duplessis, *Les emblèmes d'Alciat* (Paris, 1884); P. E. Viard, *André Alciat 1492-1550* (Paris, 1926); P. L. van Eck, Jr., "Een en ander uit de 17ᵉ eeuwse Nederlandse emblemata," [Mork's] *Magazijn* (ed. G. van Son), XXIII (1921), i, 169-178, 247-252, ii, 13-24, 65-72; Mario Praz, *Studi sul concettismo* (Milan, 1934),—an admirable introduction, which is now available in English in somewhat enlarged and improved form as *Studies in Seventeenth-Century Imagery*, I ("Studies of the Warburg Institute," III, London, 1939); E. N. S. Thompson, *Literary Bypaths of the Renaissance* (New Haven, Conn., 1924), pp. 29-67 (a suggestion of the literary influence exerted by emblems); L. Volkmann, *Bilderschriften der Renaissance; Hieroglyphik und Emblematik in ihren Beziehungen und Fortwirkungen* ("Veröffentlichungen des deutschen Vereins für Buchwesen und Schrifttum"; Leipzig, 1923),—a book of great learning dominated by the desire to connect hieroglyphics and emblems; A. G. C. de Vries, *De Nederlandsche emblemata* (Amsterdam, 1899). In the absence of a recent bibliography of emblems see *An Essay Toward a Collection of Books relating to Proverbs, Emblems, Apophthegms, Epitaphs, and Ana* (London, 1859), a catalogue of the collection of William Stirling-Maxwell.

Studies in German emblems appear to be few. Although Goedeke thinks (II, 484, § 162, III) that the genre was not popular in Germany, he was not well informed.

emblem-books calls for special studies,—notably a bibliography, a brief survey, and an evaluation of influence. Andrea Alciati's *Emblematum liber*, finished in 1521 at Milan, printed at Augsburg in 1531, and dedicated to the patrician German humanist Conrad Peutinger, is the beginning of the genre. The book is international in its origin, its later history, and its enormous influence. The first German translation (1542), for example, was printed at Paris. The artistic value of many collections of emblems and their international relations make these studies attractive. There is a special problem in the characterization of the German emblem-book. To the varieties illustrated by de Vries with Dutch examples of the genre, we must add the group of emblem-books akin to the *Album amicorum* or Stammbuch.[38] The historian of German em-

---

Volkmann's treatise is a foundation for further investigation, but leaves something to be desired. R. Sillib's brief essay, "Kurpfälzische Emblematik," *Kurpfälzer Jahrbuch,* III (1927), 210, is helpful. See also the useful bibliographical survey, A. Rümann, "Embleme-Bücher des 16. und 17. Jahrhunderts," *Philobiblion,* IX (1936), 161-178. Simpson's essay, which is mentioned below, brings a fresh enthusiasm to the subject. Although too early to be termed emblems, the pictures described in Wilhelm Fraenger, *Hans Weiditz und Sebastian Brant* ("Denkmale der Volkskunst," II; Leipzig, 1930), contribute to our understanding of the genre, see especially pp. 81-120, "Das Sinnbild."

The contemporary writings on the theory and origin of emblems are curious, but not particularly valuable. See, e.g., J. Fischart, *Kurtzer und woldienlicher Vorbericht von Ursprung, Namen und Gebrauch der Emblematen oder eingeblömeten Zierwercken,* the preface to Mathias Holzwart's *Emblematum Tyrocinia* (1581). Fischart's preface, which is typical of the many prefaces to the later emblem-books, is reprinted in J. Scheible, *Das Kloster,* X (Stuttgart, 1848), 939-948. Contemporary treatises on the theory of emblems are Henri Estienne, *The Art of Making Devises; treating of Hieroglyphicks, Symboles, Emblemes, Aenigmas, Cimiers, Cyphres and Rebus* (tr. T. Blount; London, 1648); J[ean] B[audoin], *Iconologie ou la science des emblèmes et devises* (Amsterdam, 1698). C. F. Ménéstrier, S.J., *La philosophie des images, composée d'un ample recueil de devises, et du jugement de tous les ouvrages qui ont été fait sur cette manière* (Paris, 1682), which was also issued in a Latin version, *Philosophia imaginum* (Amsterdam, 1695), is, says Praz (p. 142), the "organum" of books on the theory of emblems. Volkmann assigns (p. 104) a similar position to Ménéstrier's *L'Art des emblemes* (Lyons, 1662).

[38] Schottenloher, I, 376, nos. 9119-23. See W. D. Simpson, "David de Necker's Stammbuch of 1579," *Aberdeen University Library Bulletin,* VII (no. 43; 1931), 577-586; F. Warnecke (3d.), *Culturgeschichtliches Stamm- und Wappenbuch* (Berlin, 1894), a reprint of a text by J. T. and J. J. de Bry; R. and R. Keil, *Die deutschen Stammbücher des 16. bis 19. Jahrhunderts* (Berlin, 1893); G. Friedländer, "Von Stammbüchern und Rebus," *Festschrift zum 17. Februar, 1855* (Berlin, 1855), which last is before me only in the form of a reprint from an unidentified anniversary volume. According to a clipping from a bookseller's catalogue which I cannot identify, the first *Liber amicorum* is *New Stamm- oder Gesellenbuch,*

blems will also have to occupy himself with the origins and development of the *artes memorativae*,[39] but I have already suggested enough problems and shall not take up this interesting subject.

The Latin riddle seems to have been particularly favored by German writers of the sixteenth century, and it should therefore be of particular interest to us. Few, if any, such riddles were written in France; Sir Thomas More's experiments can probably be credited to the suggestion of continental writers and perhaps in particular to that of Erasmus; and Italian or Spanish examples are not numerous. To be sure, the most important contemporary treatise on the genre appears to be the *Ænigmata* of Lilius Gregorius Gyraldus of Ferrara, and Nicolaus Reusner's bibliography includes a few Italian names.[40]

W. A. Clouston has traced the origin of "hieroglyphic Bibles" back to Melchior Mattsperger's *Geistliche Herzens-Einbildungen/Inn Zweihundert und Fünfzig/ Biblischen Figur-Sprüchen/ angedeutet* (Augsburg, 1687), but the earlier history of the form remains obscure.[41] A

---

darein eines jeden Namen unnd Wappen geschreiben werden kan (Heidelberg: Joh. Maier in Verlegung, 1573). It is not the *Flores Hesperidum . . . oder Stamm- und Gesellenbuch* (Frankfurt a. M., G. Rabe für M. Harnisch in Heidelberg, 1573) and, "according to the Auskunftsstelle des Gesamtkataloges," is known only in one copy. Harnisch and Maier were brothers-in-law. Jost Amman's *Anthologia Gnomica. Illustres Veterum Graecae Comoediae Scriptorum sententiae, prius ab Henrico Stephano, qui et singulas Latine convertit, editae* (Frankfurt a. M., 1579) combines apophthegmatic materials with coats of arms. The library at Weimar has a large and important collection of *Stammbücher.* Compare also the medieval devices: J. von Radowitz, *Die Devisen und Motto des späteren Mittelalters; ein Beitrag zur Spruchpoesie* (Stuttgart, 1850) with a cursory but useful bibliography (pp. 6-10) including some German emblem-books. The Italian *imprese* are also connected with these materials and call for some attention.

[39] Volkmann, p. 80. The most recent work on the *artes memorativae* seems to be Helga Hajdu, "Das mnemotechnische Schrifttum des Mittelalters," *Jahrbuch des deutschen Institutes der königl. ung. Péter Pázmány Universität Budapest,* I (1936), 409-537. It surveys mnemotechnic investigation from classical antiquity to the middle of the seventeenth century.

[40] The second edition (Frankfurt a. M., 1602) of Reusner's *Ænigmatographia* is preferable to the edition of 1599. Both reprint Gyraldus' *Ænigmata* as an introduction. Reusner's excellent anthology makes it easy to investigate the genre.

[41] *Hieroglyphic Bibles; their origin and history* (Glasgow, 1894). See also A. Spamer, *Das kleine Andachtsbild vom 14. bis zum 20. Jahrhundert* (Munich, 1920), pp. 168 ff. The title-page of my copy of the *Herzens-Einbildungen* has no date and differs in this regard (but apparently in no others) from the editions cited by Clouston. Works of this sort seem to have been favored in Augsburg in these years. I should like to see M. J. Ad. Behr, *Catechismus in Emblematibus. Das ist: der durch Bilder erklärte Catechismus/Darinnen d. gantze Catechismus Lutheri/ durch Anmuthige Biblische Bilder, Figuren . . .* (Augsburg, 1718), which contains, according to a book-seller's catalogue, 35 copper-plates by J. A. Corvinus, and J. U.

"hieroglyphic Bible" is a version of the Biblical text in which pictures replace many of the nouns. The pictures are not puzzles to be interpreted as in a rebus, but are representations of the objects themselves. For *mountain* we have the picture of a mountain and for *hand*, the picture of a hand. The history of this device is yet to be traced, for I cannot believe that the idea originated with Melchior Mattsperger. Some ecclesiastical books of the early sixteenth century contained pictures which may have been of this sort, e.g., *Ars memorandi notabilis per figuras evangelistarum* (*ca.* 1470), which contains fifteen emblematical representations of events and topics in the gospels, *Tractatus colloquii peccatoris,* and *Pange lingua.*[42] The last page of the *Heures* printed for Guill. Godard (Paris, *ca.* 1515) contains a true rebus, and like the fifteenth-century *Bildercatechismus,*[43] throws no light on our problem. Possibly something might be learned by looking into the early history of illustrated school-books and the use of pictures by Comenius.[44]

English and French literary historians can turn to good surveys of the literature of travel, but the German sources, except for journeys to the Holy Land,[45] are not easily surveyed. Germany can of course

---

Kraus, *Histor. Bilder-Bibel Alten und Neuen Testaments* (Augsburg, 1705), which according to another bookseller's catalogue, has five engraved titles, five engraved frontispieces, and 135 engraved plates; his *Heilige Augen- u[.] Gemüths-Lust, Vorstellend (.) Alle Sonn- Fest- u. Feyrtägliche Nicht nur Evangelien, Sondern auch Episteln in vielen Kupfer-Stücken* (Augsburg, *ca.* 1706), which has two engraved title pages, two engraved frontispieces, and 120 engraved plates; and his *Biblisches Engel- und Kunst-Werck* (Augsburg, 1705). I have not seen R. Muther, *Die ältesten deutschen Bilder-Bibeln. Bibliographisch und kunstgeschichtlich beschreiben* (Munich, 1883). P. Schmidt, "Die Bibelillustration als Laienexegese," *Festschrift Gustav Binz* (Basel, 1935), pp. 228-239 makes some very important introductory observations regarding a very interesting subject but does not mention hieroglyphic bibles. See, further, M. Lanckorońska and R. Oehler, *Die Buchillustration des 18. Jahrhunderts in Deutschland, Oesterreich und der Schweiz* (Leipzig, 1932-34), I, Plates 1-2.

[42] I take these references from the article in the unidentified *Festschrift* of 1855 as cited in the second note preceding. For the *Ars memorandi* see F. A. Ebert, *Allgemeines bibliographisches Lexicon,* I (Leipzig, 1821), col. 107, no. 1249. Identification of the two other items I leave to the student of the subject.

[43] J. Geffcken, *Der Bildercatechismus des 15. Jahrhunderts,* I, *Die Zehn Gebote* (Leipzig, 1855).

[44] See, e.g., K. Klement, *Zur Geschichte des Bilderbuches und der Schülerspiele* (Programm; Leipzig, 1903); Leo Baer, *Die illustrierten Historienbücher des 15. Jahrhunderts; ein Beitrag zur Geschichte des Formschnittes* (Strassburg, 1903); M. Ringmann, *Die 'Grammatica figurata'* (ed. F. von Wieser; "Drucke und Holzschnitte des 15. und 16. Jahrhunderts," XI; Strassburg, 1905). For Comenius see the extensive bibliography in Č. Zíbrt, *Bibliografie české historie,* V (Prague, 1912), nos. 17, 324-30, 638.

[45] Ehrismann, pp. 521-523; Stammler, p. 520 (note on p. 420); M. Sommerfeld,

take pride in the labors of Martin Behaim in the field of cartography and those of Apian Friess in hydrography.[46] There are accounts of the "grand tour" which formed part of the liberal education of the English nobleman, but the visits of German travelers, pleasure-seekers, and scholars to Italy have not been investigated in similar fashion.[47] Inasmuch as Clark S. Northup points out (pp. 145-146) that the first books of instruction for travelers "emanated from the methodical minds of Germans," that fact might well stimulate investigation by students of German. Peter Schott's letters from Bologna, which are preserved in his *Lucubratiunculae* (1498),[48] might serve as a starting-point.

Scarcely to be considered literature are the books of magic recipes compiled in the late Middle Ages. In almost unchanged form these books are still being sold in Germany and America. Typical examples are the *Sixth and Seventh Books of Moses,* the *Secrets of Albertus Magnus,* and the *Romanusbüchlein* (not known in America).[49] Like

---

"Die Reisebeschreibungen der deutschen Jerusalempilger im ausgehenden Mittelalter," *Deutsche Vierteljahrsschrift für Literaturwissenschaft und Geistesgeschichte,* II (1924), 816-51; M. Böhme, *Die grossen Reisesammlungen des 16. Jahrhunderts und ihre Bedeutung* (Leipzig diss.; Strassburg, 1904); S. Günther, "Der Humanismus in seinem Einfluss auf die Entwicklung der Erdkunde," *Verhandlungen des 7. internationalen Geographenkongresses* [Berlin, 1899] (publ. Berlin, 1901) II, 819-844; J. Berg, *Aeltere deutsche Reisebeschreibungen* (Diss.; Giessen, 1912); V. Hantzsch, *Deutsche Reisende des 16. Jahrhunderts* ("Leipziger Studien aus dem Gebiete der Geschichte," IV; Leipzig, 1895).

[46] See A. Reichenbach, *Martin Behaim, ein deutscher Seefahrer aus dem 15. Jahrhundert* (Wurzen, 1889) and compare the review in *Mitteilungen des Vereins für die Geschichte der Stadt Nürnberg,* VIII (1889), 260-261; E. Ravenstein, *Martin Behaim, his life and his globe* (London, 1908).

[47] See Clara Howard, *English Travellers of the Renaissance* (London, 1914), and compare C. S. Northup's review in *Journal of English and Germanic Philology,* XV (1916), 144-148. Note the references to books on Italy in J. W. Spargo, *Virgil the Necromancer* (Cambridge, Mass., 1934), pp. 412, 442 ff. and compare W. Waetzold, *Das klassische Land. Wandlungen der Italiensehnsucht* (Leipzig, 1927).

[48] A copy in the Newberry Library.

[49] See editions of these works in J. Scheible, *Bibliothek der Zauber-, Geheimnis- und Offenbarungsbücher* (Stuttgart, 1849-51, in 16 parts), and *Das Kloster* (Stuttgart, 1845-49).

For an excellent survey of the problems see A. Jacoby, "Die Zauberbücher vom Mittelalter bis zur Neuzeit: ihre Sammlung and Bearbeitung," *Mitteilungen der schlesischen Gesellschaft für Volkskunde,* XXXI-XXXII (1931), 208-228. The forthcoming article "Zauberbücher" in the *Handwörterbuch des deutschen Aberglaubens* will no doubt make important contributions to our knowledge. See further Lutz Mackensen, *Die deutschen Volksbücher* ("Forschungen zur deutschen Geistesgeschichte des Mittelalters and der Neuzeit," II; Leipzig, 1927), p. 53; O. Ebermann, "Albertus Magnus," *Handwörterbuch des deutschen Aberglaubens,* I (Berlin,

these, oneiromantic guides are compiled in the late Middle Ages in imitation of much older models. The history of these books is little known. Internal evidence would probably show when and where they were compiled. Comparison with collections of popular charms and incantations or with superstitious interpretations of dreams will probably give some impression of the influence which these books exerted on popular tradition and belief. No one appears to have used the oneiromantic materials in interpreting the dreams in the vernacular literatures of Western Europe.[50]

Closely associated with books of magic are books of charms and incantations, and many formulae now found in independent use are derived from books of magic. The history of these formulae and of the books containing them are interesting undertakings.[51] An example of

---

1927), 24, § 35 (this section deals rather briefly with the magical works ascribed to Albertus Magnus and will be enlarged in the supplement).

As examples of historical accounts of this sort of literature see Johannes Bolte's survey of books of divination: "Zur Geschichte der Losbücher," in *Georg Wickrams Werke,* IV ("Bibliothek des Literarischen Vereins," CCXXX; Tübingen, 1913), 276-347, and "Zur Geschichte der Punktier- und Losbücher," *Jahrbuch für historische Volkskunde,* I (1925), 185-214. Oskar Ebermann has written the history of a comparatively recent book of recipes; see "Le Médecin des Pauvres," *Zeitschrift des Vereins für Volkskunde,* XXIV (1914), 134-162.

For the bibliographical background see J. G. T. Grässe, *Bibliotheca magica et pneumatica, oder Bibliographie des Zauber-, Wunder-, Geister- und sonstigen Aberglaubens* (Leipzig, 1843); K. Sudhoff, *Deutsche medizinische Inkunabeln* ("Studien zur Geschichte der Medizin," II-III; Leipzig, 1908); *Bibliotheca pneumatica,* a catalogue (no. 31 ff.) issued by the bookseller J. Rosenthal; A. L. Caillet, *Manuel bibliographique des sciences psychiques ou occultes* (Paris, 1912). Indispensable for historical information is Lynn Thorndike, *A History of Magic and Experimental Science* (New York, 1923-34). Compare also W.-E. Peuckert, *Pansophie: ein Versuch zur Geschichte der weissen und schwarzen Magie* (Stuttgart, 1936), which deals primarily with German materials of the sixteenth and seventeenth centuries.

[50] See, e.g., G. D. Kelchner, *Dreams in Old Norse Literature and their Affinities in Folklore* (Cambridge, Eng., 1935). In my notice of this book (*Modern Philology,* XXXIII [1935-36], 212-213) various studies in the literary use of dreams are collected. Add to them: Otto Gotthardt, *Ueber die Traumbücher des Mittelalters* (Programm, Eisleben, 1912); F. Fürbringer, *De somniis in romanorum poetarum carminibus narratis* (Diss.; Jena, 1912) and Wilhelm Schmitz, *Traum und Vision in der erzählenden Dichtung des Mittelalters* ("Forschungen zur deutschen Sprache und Dichtung," V; Münster i. W., 1934).

[51] For the orthodox Christian formulae see Gelasius di Cilia, *Locupletissimus thesaurus varias selectissimas benedictiones, conjurationes, exorcismos, absolutiones, . . . Locupletior et correctior redditus* (Augsburg, 1716). For collections of charms see F. Ohrt, *Danmarks trylleformler* (Copenhagen, 1917-21); A. C. Bang, *Norske hekseformularer og magiske opskrifter* ("Skrifter udgivne af Videnskabsselskabet i Christiania;" Oslo, 1901-2); E. Linderholm, "Signelser ock besvär-

the sort of studies which might be undertaken is the history of the exegesis and use of the 108th Psalm (now the 109th). This was freely used against thieves in the Middle Ages, but the circumstances of its use are not fully known.[52]

An effective survey of prophetic literature in post-medieval Germany is lacking, perhaps because there is no text so important for Germany as the *Prophécies de Nostradamus* was for France. A single distinguished writer or work has often inspired the discussion of a genre. There were, to be sure, prophecies and writings modelled on prophecies which made a great stir in Germany at this time. I think, for example, of the *Reformation des Kaisers Sigismund,* which sought to give a plan for society, the *Wunderliche Weissagung* (derived ultimately from Joachim of Flora), which brought the condemnation of the city council at Nuremberg upon Andreas Osiander and Hans Sachs, and many writings of the Anabaptists (for example, Leonard Jobst of Strassburg). Significant as these may have been in one way or another, none of them enjoyed so long and so interesting a life as the *Prophécies de Nostradamus.* Although the *Sibyllenweissagung,* a work ultimately of classical origin, was reprinted many times,[53] the editions do not appear

jelser från medeltid ock nytid," *Svenska landsmål ock svenskt folkliv,* "Bilagor," 1927, no. 2 (Whole Series, no. 176), 1920, no. 2 (Whole Series, no. 185). Unfortunately, there is no standard collection of charms in either English or German. *Sapienti sat.* A good introduction to the types of German charms is an annotated edition of a collection in J. Lefftz, "Alte Heilsegen und Beschwörungsformeln; ein Beitrag zur religiösen Volkskunde des Elsass," *Archiv für elsässische Kirchengeschichte,* VII (1932), 189-226. An index to English or German charms would be a very useful undertaking.

For the history and interpretation of charms see Ferdinand Ohrt, *Da signed Krist—* (Copenhagen, 1927) and articles in the *Handwörterbuch des deutschen Aberglaubens* by Ebermann, Jacoby, and Ohrt. Ohrt's brief introduction—*Trylleord* ("Danmarks Folkeminder," XXV; Copenhagen, 1922)—is admirable.

[52] See Archer Taylor, "The Judas Curse," *American Journal of Philology,* XLII (1921), 236-237.

[53] Fundamental to further investigation is W.-E. Peuckert's brief and illuminating "Sibylle" in *Handwörterbuch des deutschen Aberglaubens,* VII (Berlin, 1936), cols. 1656-59. His *Sibylle Weiss* has not been published. See also L. Darnedde, *Deutsche Sibyllen-weissagung* (Greifswald diss.; Charlottenburg, 1933). Another work of similar nature is available in a modern edition with rich annotations; see P. Piur (ed.). *Oraculum angelicum Cyrilli* in K. Burdach, *Vom Mittelalter zur Reformation,* II, iv (Berlin, 1912), 221-343.

Important works for the materials and background of prophecy in the sixteenth century are W.-E. Peuckert, "Deutsche Volkspropheten," *Zeitschrift für die alttestamentliche Wissenschaft,* N.F. XII (1935), 35-54 (a characterization of the psychological peculiarities of these figures); J. Rohr, "Die Prophetie im letzten Jahrhundert vor der Reformation als Geschichtsquelle und Warnung," *Historisches Jahrbuch,* XIX (1898), 29-56, 547-566; A. M. Warburg, "Heidnisch-antike Weis-

to vary greatly. This work has been fully studied. On the other hand, J. L. Lichtenberg's prophecies, which were widely circulated in the sixteenth century, are yet to be investigated.[54] Prophecies were freely used in the perpetual calendar (*Praktik*) and gave rise to satirical parodies by Rabelais and, more or less directly dependent on him, to those by Johannes Nas and Johann Fischart. Curiously enough, Fischart took a great deal from the writings of his opponent, Nas. Much of this prophetic literature derives ultimately from the Apocalypse, various pseudo-apocalyptic writings, and writers and seers like Joachim of Flora. It remains to be learned how much of this prophetic writing is essentially German. Probably the bulk of it, like the inspiration to write it, is of international origin.

Almanacs and calendars, which have much in common with prophecies, contain a surprising amount of cultural information. We need a good historical account of the genre. Good bibliographies of English and American almanacs are available; the German materials are less well catalogued.[55] Admirable investigations—notably that by G. L. Kittredge—suggest problems and ways to solve them.[56]

---

sagung im Wort und Bild zu Luthers Zeiten," *Sitzungsberichte der Heidelberger Akademie, philosophisch-historische Klasse,* XI (1920), no. 26; H. Grundmann, "Die Pabstprophetien des Mittelalters," *Archiv für Kulturgeschichte,* XIX (1928-29), 77-138; Heinrich Werner, *Die Flugschrift 'Onus ecclesiae' mit einem Anhang über soziale und kirchenpolitische Prophetien* (Diss.; Giessen, 1900). Stammler, p. 462 (note on p. 16). Peuckert's various articles, "Prophete" and "Prophetie," in *Handwörterbuch des deutschen Aberglaubens,* VII (1935-36), cols. 338-366 and "Weissager" und "Weissagung," *ibid.,* IX (1938), *passim* are indispensable.

For a survey of prophetic writing see H. J. Forman's entertaining work, *The Story of Prophecy in the Life of Mankind from Early Times to the Present Day* (New York, 1936). A. Ritter collects the German materials in convenient form in *Collectio vaticiniorum das ist, Propheceien vnd Weissagungen* (Berlin, 1923). In studying these matters we can range far afield; see, e.g., W.-E. Peuckert, "Germanische Eschatologien," *Archiv für Religionswissenschaft,* XXXII (1935), 1-37. Bibliographical information may be found in a variety of places, e.g., A. L. Caillet, *Manuel bibliographique des sciences psychiques ou occultes* (Paris, 1912).

[54] J. Franck, *Allgemeine deutsche Biographie,* XVIII (Leipzig, 1883), 538.

[55] For bibliographies of English and American almanacs see E. F. Bosanquet, *English Printed Almanacs and Prognostications; a bibliographical history to the year 1600* ("Bibliographical Society, Illustrated Monographs," XVII; London, 1917), and the additions in *The Library,* 4th Ser., VIII (1928), 456-477; H. A. Morrison, *Preliminary Check List of American Almanacs (1630-1800)* (Washington, D.C., 1907). For the titles of German almanacs see K. Sudhoff, *Deutsche medizinische Inkunabeln* ("Studien zur Geschichte der Medizin," II-III; Leipzig, 1908), pp. 265-271, "Praktiken und Prognostikationen," and the works cited below.

[56] For discussions of the cultural elements in almanacs see G. L. Kittredge, *The Old Farmer and his Almanac* (Boston, 1904); E. F. Bosanquet, "English Seventeenth-Century Almanacks; (1) Their History, (2) As Books of Reference, (3) As

24. *The Literary History of Jest-Books.*—Among the various literary species of the late fifteenth century and the whole of the next centuries, the jest in prose—very rarely in verse—offers perhaps the simplest and yet the most varied problems. My interest in these problems and the abundance of materials within our reach lead me to deal with the literary history of jest-books at considerable length. I shall have occasion to point out the need for new editions, the definition of genres, the characterization of types of jest-books, the search for sources, and many another bit of information.

In the description of problems concerned with Renaissance jest-books I shall not stress the antecedents of the Renaissance jest. The medieval short story exhibits many varieties,—the *bispel,* the fable, the exemplum (often in Latin or German prose), the humorous tale, the legend, and the historical anecdote. Except for the *bispel,* these varieties are perhaps adequately described for our purposes.[57] The selection of medieval Ger-

a Medium for Advertisement, (4) The MS Notes in Them by Contemporary Owners," *The Library,* 4th Ser., X (1930), 361-397; G. Hellmann, "Die Meteorologie in den deutschen Flugschriften und Flugblättern des 16. Jahrhunderts; ein Beitrag zur Geschichte der Meteorologie," *Abhandlungen der preusissischen Akademie der Wissenschaften, physikalisch-mathematische Klasse,* 1921, no. 1, and "Versuch einer Geschichte der Wettervorhersage im 16. Jahrhundert," *ibid.,* 1924, no. 1 (primarily a bibliography); *Meteorologische Volksbücher* (2d ed.; Berlin, 1895); *Beiträge zur Geschichte der Meteorologie,* I-V ("Veröffentlichungen des königlich preussischen meteorologischen Instituts," CCLXXIII ff.; Berlin, 1914 ff.). A larger scene is surveyed in G. Bilfinger's works. Perhaps the best small book to be used in conjunction with Hellmann's *Volksbücher* is W. Uhl, *Unser Kalender in seiner Entwicklung von den ältesten Anfängen bis heute* (Paderborn, 1893). See also L. Sig, *Vorgregorianische Bauernkalender; ein Beitrag zur christlichen Kalenderkunde* (Programm; Strassburg, 1905).

For editions of old calendars see P. Heitz and K. Haebler, *Hundert Kalenderinkunabeln* (*Strassburg,* 1905). A manual of these materials is Eucharius Rösslin, *Kalendar mit allen astronomischen Haltungen* (1533). Published by Christian Egenolf, who issued many convenient compendia, Rösslin's *Kalendar* contains information about the influence of the stars, the value of the astrolabe, and the superstitions associated with the calendar and the weather. Remember also that Melanchthon wrote a calendar in Latin verse.

For an example of literary studies in almanacs see Adolf Hauffen, "Fischart-Studien, IV," *Euphorion,* V (1898), 25-47, 226-256. It is given in condensed form in his *Johann Fischart* (Berlin, 1922), I, 143-153, II, 401-402. This essay contains an extensive bibliography.

[57] See H. H. Borcherdt, *Geschichte des Romans und der Novelle in Deutschland,* I, *Vom frühen Mittelalter bis Wieland* (Leipzig, 1926); H. Weisser, *Die deutsche Novelle im Mittelalter auf dem Untergrund der geistigen Strömungen* (Freiburg, i.Br., 1926). On the *bispel* see Ehrismann, p. 344; on the fable see W. Kayser, "Die Grundlagen der deutschen Fabeldichtung des 16. und 18. Jahrhunderts," [Herrig's]

man tales in print provides an ample background for the student of the Renaissance jest. At the height of Romantic interest in medieval studies, Johann Nepomuk Graf von Mailáth and J. P. Köffinger called attention to the genre by printing selections from one of the most important medieval anthologies of tales in verse.[58] During the next generation, several such tales were issued separately. Finally, in 1850, Friedrich von der Hagen printed a round hundred stories with scholarly discussions of origins and of texts.[59] A generation later, Heinrich Lambel printed a good anthology of tales.[60] Today, critical editions of texts have been prepared and something of a start has been made in the investigation of Der Stricker, the most voluminous and most interesting writer of tales.

The German jest-book, with which we are particularly concerned, is a genre with its beginnings in the last years of the fifteenth century. It appears to have had no significant relations to the medieval tales in verse except in so far as the medieval tale drew more frequently upon oral tradition. The genre of the jest-book approached its end in the early years of the seventeenth century. We have therefore to consider the two centuries of its history.

Thanks to Herman Oesterley, Johannes Bolte, and Albert Wesselski, the German jest-books of the sixteenth century are available in admirably annotated editions, and the few remaining gaps can be easily filled. Although the German collections issued in the first seventy years of the century are for the most part accessible, the early Latin collec-

---

Archiv für das Studium der neueren Sprachen, CLX (1931), 19-33; on the exemplum see M. D. Howie, *Studies in the Use of Exempla* (Diss.; London, 1923); J. T. Welter, *L'exemplum dans la littérature réligieuse et didactique du moyen-âge* (Paris, 1927). Joseph Bédier's *Les Fabliaux* (Paris, 1893; 2d ed., 1895; later editions unchanged), has been a powerful stimulus to the study of the humorous tale. Few of its readers have consulted the important critical remarks of W. Cloetta, [Herrig's] *Archiv für das Studium der neueren Sprachen,* XCIII (1894), 206-226, and F. von der Leyen, *ibid.,* CXVI (1906), 292-300.

[58] *Koloczaer Codex altdeutscher Gedichte* (Pesth, 1817). There is a copy in the University of Chicago Library. Graf von Mailáth published translations of some of the tales in *Auserlesene altdeutsche Gedichte* (Stuttgart, 1819).

[59] *Gesammtabenteuer. Hundert altdeutsche Erzählungen: Ritter- und Pfaffen-Mären; Stadt- und Dorfgeschichten; Schwänke, Wundersagen und Legenden* (Stuttgart, 1850). The demands of scholars soon called for more than von der Hagen offered, but at the time of publication his notes were all that could be expected. A new edition of *Gesammtabenteuer* by H. Niewöhner (Berlin, 1937 ff.) is now appearing.

[60] *Erzählungen und Schwänke* ("Deutsche Classiker des Mittelalters," XII; 2d ed.; Leipzig, 1883).

tions are still imperfectly known. Johann Adelphus Muling's *Margarita facetiarum* (1508),[61] with its appendix of "Scommata" attributed to Johannes Geiler von Kaisersberg, ought to be republished or excerpted and described. Beyond Goedeke's conjecture that it may have found its way into the British Museum, no one seems to know anything about Chr. B. Hyrtwyl, *Etlich Historien vnnd fabeln gantz lustig zu lesen* (1512).[62] Collections belonging to the early years of the sixteenth century—a time when the genre was taking shape—must be accurately known before a literary history of the genre is possible. An insufficiently known jest-book of the middle of the century is Nicodemus Frischlin's *Facetiae*.[63] It was rather widely circulated and can probably be taken as representative of the current taste in jests. Its interest lies in its possible value as an anthology of hackneyed jests; one would not turn to it for novelties of any kind. Bernardino Ochino's *Apologe*,[64] on the other hand, is important because it was first issued in Italian and was then re-issued in an enlarged form in Germany (1556, 1559). It is therefore an example of the communication of materials between Italy and Germany. These and other jest-books published in the last quarter of the sixteenth century, and many of those published in the seventeenth century are imperfectly known to us. Even the titles of these collections have been listed only in general bibliographies. To be sure, the individual collections may be relatively unimportant compilations of older materials, but even so, the fact remains to be established. We cannot estimate the significance and influence of these books or fix their position in the history and development of the genre until we know something about their contents, sources, purposes, and style. Two generations ago, Wilhelm Scherer stated the tasks to be done briefly and emphatically: "Der Grundstock dieser kleinen Erzählungen war zu classificiren, auf ihren Ursprung anzusehen, dann zu beobachten, wie weit er bleibt und wiederkehrt, wie weit er sich verliert, wie weit er sich vermehrt; wie viel aus der schriftlichen Ueberlieferung, wie viel aus dem

---

[61] The *Margarita* is in the Newberry Library. On Muling see Stammler, p. 469 (note on p. 57); J. Knepper, "Ein elsässischer Arzt der Humanistenzeit als deutscher Poet," *Jahrbuch für Geschichte, Sprache, und Litteratur Elsass-Lothringens,* XVII (1901), 17-24.

[62] *Grundriss,* I, 375, no. 13.

[63] An edition published before 1560 and the editions of 1600, 1615, and 1619 are in the University of Chicago Library. On Frischlin see D. F. Strauss, *Leben und Schriften des Dichters und Philologen Nicodemus Frischlin* (Frankfurt a. M., 1855).

[64] Ed. K. Amrain; "Der Volksmund," VII-VIII; Leipzig, 1907. Ochino's *Apologe* is a source of criticisms of the church.

Leben stammt. Der lokale und litterarische Gesichtskreis jeder Sammlung war zu erforschen u.s.w."[65]

A complete new edition of an unpublished jest-book is often unnecessary. Analyses like A. L. Stiefel's investigations into the anonymous *Schertz mit der Warheyt* (1550), a hodge-podge of contemporary collections, T. F. Dunn's study of the fourth book of the *Mensa philosophica* (*ca.* 1492), and Albert Wesselski's summary of the *Emplastrum cornelianum* (1605) by Johann Sommer satisfy our needs.[66] Such studies may lead to new discoveries. Although Heinrich Kurz gave abundant notes on the fourth book of Burkhard Waldis's *Esopus* (1547), its sources are not yet fully known and the author's purposes are not clearly perceived.[67]

We have a good bibliography of the original texts and the modern editions in H. Hayn and A. N. Gotendorf, *Bibliotheca germanorum erotica et curiosa.*[68] This work indicates where the original texts, which often exist in very few copies, may be found. Oesterley, Bolte, and Wesselski have given us admirably annotated modern editions. Finally we have many preliminary studies of various sorts.[69] In perhaps no

---

[65] *Die Anfänge des deutschen Prosaromans und Jörg Wickram von Colmar* ("Quellen und Forschungen zur Sprach- und Culturgeschichte der germanischen Völker," XXI; Strassburg, 1877), pp. 20-21. I have omitted a footnote not pertinent in this connection.

[66] A. L. Stiefel, "Ueber das Schwankbuch 'Schertz mit der Warheyt,'" [Herrig's] *Archiv,* XCV (1895), 55- 106; T. F. Dunn, *The Facetiæ of the 'Mensa philosophica'* ("Washington University Studies," no. 5; St. Louis, Mo., 1934); A. Wesselski, "Johann Sommers 'Emplastrum cornelianum' und seine Quellen," *Euphorion,* XV (1908), 1-19. An old study is Franz Schnorr von Carolsfeld, "Ueber 'Klaus Narr' und M. Wolfgang Büttner," *Archiv für Litteraturgeschichte,* VI (1876-77), 277-329.

[67] Ernst Martens, *Entstehung des Esopus von B. Waldis* (Diss.; Göttingen, 1907), pp. 75-80.

[68] Third ed.; Munich, 1912-29. See also Goedeke, II, 457-473, § 159. Melander's curious contemporary bibliography of Renaissance jest-books extends only to "O" in the editions within my reach; see F. Gerhard, *Joh. Peter de Memels 'Lustige Gesellschaft'* (Halle, 1893), p. 16.

The *Volksbücher,* which belong primarily to another genre, are also carefully listed. See P. Heitz and F. Ritter, *Versuch einer Zusammenstellung der deutschen Volksbücher des 15. und 16. Jahrhunderts nebst deren späteren Ausgaben und Literatur* (Strassburg, 1924) and compare an important review in *Zeitschrift des Vereins für Volkskunde,* XXXV-XXXVI (1925-26), 128. Only the Italian *novelle* have been listed with equal care.

[69] See as a general introduction: Gustav Bebermeyer, "Facetie," in *Reallexikon der deutschen Literaturgeschichte,* I, 340-344, and "Schwank" in *ibid.,* III, 208-213. Compare also Ignaz Hub, *Die komische und humoristische Literatur des 16. Jahrhunderts* (Strassburg, 1856-57); H. Gumbel, "Zur deutschen Schwankliteratur im 17. Jahrhundert," *Zeitschrift für deutsche Philologie,* LIII (1928), 303-346; Heinz

other movement or genre of literature in the fifteenth and sixteenth centuries, except that of the lyric, is the student provided with such satisfactory tools.

Kindermann, *Die deutschen Schwankbücher des 16. Jahrhunderts* ("Heimatblätter des deutschen Heimatbundes Danzig," VI, no. 3; Danzig, 1929) ; G. Kuttner, *Wesen und Formen der deutschen Schwankliteratur des 16. Jahrhunderts* ("Germanische Studien," CLIII; Berlin, 1934). Compare K. Herz, *Soziale Typen in den Prosaschwänken des 16. Jahrhunderts* (MS diss.; Frankfurt a. M., 1925).

The problems in the *Volksbücher* are somewhat different from those in the jest-books. Consult such general works as Joseph Görres, *Die teutschen Volksbücher: nähere Würdigung der schönen Historischen, Wetter- und Arzneybüchlein, welche theils innerer Werth, theils Zufall, Jahrhunderte hindurch bis auf unsere Zeit erhalten hat* (Heidelberg, 1817) ; R. Benz, *Geschichte und Aesthetik der deutschen Volksbücher* (Jena, 1924) ; Lutz Mackensen, *Die deutschen Volksbücher* ("Forschungen zur deutschen Geistesgeschichte," II; Leipzig, 1927) ; F. Podleiszek, *Die Kulturentwicklung vom Mittelalter zur Neuzeit in den deutschen Volksbüchern des 15. und 16. Jahrhunderts* (Diss.; Vienna, 1929. Although this dissertation was not published, the results are available in the prefaces to the author's *Anfänge des bürgerlichen Prosaromans in Deutschland* [Leipzig, 1933] and *Volksbücher von Weltweite und Abenteuerlust* [Leipzig, 1936], both in the series "Deutsche Literatur") ; W.-E. Peuckert, "Der Ausgang des Mittelalters und das Volksbuch," *Zeitschrift für Deutschkunde,* L (1936), 663-676. Typical studies are W. Hesse, *Das Schicksal des Lalebuches in der deutschen Literatur* (Diss.; Breslau, 1929) ; W. Hilsberg, *Der Aufbau des Eulenspiegel-Volksbuchs von 1515* (Diss.; Hamburg, 1933) ; F. F. Siggelkow, *Studien zu den mittelniederdeutschen Volksbüchern* (Diss.; Greifswald, 1930) ; H. Tiedge, *Jörg Wickram und die Volksbücher* (Göttingen diss.; Hannover, 1904). For a statement of problems see F. Stroh, "Volksbuchprobleme," *Dichtung und Volkstum,* XXXVI (1935), 78-87. A comparison of the results in R. Paulli's "Folkebøgernes historie" and "Folkebøgernes illustrationer" in *Danske folkebøger fra 16. og 17. aarhundrede,* XIII (Copenhagen, 1936), 171-364 with the German investigations is instructive. I shall indicate only one problem in the study of the *Volksbuch*. No one has stopped to resolve the conflict of opinions regarding the source of the *Volksbuch Griselda*. Some have maintained that it was derived from Steinhöwel's translation and others from that of Nikolaus von Wyle. See P. Heitz and F. Ritter, *Versuch einer Zusammenstellung der deutschen Volksbücher des 15. und 16. Jahrhunderts* (Strassburg, 1924), p. 63, n. 1.

The problems of the origins of the novel have only a little in common with the history of the jest-book. Consult F. Bobertag, *Geschichte des Romans und der ihm verwandten Dichtungsgattungen, I, Bis zum Ausgang des 18. Jahrhunderts* (Berlin, 1881-84), and the searching criticism of Wilhelm Scherer, *Die Anfänge des deutschen Prosaromans und Jörg Wickram* ("Quellen und Forschungen zur Sprach- und Culturgeschichte der germanischen Völker," XXI; Strassburg, 1877).

Compare the surveys of the jests and jest-books in other countries, e.g., L. di Francia, *Novellistica,* I ("Storia dei generi letterari italiani," XI; Milan, 1924) ; Rudolf Besthorn, *Ursprung und Eigenart der älteren italienischen Novelle* ("Romanistische Arbeiten," XXIV; Halle, 1935) ; Giambattista Marchesi, *Per la storia della novella nel secolo XVII* (Rome, 1897) ; M. Menéndez y Pelayo, *Orígenes de la*

The German jest-book springs from many sources—the fable, the facetia, the exemplum, the traditional tale, and the Italian novella. Its relations to the fable are tenuous and are broken almost at the start. In general, the jest-books included comparatively few fables, but the collections of fables endeavored on occasion to gain a wider audience by taking up narrative materials belonging to the jest-books. The moralizing tag which often appears along with jests in the early collections belongs probably to the exemplum rather than the fable, but this origin remains to be demonstrated. The stream which the Latin facetia poured into the jest-book was large, but its full extent and nature have not been perceived. Besides making a contribution to the subject-matter of the jest-books, the facetia may have led the authors to seek elegance of style. As we know, the aim of the humanists who wrote facetiæ was to create a polished narrative. The position and importance of Sebastian Brant's *Liber faceti* (1496) is yet to be made out. Stammler (p. 192) says that he was writing a book for his son to provide instruction in the aspects of life and conduct that were neglected in the moral verses of the pseudo-Cato. His inclusion of thirty-five loose tales from the facetiæ of Poggio was intended, Brant said, to illuminate the weaknesses of mankind. In the history of the German adaptations of Latin facetiæ, the place of Otmar Nachtigall, sometimes called Luscinius, is still to be fixed.[70] About the beginning of the sixteenth century, the Latin facetia seemed to be establishing itself in German literature. The second quarter of the century saw virtually no collections of this sort, and after the middle of the century Michael Lindener, the author of the *Rastbüchlein* (1558) and the *Katzipori* (1558), sought to re-establish the facetia in German literature.[71] Although the historical

---

novela, I-IV ("Nueva biblioteca de autores españoles," I, VII, XIV, XXI; Madrid, 1905-15), especially the preface to Vol. I; L. Sainéan, *Problèmes littéraires du 16ᵉ siécle* (Paris, 1927), which is particularly useful for the variety of problems discussed; Pietro Toldo, *Contributo allo studio della novella francese del XV e XVI secolo* (Rome, 1895) ; Ernst Schulz, *Die englischen Schwankbücher bis herab zu Dobson's 'Drie Bobs' (1607)* ("Palaestra," CXVII; Berlin, 1912).

[70] See, e.g., Charles Schmidt, *Histoire littéraire de l'Alsace* (Paris, 1879), II, 174-208; H. A. Lier, "Ottmar Nachtigalls 'Ioci ac sales mire festivi.' Ein Beitrag zur Kenntnis der Schwankliteratur im 16. Jahrhundert," *Archiv für Literaturgeschichte,* XI (1882), 1-50; K. Hartfelder, *Zeitschrift für die Geschichte des Oberrheins,* XLV (1891) ; 168-170; E. Schröder, "Beiträge zum Lebensbilde Dr. Otmar Nachtgalls," *Historisches Jahrbuch im Auftrage der Görresgesellschaft,* XIV (1893), 83-106.

[71] Bebermeyer in *Reallexikon der deutschen Literaturgeschichte,* III, 212. Compare also his article "Facetie" in *ibid.,* I, 340-344; K. Vollert, *Zur Geschichte der lateinischen Facetiensammlungen des 15. und 16. Jahrhunderts* ("Palaestra," CXIII; Berlin, 1912).

study of the German-Latin facetia has been prosecuted with vigor and and success, the subject is not exhausted. A review of the connections of the facetia and the jest would throw light on the development of the jest-book as a genre.

We should not fail to recognize that the facetia exerted an indirect influence on collections of jests through the collections of table-talk. Desiderius Erasmus established a tradition of easy talk in his *Colloquia familiaria* (1524) ; Conrad Peutinger maintained at Augsburg a table in the classical manner; Luther's remarks at dinner were carefully written down, but were not published for a generation (1566). Such is the background of the collections of jests designed to provide materials for table-talk. The pattern is already established in the anonymous *Mensa philosophica* of the late fifteenth century. The first three chapters of this work constitute a serious treatise on dietetics. The fourth chapter, "De honestis jocis," which is by another hand, is a compilation of jests descended largely from the exemplum-books, and arranged in the manner characteristic of collections of exempla. Later jest-books under the influence of the tradition of table-talk are Johannes Peregrinus, *Convivalium sermonum liber* (1542), Johann Gast, *Tomus primus convivalium sermonum* (1542), which was enlarged to two voumes in 1548, later to three volumes, and finally changed its name to *Florilegium historicum* etc. (1686), and various works by Gaspar Ens, *Pavsilypsus* (1631) and *Epidorpidum libri IV* (1648).[72]

As early as Heinrich Bebel's Latin collection of jests (1508), almost the first collection to be made in Germany and definitely influenced by the Latin facetia current in Italy and humanistic models, we find an admixture of German traditional stories. In all the later German jest-books, we find a similar admixture. The extent and nature of the contribution of German tradition to the stock of the jest-book remains to be made out. After the middle of the sixteenth century, a departure from the conventional materials is seen in the inclusion of historical incidents. This is typical of Hans Wilhelm Kirchhof's *Wendunmut* (1563-1603). The title is similar to those of *Schimpf und Ernst* (1522) and *Schildwacht* (1560) and many another jest-book of the period in

---

[72] These works are in the University of Chicago Library. Gast, vol. I is the second edition (1549) bound with vol. II (1st ed., 1548) ; it may be compared with the edition of 1566 and the *Florilegium* (1686).

As an example of the interest in table-manners, see J. W. Stuck, *Antiquitatum convivalium libri III in quibus Hebraeorum, Graecorum, Romanorum aliarumque nationum antique conviviorum genera, nec non more, consuetudines, ceremoniaeque conviviales etc. multa grammatica, physica, medica, ethica, oeconomica, politica etc. jucunda simul et utilia tractantur* (Zürich, 1582).

suggesting that the purpose is to amuse the reader, but the contents have changed greatly. Although the modern reader may correctly interpret *Schimpf* as *jest*, he is not likely to perceive that *Schimpf und Ernst* is a survival of a medieval conventional phrase belonging to the language of tournaments.[73] The title "Schimpf und Ernst" suggested titles for many later collections, e.g. J. de Brune, *Jok en Ernst, dat is: allerlei deftige Hofredenen, Quinkslagen, Boeteryen etc. gevvnden . . . van Prinssen, Mevrouwen etc.*[74]

By the middle of the sixteenth century—and perhaps earlier, German collectors of jests drew directly upon vernacular Italian collections. The extent and nature of this influence are yet to be discovered. Characterizations of the contents and sources of the German jest-books are greatly needed to clarify the history of the genre; they can be easily made with the excellent annotated editions at our disposal.

An important source from which German jest-books of the sixteenth century descend is the medieval exemplum or illustrative tale for use in sermons. Characteristic details of the collections of exempla persist in the epoch-making *Schimpf und Ernst* (1522) of Johannes Pauli. The title shows clearly that a didactic purpose—a purpose appropriate enough for a Franciscan monk—guided him in part. The arrangement of the jests according to topics and the moralizing tags descend directly from collections of exempla. The materials, too, are taken in large part from such collections. These and other characteristcs belonging to collections of exempla are still found in jest-books compiled after the middle of the sixteenth century. In this connection, I may mention the possibility of studying the moralizing tags attached to the stories. No one has, so far as I am aware, compared the various moralizations attached to a particular story and endeavored to draw some inferences from the materials. Such a study would provide a background for comment on the use of moralizations in the early jest-books.[75]

In the seventeenth century, the jest-books in German and Latin became mere collections of bons mots, epigrams, and apophthegms with a constantly declining proportion of narrative materials. This transformation did not so rapidly overtake the Latin collections illustrated by such little-known works as the *Jocoseria* (1605) of Otto Melander, the *Pia hilaria* (1622) of Angelinus Gazaeus with a rare, spurious second part (1638), and the longlived *Democritus ridens* (1649) ascribed to J. P.

[73] E. Wiessner, *Kommentar zu Heinrich Wittenweilers 'Ring'* ("Deutsche Literatur"; Leipzig, 1936), p. 61 (note on ll. 1193 ff.).

[74] Amsterdam, 1650.

[75] See L. K. Born's instructive comment on the interpretations attached to stories by Ovid in "Ovid and Allegory," *Speculum*, IX (1934), 373-379.

Lange.[76] The history of these Latin collections is yet to be written. As an example of the details to be considered, note that, according to Brunet, the *Facetiæ facetiarum* of 1645 contains six items not in the edition of 1615, and conversely, the edition of 1615 contains three items which were not reprinted in the later issue.[77] More difficult than a history of the Latin collections would be an account of the German jest-books such as *Lyrum Larum* (*ca.* 1670), *Der Geist von Jan Tambour* (1652),[78] *Der Geist von Jan Trompeter* (*ca.* 1668), Christophorus Friedrici (pseud.), *Oel und Wein* (1719), and the like.[79] In this field, Hayn and Gotendorf's bibliography is an indispensable guide.

A new form of jest-book established itself in the sixteenth century, although examples had been known in German literature from the days of Der Stricker's *Pfaffe Amis* (*ca.* 1225), the jests about Neidhart (13th cent.), and the internationally known *Salomon and Marcolphus,* which came to Germany about 1482. This form is marked by the concentration of a single type of narrative about a central figure. It comes to a climax in *Kalenberger* (*ca.* 1473), *Eulenspiegel* (1515), *Peter Leu* (1550), which calls itself a "second Kalenberger," *Finkenritter* (1560), and *Lalebuch* (1597) soon rebaptized as *Schiltbürger* (1598).[80] The geographical distribution of these books has not yet been described, but it appears to differ from that of the jest-books previously described. Tales similarly grouped about one figure are found in other lands and ages. The stories about Nasreddin form a cycle in the Levant, and stories about fools have always grouped themselves together. Ra-

---

[76] The editions of *ca.* 1600, 1604-5 (vol. 3 lacking), 1605 ("Centuria secunda" only), 1611, 1617, 1626, and 1643 of Melander, the first part of Gazaeus (1657), and the editions of 1649, 1696, 1701, and 1754 of *Democritus ridens* are in the University of Chicago Library. I have the *Pia hilaria* (editions of 1622, 1629, and 1657) and the spurious second part (editions of 1638 and 1657). On Melander see E. Schröder, "Otto Melander von Mederhone und sein Buch von Schimpf und Ernst," *Das Werratal,* II (1925), 4-6. Melander's jest-book was one of the few issued in a German edition. *Die Kunst der Vergnüglichkeit* (1678. Copy in the University of Chicago Library), ascribed to J. Lange, is a book of moralizing; it has no connection, as one might possibly have suspected, with the *Democritus ridens* ascribed to J. P. Lange.

[77] The University of Chicago Library has the editions of 1615 and 1657.

[78] Ascribed to J. P. Meerhuysen; see H. J. A. Ruys, *Nieuw nederlandsch biographisch Woordenboek* (Leiden, 1921), V, 338-340.

[79] I have named as examples only works which are in the University of Chicago library. Volumes II and III of *Oel und Wein* are lacking.

[80] For bibliographical references to these works see P. Heitz and F. Ritter, *Versuch einer Zusammenstellung der deutschen Volksbücher des 15. und 16. Jahrhunderts nebst deren späteren Ausgaben und Literatur* (Strassburg, 1924). Compare also Ehrismann, p. 521.

belais used a folk-tale of Gargantua which was probably of a cyclical type. Although not a collection of stories, Brant's *Narrenschiff* has some similarity to jest-books dealing with a single character. On the whole, the jest-books with a single hero and a single type of tale stand apart from the ordinary jest-book. Borrowings of stories from one class to the other have not been frequent. Conceivably one might write a literary history of the jest-book with a single hero and compare with the type such collections of materials on a single theme as the *Faustbuch* and the *Narrenschiff*. The history might end with *Münchhausen* or even with Wilhelm Busch's *Max und Moritz,* the progenitors of the Katzenjammer Kids.

The geography of the jest-books is still largely unexplored. At the beginning of the sixteenth century, Alsatian writers—Sebastian Brant, Johann Adelphus Muling, and Johannes Pauli—and the Swabian Heinrich Bebel compiled jest-books, and in the middle of the century, such writers as Jörg Wickram and Martin Montanus continued the tradition. In other parts of Germany few jest-books were compiled. Jest-books imply the existence of a bourgeois audience with time to read. Such an audience was to be found in Southern Germany. The study of the geographical aspect of the jest-book is yet to be undertaken in an effective way. An even more obscure chapter is that of the religious affiliations of the compilers.

Concluding the subject of the jest-books, I mention the problem of their international relations. As we have seen, the earliest jest-books in Germany were connected with Latin religious stories or exempla and Latin rhetorical exercises or facetiæ. I have raised the questions of the extent and the nature of the influence of native oral tales and the Italian novelle. In all this discussion, the German jest-book has been considered as the borrower and not the lender. During its later history—particularly after say 1570,—the German jest-book becomes a model and a source for jest-books in the Netherlands and Scandinavia. Such collections as the *Wechkorter,* the *Tidsfordriv,* and the *Geest van Jan Tamboer* are closely connected with German jest-books. These relations are yet to be summarized.

The identification of jest-books which are cited by short titles or paraphrases of the true titles is often difficult. Some of the most distinguished scholars in our field have endeavored without success to identify the *Buch der kleinen warheit* used by the Meistersinger of the early sixteenth century.[81] Possibly a systematic comparison of the tales ascribed to it with the collections available to the Meistersinger will identify it as one of the familiar collections of the age.

[81] See my *Literary History of Meistergesang* (New York, 1937), p. 111, n. 63.

25. *The History of a Theme.*—A commonplace of literary history is the assertion that post-medieval German authors avidly sought new themes. The assertion is indeed true : many old themes persist in the latter period and many new ones appear in the rising tide of drama and jest. From this fact springs a type of investigation characteristic of the study of post-medieval German literature : the employment of such themes as Griselda, the Prodigal Son, or the peasant is traced through a series of literary works. In treating such problems of literary history, we must seek far more than a compilation of titles illustrating the theme and a tabulation of the differences and similarities exhibited by various texts. Compilations and tabulations, useful as they are, will scarcely supply more than the scaffolding on which to erect a structure of enduring worth. We must add the building; to change the figure, we must illuminate and interpret the variations and resemblances in the light of a full knowledge of the authors and their environments.

By way of preliminary illustration of the treatment of the history of themes, let us first take examples from a later period, one nearer our own. The Romanticists employ some themes from Scandinavian story. With this fact in mind we are immediately confronted by such questions as: What Scandinavian themes are used? Do they belong to any specific classes? When in the course of the Romantic movement do they appear? What authors use them? What relation has their use to the various typical Romantic notions, and particularly to the Romantic interest in Germanic antiquity? Can we recognize any work as giving an initial impetus or as changing the course of the current? In the light of answers to such questions, we can interpret the cultural and historical values of such a book as Fouqué's *Sigurd der Drachentödter* (1808). In this case, to be sure, we must consider whether the interest in a Scandinavian subject or in the German *Nibelungenlied* inspired the choice of the theme, and assign, if need be, to each motive its proper value.[82]

If we do not limit ourselves to a single epoch, we may ask: In what different ways have various ages conceived the same theme? An answer is but the idle accumulation of facts unless it relates the differences to the respective ages or estimates the literary and esthetic worth of the variations, and by this means enriches and enlarges our knowledge and appreciation of literature. The theme of Pygmalion and Galathea offers variations which will illustrate my point. Thus, Francis Bacon uses the theme as an example of the scholastic fault of preferring verbal analysis to the observation of things. "Of this vanity, Pygmalion's frenzy is a

[82] J. Krejčí, "Nordische Stoffe bei Fouqué," *Vierteljahrschrift für Litteraturgeschichte*, VI (1893), 553-570 deals chiefly with the manner of Fouqué's treatment and less with his sources and the reasons for his familiarity with them.

good emblem; for words are but the images of matter, and except they have life of reason and invention, to fall in love with them is all one as to fall in love with a picture."[83] In the middle of the eighteenth century, the theme is used to reflect notions of social classes conceived in the surging currents which swept away the ancien régime. In modern times, the theme owes its popularity largely to Jean Jacques Rousseau, directly or indirectly, and his influence can be perceived easily in the eighteenth-century versions with a pastoral coloring. Karl Leberecht Immermann's *Der neue Pygmalion* (1825, revised in 1829) adapts the old theme to the modern question whether a man in a higher social and intellectual position should and could marry the woman of his choice.[84] This question interested Immermann's contemporaries, and appears again and again in the works of George Sand and the Young Germans. A century later, when Bernard Shaw dramatizes the old story, he reflects a new attitude determined by the preoccupation of his age with social problems. He deals with the rehabilitation of the lower classes and has of course no occasion to utilize the pastoral or feministic traits of the older versions. The scientific attitude of the nineteenth century enlarged the domain of the symbol. Faust is not a medieval philosopher, but a builder of canals and a drainer of swamps. The additions to our positive knowledge did not destroy myths, but led to their more pregnant application.[85]

In studying the history of a theme, one may ask also why the artistic possibilities which seem to be inherent in a particular subject have never found adequate expression. Sophonisba, for example, has never provided the theme for a really great drama, but the theme may deserve a better fate than it has had. How and why have writers failed to achieve the realization of its possibilities? Such a critical problem might well be difficult to anchor and should not be undertaken by one not aware of the difficulties involved. Does the fault lie in the writers, or is it in the theme?

One can consider also the essential nature of the various genres by comparing dramatic, lyric, and epic treatments of the same theme. How does it come about that a particular theme ordinarily lends itself to effective treatment in only one of these genres? Such are large questions in the field of comparative literature, but we cannot linger over them.

The famous Dutch morality called in English *Everyman* may serve

---

[83] Quoted from Jerome Frank, *Law and the Modern Mind* (New York, 1930) pp. 89-90.

[84] Harry Maync, *Immermann: der Mann und sein Werk im Rahmen der Zeit- und Literaturgeschichte* (Munich, 1921), pp. 170-174.

[85] L. Mumford, *Technics and Civilization* (New York, 1934), p. 331.

as an illustration of a certain type of problem in the history of themes. Until now, the scholarly discussions of this morality have dealt primarily with the priority of the Dutch or English text and with the inter-relations of the many later versions in Latin and German. The ultimate source is Oriental—perhaps Hindu—but a late medieval adjustment to the characteristic doctrines of Catholicism has greatly modified the original theme. Although *Everyman* is in essence a Catholic mystery play, it enjoyed a great success in Protestant Germany long after the Reformation. We may therefore ask: What significance have these survivals? From what cultural influences do they spring? How does the content or the purpose of the play change to adapt itself to new surroundings? The numerous discussions[86] of *Everyman* will supply materials for answering these questions. We do not need additional studies in the relationships of these texts, for such matters are comparatively clear. We do not need an interpretative history of this extraordinarily popular mystery play. For the present, at least, the reader is lost in details.

Studies in comparative literature might deal with the various classes of subjects used in drama. For example, J. E. Gillet has admirably reviewed the use of Biblical themes in post-medieval German drama.[87] There is room, to be sure, for a much more exhaustive treatment and for similar studies in other classes of subjects. One might examine the themes taken from classical Latin or Greek literature or from national history. All such studies must be carried out with full knowledge of the

---

[86] The following references are particularly helpful in summarizing and interpreting the cultural background of the various versions of *Everyman:* K. Goedeke, *Every-Man, Homulus und Hekastus* (Hanover, 1865) ; J. Bolte, *Jahrbuch des Vereins für niederdeutsche Sprachforschung,* XI (1885), 151-156, 176, his editions of *De düdesche Schlömer* (Norden, 1889), pp. *15-*45 and *Drei Schauspiele vom sterbenden Menschen* ("Bibliothek des Literarischen Vereins," CCLXI-XLXX; Leipzig, 1927), pp. v-xxii; *Archiv für das Studium der neueren Sprachen,* LXXXVIII (1892), 413-415; Roersch, *ibid.,* CXIII (1904), 13-16; K. T. Gaedertz, "Ein Münchner Mysterienspiel in 1510," *Magazin für die Litteratur des In- und Auslands* (1890), 527-529, 544-546; W. Brecht, "Die Vorläufer von Hofmannsthals 'Jedermann,'" *Oesterreichische Rundschau,* XX (1924), 271-287; Herbert Lindner, *Hugo von Hofmannsthals 'Jedermann' und seine Vorgänger* (Diss.; Leipzig, 1928) ; Eckhardt, *Englische Studien,* LXVIII (1933), 195-197. Compare further the various texts cited in W. Stammler, *Von der Mystik zum Barock,* pp. 270, 325, 332, 347, 352, 538 (note on 1589), the new manuscript version printed by L. Willems in the *Verslagen en Mededeelingen van het Vlaamsche Academie,* 1933, pp. 971-1009, and the edition in J. Endepols, *Den spyeghel der salcheyt van Eleckerlijc* ("Lyceum-Herdrukken," IX; 3d ed.; Groningen, 1932).

[87] "The German Dramatist and His Bible," *PMLA, XXXIV* (1919), 465-493.

background of cultural and political history as well as of literary and religious traditions.

In studying the stories dealt with in post-medieval German literature, one may ask: What stories are told? Which ones are newly introduced? What new treatments of familiar subjects occur? What old subjects are neglected? To such questions we have no satisfactory answers, either for movements such as humanism and the Reformation or for genres such as the drama, the jest, or the folk-song. If we seek to answer these questions in a strictly literal sense, we are, to be sure, undertaking a contract at once large and scarcely worth attention. Yet we can investigate these matters in such a way as to throw light on the material and the age. In other words, we should seek to learn whether the proportion of stories derived from classical sources is large, whether such stories are quickly transferred to new uses from the books made accessible by the efforts of the humanists, and so on. What subjects that enjoyed wide popularity in the twelfth and thirteenth centuries are still used in the fourteenth and fifteenth? What old subjects have fallen from favor? The task is one of characterizing groups of materials rather than tabulating and indexing separate stories. The medieval exemplum, for instance, employs a rather definite body of materials and disregards at the same time various other groups of subjects. How much of the material characteristic of exempla is used in the fourteenth and fifteenth and sixteenth centuries? Such questions require a sensitiveness to the tempers of both periods to the types compared as well as an accurate knowledge of the materials.

Certain themes are or become typical of particular epochs or movements. Griselda begins her triumphant career in the Renaissance and owes a share of her popularity to the prominence of Petrarch and Boccaccio, who supplied her story to the world. Yet it is not solely the conspicuous position of these authors which made Griselda acceptable to the Renaissance. There is something in the story itself that appealed to the age. The story of Griselda calls for interpretation in this light much more than as an example of the variations which a tale may undergo. Study of the versions of a story has been devoted too much to tabulating the differences exhibited by the versions and too little to interpreting these differences as throwing light on the age or on some literary or cultural problem. Everyone knows that the theme of the unmarried mother or the "demonic" personality is characteristic of Storm and Stress, or that the conflict of generations has been treated again and again in the last thirty years. We can often explain the popularity of a particular story by referring to a characteristic idea of an age. The parable of the Prodigal Son, which illustrates the doctrine of salvation through faith, and that of Susanna, which represents the Lutheran church attacked by unjust judges, enjoyed high favor with Protestant authors.[88] Some themes—the Prodigal Son, Griselda, and Judith, for example—have been amply dicussed, whereas others—Daniel, Lazarus, and Tobias for example—have been comparatively neglected.[89]

[88] On the Prodigal Son see W. Scherer, *Die Anfänge des deutschen Prosaromans und Jörg Wickram von Colmar* ("Quellen und Forschungen zur Sprach- und Culturgeschichte der germanischen Völker," XXI; Strassburg, 1877), pp. 50-51; H. Holstein, *Das Drama vom verlorenen Sohn* (Programm; Geestemünde, 1880), and in fuller form as a book with the same title (Halle, 1880), which is reviewed at length by Karl Goedeke, *Göttingische gelehrte Anzeigen,* 1880, i, 655-662; F. Spengler, *Der verlorene Sohn im Drama des 16. Jahrhunderts* (Innsbruck, 1888), which is reviewed by A. von Weilen, *Anzeiger für deutsches Altertum,* XVI (1890), 113-119; A. Schwenkendieck, *Bühnengeschichte des verlorenen Sohnes in Deutschland,* I ("Theatergeschichtliche Forschungen," XL; Leipzig, 1930); W. Flemming (ed.), *Das Ordensdrama* ("Deutsche Literatur," Barock," II; Leipzig, 1930), p. 29; W. Beemelmann, "Bilder aus dem Kölner Volksleben des 16. Jahrhunderts; Aufführungen des verlorenen Sohnes," *Jahrbuch des Kölner Geschichts-Vereins,* XIII (1933), 135-152 (cf. E. Schröder, *Anzeiger für deutsches Altertum,* LII [1933], 157); Kurt Michel, *Das Wesen des Reformationsdramas entwickelt am Stoff des verlorenen Sohns* (Giessen diss.; Düren, 1934); A. Dörrer, "Der verlorene Sohn," *Germanisch-romanische Monatsschrift,* XXIV (1936), 21-35. A comparison of these studies is very instructive. Although the discussions of the theme have been numerous, the significance of the pictorial tradition might still be discussed. See, e.g., M. Geisberg, "Der verlorene Sohn aus dem Verlage Jobst de Negkers im Kupferstichkabinett," *Mitteilungen aus dem sächsischen Kunstsammlungen,* II (1911), 25-30. Johannes Meder's sermons on this theme—*Quadrigesimale de filio prodigo* (1495)—are illustrated with interesting woodcuts. I cannot say whether these illustrations are the same as the eighteen in his *Parabola fillii glutonis profusi* (1510), which is cited in G. W. Panzer, *Annales typographici,* IX (Nuremberg, 1801), 392; J.-C. Brunet, *Manuel du libraire* (5th ed.; Paris, 1862), III, cols. 1565-66.

On Susanna see R. Pilger, "Die Dramatisierungen der Susanna im 16. Jahrhundert," *Zeitschrift für deutsche Philologie,* XI (1880), 129-217, with additions by K. Goedeke, *Göttingische gelehrte Anzeigen,* 1880, i, 641-655; *The Book of Tobit and the History of Susanna, Reprinted from the Revised Version of the Apocrypha, with an Introduction by Dr. Montague R. James* (London, 1929); J. H. Mozley, "Susanna and the Elders: Three Medieval Poems," *Studi medievali,* n.s., III (1930), 27-52.

[89] On Lazarus see E. Nahde, *Der reiche Mann und der arme Lazarus im Drama des 16. Jahrhunderts* (Diss.; Leipzig, 1928); P. Harder, "Die Schuld 'des reichen Mannes' in Urteilen der späteren Literatur," *Beiträge zur Geschichte der deutschen Sprache,* L (1927), 132-142; A. Freybe, "Georg Rollenhagens Leichenpredigt zum Begräbnis des reichen Mannes, ein parodistisches Meisterstück," *Neue kirchliche Zeitschrift,* III (1892), 989-1008; H. Gressmann, "Vom reichen Mann und armen Lazarus; eine literaturgeschichtliche Studie mit ägyptologischen Beiträgen von G. Möller," *Abhandlungen der königlich preussischen Akademie,* 1918, no. 7; J.

Perhaps we can associate the popularity of the theme of Dives and Lazarus with the discussion of problems involved in the secularization of poor-relief. Probably something can still be said about the theme of the seven or ten ages of man: Shakespeare used it in *As You Like It,* and medieval artists frequently depicted it in mural decorations. Its form—a series of tableaux—made it suitable for dramatic presentation in a simple review introduced by a herald.[90]

26. *The History of Literary Conventions.*—Closely allied to the history of a theme is the history of a literary convention. The distinction between a theme and a literary convention is unimportant and often difficult to make. The often-described verse about the Virgin Mary[91] forms one of the subjects or conventions of medieval lyric poetry. Its history in the medieval period has been written, but its survival in the sixteenth century is insufficiently known. In the hands of the Meistersinger, Mary-verse is a survival of a medieval fashion. Regarding its use in other circles we know very little. It is not a matter of particular consequence

---

Bolte (ed.), *Georg Rollenhagens 'Spiel vom reichen manne und armen Lazaro'* ("Neudrucke deutscher Literaturwerke aus dem 16. und 17. Jahrhundert," CCLXX-CCLXXIII; Halle, 1929), pp. xiv-xvi.

Pictorial representations are often important for their relations to literary treatments of a theme. See as an illustration O. Thulen, *Johannes der Täufer* (Leipzig, 1930), and the discussion below, pp. 146-148.

On the use of the name Daniel for Luther see W. Gussmann, *D. Johann Ecks vierhundert und vier Artikel zum Reichstag von Augsburg 1530* ("Quellen und Forschungen zur Geschichte des Augsburger Glaubensbekenntnisses," II; Cassel, 1930), "Exkurs I." In 1520, Luther called the Pope a "Daniel zu Babylonien"; see K. Sang, *Die appellative Verwendung von Eigennamen bei Luther* ("Giessener Beiträge zur deutschen Philologie," II; Giessen, 1921), p. 61.

[90] See Gustav Roethe, *Die Gedichte Reinmars von Zweter* (Leipzig, 1887), p. 619 (note on stanza 200); A. Englert, "Die menschlichen Altersstufen in Wort und Bild," *Zeitschrift des Vereins für Volkskunde,* XV (1905), 399-412; A. Wesselski, *Heinrich Bebels Schwänke* (Munich, 1907), II, 135 (note on III, 103); F. Boll, "Die Lebensalter: ein Beitrag zur antiken Ethnologie und zur Geschichte der Zahlen," *Neue Jahrbücher für das klassische Altertum,* XXXI (1913), 89-145. Older references of less importance are Hoffmann von Fallersleben, H. F. Massmann, and F. J. Mone in [Mone's] *Anzeiger für Kunde des deutschen Mittelalters,* I (1832), cols. 253-54, 300, II (1833), cols. 13-14, 183-184; K. Bartsch (ed.), *Germanistische Studien* (Vienna, 1872), I, 6, n. 12. I have not seen A. Hauffen, "Die Altersstufen im deutschen Volkslied in Böhmen," in *Festschrift des Zweigvereins Reichenberg* (Reichenberg, 1912), cited in A. Hauffen, *Bibliographie des deutschen Volksliedes in Böhmen* (Prague, 1913), p. 9, no. 47 a; and a Russian work by J. A. Shl'apkin (St. Petersburg, 1909), cited in *Zeitschrift des Vereins für Volkskunde,* XXII (1911), 317.

[91] I have collected references in my *Literary History of Meistergesang* (New York, 1936), pp. 84, 86, n. 17.

whether we consider the Dance of Death to be a theme or a convention. In some instances, we discern a relationship in subject-matter between two versions of the Dance of Death; elsewhere, we see that a conventional framework is being used. In formulæ, stylistic details, and metre the term "literary convention" can be used without confusion.

Traditional folksong is often a repository of literary ideas and conventions which have trickled down to the folk. The identification of such survivals, the tracing of the paths which they have traversed, and the interpretation of the changes which they have undergone are instructive undertakings of no great difficulty. Such accounts of the development of details in folksong may throw light on the origin and date of a song and reveal the extent and nature of influences on the popular mind. New aesthetic values may arise in the rehandling of these details by oral tradition. Thus, for example, the notion of the Dance of Death—a literary and pictorial convention which swept over Europe in the late Middle Ages—persists in a number of German and other popular songs.[92] No one has yet investigated the characteristics of this particular

---

[92] See T. Odinga, *Vierteljahrschrift für Literaturgeschichte,* IV (1891), 152-155; L. E. Broadwood, *Journal of the Folksong Society,* I (1902), 169, and *ibid.,* II (1905), 137-139, no. 7; K. Hübl, "Ein Totentanz," *Ostböhmische Heimat,* II (1927), 52, as cited in A. Hauffen and G. Jungbauer, *Bibliographie der deutschen Volkskunde in Böhmen* ("Beiträge zur sudetendeutschen Volkskunde," XX; Reichenberg, 1931), p. 194, no. 3019; P. Eisner, *Volkslieder der Slawen* (Leipzig [1926]), pp. 253-254; H. Grüner Nielsen, *Danske Viser,* V (Copenhagen, 1922-27), 35-36, no. 92; O. Böckel, *Handbuch des deutschen Volkslieds* (Marburg, 1908), pp. 108-110; K. Hennig, *Die geistliche Kontrafaktur im Jahrhundert der Reformation* (Halle, 1909), pp. 22-23, no. 21; L. Erk and F. M. Böhme, *Deutscher Liederhort* (Leipzig, 1894), II, 795-800, no. 1059, III, 375, no. 1534 A, and 850-53, nos. 2153-55; Johannes Bolte, *Zeitschrift des Vereins für Volkskunde,* XXVI (1916), 178, no. 43, and *ibid.,* XXXVII-XXXVIII (1927-28), 245, no. 43, and "Zum siebenbürgischen Königsliede," *Das deutsche Volkslied,* XXVIII (1926), 96-97; Otto von Greyerz, *Schweizerisches Archiv für Volkskunde,* XXV (1925), 161-179, and *Das Volkslied der deutschen Schweiz* ("Die Schweiz im deutschen Geistesleben," XLVIII-XLIX; Frauenfeld, 1927), p. 57; G. Kalff, *Het Lied in de middeleeuwen* (Leiden, 1883), p. 56-57, 114-116, 202-203, 527-528.

For a general bibliographical introduction to the Dance of Death see my notes in *Modern Philology,* XXX (1933), 325-328. Compare further A. Vicard, *Les fantômes d'une danse macabre* (Le Puy-en-Velay, 1918); H. T. Bossert, *Ein altdeutscher Totentanz* ("Wasmuths Kunsthefte," II; [Berlin, n.d. = 1919]); *The Dance of Death from the XIIth to the XXth Century . . . ; the notable collection of Miss Susan Minns* (New York, 1922), an auction catalogue of a very valuable collection; *Doodendans: catalogus der verzameling Reichelt* (Amsterdam, 1923); H. Thule, *Studien zur Geschichte des Totentanzes* (Diss.; Giessen, 1923), which is available only in an extract of 14 pp.; E. Vouilliéme, "Zur Bibliographie H. Knoblochtzers in Heidelberg; Der Totentanz," *Bok- och bibliothekshistoriske*

survival and identified the various forms of the Dance of Death represented in folk-song. The task need not lead the student into the complicated and unsolved problems of the origin and dissemination of the
Dance of Death; but he will need to be acquainted with its various
types.

Another survival of earlier ways of thinking is the use of colors in
folk-song. A good deal has been done in the investigation of the medieval
symbolism of colors, and—although many texts connected with the
subject remain to be extracted from manuscripts and printed,—the outlines are fairly clear.[93] The persistence of these types of medieval

---

studier tillägnade Isak Collijn på hans 50-årsdag (Uppsala, 1925) ; Ehrismann,
pp. 580-582; Florence Whyte, *The Dance of Death in Spain and Catalonia* (Bryn
Mawr diss.; Baltimore, 1931), a competent and thorough piece of work; L. P.
Kurtz, *The Dance of Death* ("Publications of Institute of French Studies"; New
York, 1934), a superficial work. The dissertation by E. Vallazza, *Die mittelalterli-
chen Totentänze in Frankreich, Italien und Spanien* (Innsbruck, 1932), which is
occasionally cited, has not been printed. Fundamental to further investigation is
S. Kozáky, *Geschichte des Totentanzes,* I ("Bibliotheca humanitatis historica," I;
Budapest, 1936) ; only the first volume which deals with the origins of the theme,
has yet appeared.

Two interesting examples of the Dance of Death in German literature have
not been fully described: a version with an introduction by Caspar Scheit published in 1557 and now preserved only in later editions (see K. Hedicke, *Caspar
Scheits 'Frölich Heimfart' nach ihren geschichtlichen und litterarischen Elementen
untersucht* (Diss.; Halle, 1903), p. 2, note "f"), and an anonymous Meisterlied,
"Ein Lied von dem Tod," cited in Goedeke, I, 319, No. 84. Joachim von Watt's
dialogue with Death is allied to the Dance of Death (see Hans Rupprich, *Humanismus und Renaissance in den deutschen Städten* ["Deutsche Literatur," Leipzig,
1935], p. 53) ; it has not been reprinted.

[93] See H. Niewöhner in *Verfasserlexikon,* I, cols. 602-606, "Die sechs Farben"
(several unprinted texts are cited) ; W. Seelmann, *Jahrbuch des Vereins für
niederdeutsche Sprachforschung,* VIII (1882), 73-85, XXI (1898), 162, XXVIII
(1902), 118-156; Ehrismann, p. 688; W. Gloth, *Das Spiel von den sieben Farben*
("Teutonia," I; Königsberg, 1902) ; Uhland, *Schriften zur Geschichte der Dichtung
und Sage* (Stuttgart, 1866), III, 430-434; P. Strauch (ed.), *Der Marner* ("Quellen
und Forschungen zur Sprach- und Culturgeschichte der germanischen Völker,"
XIV; Strassburg, 1876), p. 149 (note on V, 14) ; K. Matthaei, *Das weltliche
Klösterlein* (Diss.; Marburg, 1907) ; W. von Wickede, *Die geistlichen Gedichte des
Cgm. 714* (Rostock diss.; Hamburg, 1909), pp. 69-76; E. Pflug, *Suchensinn und
seine Dichtungen* ("Germanistische Abhandlungen," XXXII; Breslau, 1908), pp.
44-45; K. Stejskal (ed.), *Hadamars von Laber Jagd* (Vienna, 1880), p. 198, str.
242; C. Haltaus (ed.), *Liederbuch der Clara Hätzlerin* ("Bibliothek der gesammten deutschen National-Literatur," VIII; Quedlinburg, 1840), pp. lv, 168-170, no.
21; W. Wackernagel, "Die Farben- und Blumensprache des Mittelalters," *Kleine
Schriften,* I (Leipzig, 1872) 142-240; H. Becker, *Zeitschrift für deutsche Philologie,* LIII (1928), 165, n. 18; H. Grüner Nielsen, *Danske Viser* (Copenhagen,
1922-27), V, 405-406, no. 288.

symbolism of color in the folk-songs of the fifteenth and sixteenth centuries as well as in modern folk-songs might be studied.

27. *The History of Stylistic Devices and the Study of Technique.*— The study of stylistic peculiarities may concern itself either with the history of a stylistic device or with the analysis and description of the technique to accomplish a purpose. The history of a stylistic device, which is after all indistinguishable from the history of a literary convention, may deal with a detail or an entire literary form.

The English and German ballads containing riddles constitute a very curious literary genre.[94] Knowledge of such ballads appeared to be limited to English and German tradition, with the possible exception of the Scandinavian "Sven Vonved."[95] After we have described the genre, the first problem is to ascertain the significance of this peculiar limitation on the currency of the form. The facts thus discovered may have some bearing on the pointless dispute over "ballad origins." Another and relatively simple problem exists in the riddles found in these ballads. This history is yet to be traced. Apparently they have ancient ritualistic connections, for similar riddles—and even some identical ones—can be found as early as the *Rigveda*. The fourteenth-century German "Traugemundslied" is scarcely a ballad, but it cannot be separated from this group of riddle-ballads. The wanderer Tragemund or Trougemund—his name may be a corruption of a word akin to "dragoman" in some earlier form—answers a number of enigmatic questions, e.g. "What is greener than grass?" In English, the questions— many of them identical with the German ones—are enclosed in a narrative frame: the suitor or the heroine must answer the questions in order to meet a test.

See also such studies as M. Jacobsohn, *Die Farben in der mittelhochdeutschen Dichtung der Blütezeit* (Diss.; Greifswald, 1915) ; E. Schwenter, *Eine sprachge-schichtliche Untersuchung über den Gebrauch und die Bedeutung der altgermanischen Farbenbezeichnungen* (Diss.; Göttingen, 1915) ; Berkusky, "Zur Symbolik der Farben," *Zeitschrift des Vereins für Volkskunde*, XXIII (1913), 146-163, 250-265; R. Hochegger, *Die geschichtliche Entwicklung des Farbensinnes* (Innsbruck, 1884) ; and the various articles on the colors in the *Handwörterbuch des deutschen Aberglaubens*.

As an example of a folk-song in which the symbolism of the colors might be interpreted see F. M. Böhme, *Altdeutsches Liederbuch* (Leipzig, 1877), pp. 289-290, no. 206.

[94] Ehrismann, pp. 352-354; F. J. Child, *English and Scottish Popular Ballads* (Boston, 1882-98), Nos. 1, 2, 44 (with the headnotes) ; L. Uhland, *Schriften zur Geschichte der Dichtung und Sage* (Stuttgart, 1866), III, 181 ff.; F. B. Gummere, *The Popular Ballad* (Boston, 1907), pp. 96, 135-142, 291; H. Grüner Nielsen, *Danske Viser,* V (Copenhagen, 1922-27), 232-233, no. 156.

[95] Svend Grundtvig (ed.), *Danmarks gamle Folkeviser,* I (Copenhagen, 1853), 235-250, no. 18.

A stylistic device or literary convention characteristic of the fifteenth and sixteenth centuries is the personification "Hans Unmut" and the like.[96] In the Middle Ages, we find personification of abstractions with the title "Lord" or "Lady," e.g. Frau Sælde. Personification in the form of a full name and without a title is, I believe, an invention of the late fifteenth or early sixteenth century, but the origin and history of the device are yet to be written. The examples in proverbs can be easily found and will probably suggest the outlines of the historical development. These aspects of the literary use of names involve also the emotional coloring attached to names. Information about this detail is difficult to find. We attach definite emotional connotations to Percival, Leroy, Claude, and many another name. What was the connotation of a particular name in the fifteenth or sixteenth century,—or even much later? [Ernst Heimeran's] *Namens-Büchlein*[97] attempts for the first time, so far as I am aware, to collect the examples of German names in literature and history. A very interesting problem pertaining to these remarks is the name of Faust in Goethe's drama. In the absence of more definite information, I assume that Goethe substituted Heinrich for the traditional Johann. If this assumption is correct, the change reflects Goethe's attitude toward the two names. In any event, the change calls for discussion and interpretation. The problem is difficult, but not impossible of solution.[98]

[96] P. Strauch (ed.), Caspar Scheit, *Die fröhliche Heimfahrt* ("Schriften des wissenschaftlichen Instituts der Elsass-Lothringer im Reich"; Berlin, 1926), p. 124, 1. 1906. See K. Burdach, *Vorspiel,* I (Halle, 1925) 51-52; J. Leopold, "Eigennamen als Gattungsnamen in Redensarten und Sprichwörtern," *Taalstudie,* IV (1881), 218-236. For the medieval background see R. Galle, *Die Personification (als poetisches Kunstmittel und ihre Verwendung in der mittelhochdeutschen Dichtung bis zum Beginne des Verfalles)* (Leipzig diss.; 1888). I have collected examples of "Sir Penny" in *Modern Philology,* XXXIV (1936), 202.

[97] Munich, [1933]. Studies in which somewhat similar materials are collected and described are T. Hjelmqvist, *Bibelgeografiska namn med sekundär användning i nysvenskan* (Lund, 1901), and *Förnamn och familjenamn med sekundär användning i nysvenskan* (Lund, [1903]); R. O. Frick, "Les prénoms à la Côte-aux-Fées quelque trois siècles durant," *Schweizerisches Archiv für Volkskunde,* XXXVI (1937), 1-31.

[98] Willi Krogmann suggests that Goethe took the name Heinrich from a ballad; see *Untersuchungen zum Ursprung der Gretchentragödie* (Rostock diss.; Wismar, 1928), p. 29. Notwithstanding its title, Edward Schröder's essay "Von der Verbreitung des Namens Heinrich und vom Schicksal der Fürstennamen überhaupt," *Deutsche Namenkunde* (Leipzig, 1938), pp. 74-77 (reprinted from *Zeitschrift des Harzvereins,* LXX [1937], 23-26) contains only the remark that the name Heinrich owes its currency to Emperor Heinrich I; the article deals more extensively with other princely names.

A good example of the methods to be employed in determining the currency

The persistence of metrical conventions in folk-song is easily recognized. Carl Colditz, for example, traces the history of a special stanza in five lines—the Morolf stanza as it is called from its use in the Middle High German epic of *Salman und Morolf*—from the first appearance of the stanza in folk-song about the middle of the fifteenth century until its disappearance about three centuries later.[99] The Morolf stanza is first used in a pilgrim's song and is later adapted to the ballad about the bandit Lindenschmid (d. 1490). This ballad and the familiar song "Es kommt ein frischer Sommer daher" supply a constantly-repeated impetus to the use of the stanza, and it becomes a typical form for hymns and historical songs. Something similar might perhaps be done with the curious stanza of thirteen lines used in the *Eckenlied*.[100] In general, the peculiar stanzaic forms found in popular song call for historical study. In my *Literary History of Meistergesang*,[101] I have commented on the need for studies in the history of metrical conventions and I shall not repeat what was said there. The problems can be stated in simple terms; their solution will help us in understanding the literary activities of the age. I have also commented on the need for an account of the "Three's" and "Four's" which are frequently found in the literature of the sixteenth century.[102] The example which immediately comes to mind is the anonymous "Trias romana," a savage and witty criticism of Rome. The form is derived ultimately from a pattern of Hebrew riddles (Prov. 30:18), but in Europe, it loses much of its enigmatic character and becomes a formula for proverbs. Whole books in "Three's" and "Four's" are composed in France and England.

Many treatises list the conventional elements of medieval and earlier German poetry, but they are for the most part catalogues without any

---

and connotation of proper names is Professor John A. Walz's comment on the use of Grete in the sixteenth century; see "A German Faust Play of the Sixteenth Century," *Germanic Review*, III (1928), 11-12. In his edition of the *Narrenschiff*, Friedrich Zarncke remarks that this pejorative connotation of Grete was Low German in origin and was later introduced into High German; see the note on "Vorrede," 1. 114. J. C. Dolz, *Die Moden in den Taufnamen* (Leipzig, 1825) is pertinent to the study of such connotations.

[99] "Ueber die Anwendung der Morolfstrophe im Mittelalter und im deutschen Lied," *Modern Philology*, XXXI (1933-34), 243-252.

[100] I have collected references in my *Literary History of Meistergesang* (New York, 1937), pp. 72-73.

[101] See, *e.g.*, the remarks on *Hort* on p. 61.

[102] *The Proverb* (Cambridge, Mass., 1931), pp. 160-164; T. Hampe, *Euphorion*, IV (1897), 28; W. Uhl, *Die deutsche Priamel* (Leipzig, 1897), pp. 175-176. See also my article "Problems in the Study of Riddles," *Southern Folklore Quarterly*, II (1938), 6-7.

interpretations of the materials collected.[103] Ludwig Uhland's fragmentary history of German folk-song is a notable exception to the rule, but after a century there is much to be added to it. Recent efforts to find traces of materials and literary conventions much older than the fifteenth century or even the Middle Ages are very interesting.[104] No one has followed the hint which John Meier threw out long ago when he called attention to the extensive use of parallelism—a striking peculiarity of old Germanic verse—in folk-song of a much later period.[105] A comparatively easy task would be the tracing of the history of conventional signatures attached to folk-songs, particularly historical songs, of the late medieval period.[106] When and how did this device come to be used? What forms does it take? To what varieties of songs is it attached?

A stylistic investigation of larger scope than any I have thus far mentioned is the problem of the technique used in propaganda after 1520. How were the broadsides composed? How were they adapted to various audiences? What means were chosen to appeal to the common man? The investigation is an interesting one. Propaganda was, in 1520, a new thing or at least its methods and aims differed greatly from the literature of the immediately preceding epoch. How did the methods of Catholics and Protestants differ? For example, my impression is that Protestants used the dialogue (*Gespräch*) freely in controversy and Catholics did not. If this impression is correct, how did this limitation come about?

28. *The Geography of Ideas and Literary Forms.*—Studies in the geography of ideas and literary forms are instructive and can often be presented as maps with explanatory comment. Representation on a map forces one to formulate clearly the results of an investigation. It often

---

[103] See, e. g., R. M. Meyer, *Die altgermanische Poesie nach ihren formelhaften Elementen beschrieben* (Berlin, 1889) ; A. Daur, *Das alte deutsche Volkslied nach seinem festen Ausdrucksformen betrachtet* (Leipzig, 1909) ; Adele Stöcklin, *Die Schilderung der Natur im deutschen Minnesang und im älteren deutschen Volkslied* (Basel diss.; Strassburg, 1913). Compare Ehrismann, pp. 197-198.

[104] See, e.g. Beyschlag, "Zeilen- und Hakenstil. Seine künstlerische Verwendung in der Nibelungenstrophe und im Hildebrandston," *Beiträge zur Geschichte der deutschen Sprache,* LVI (1932), 220-332; Hermann Schneider, "Usprung und Alter der deutschen Volksballade," *Vom Werden des deutschen Geistes; Festgabe Gustav Ehrismann . . . dargebracht* (Berlin, 1925), pp. 112-124.

[105] *Literaturblatt für germanische und romanische Philologie,* XVI (1895), cols. 260-261 ; "Zum Hildebrandslied," *Festgabe Philipp Strauch . . . dargebracht* ("Hermaea," XXXI; Halle, 1932), pp. 45-48.

[106] I note many signatures to the texts in J. Görres, *Altteutsche Volks- und Meisterlieder aus den Handschriften der Heidelberger Bibliothek* (Frankfurt am Main, 1817).

discloses connections which might otherwise have been obscure. Although the cartographic representation of materials in the humanities and particularly in literary history has not developed a wholly satisfactory technique, it has many advantages and should be used more freely than it is at present. The recent developments in linguistic atlases can teach students of literature much, and the smaller maps used in studies in folklore often suggest ways and means of depicting the results of an investigation.

Some geographical investigations of literature have enlarged our knowledge, others have raised questions for further study, and few have been utterly valueless. For example, our notions of currents in Middle High German literature would be clearer than they often are, if we kept in mind the distinguishing features of Rhenish, Thuringian, Swabian, and Bavarian-Austrian writers.[107] Gustav Roethe's description of the differences between the Upper German and Middle German fashions of writing didactic verse in the Middle Ages is an early example of geographical analysis.[108] He did not draw a map. Recently, Josef Nadler has described German romanticism as a movement of East German origin.[109] He, too, did not represent his results on a map.

In the investigation of our period, maps indicating the distribution of characteristic literary phenomena will give us new information. Students should always have a good atlas within reach. In Lutz Mackensen's *Deutscher Kulturatlas*,[110] the first effort to depict cartographically humanistic materials, students will find much of interest. I have already mentioned the possibilties of using a map in the study of a saint's life and in the history of jest-books. Particularly attractive problems involving the drawing of a map are the dissemination of the religious drama (especially in its later forms), the rise of the humanistic and Protestant theater and drama, and the choice of subjects in the Protestant drama of the sixteenth century. A minor problem of some importance is the dissemination of Meistergesang. It appears that Danzig is the only city in Northern Germany where Meistergesang is said to have been practised. The evidence is of doubtful value, but it

---

[107] See a good bibliography of the theory of the cartographic presentation of humanistic subjects in Eberhard Freiherr von Künssberg, *Rechtliche Volkskunde* ("Volk," III; Halle, 1936), pp. 7-8, n. 1, especially H. Aubin, "Methodische Probleme historischer Kartographie," *Neue Jahrbücher für Wissenschaft und Jugendbildung*, V (1929), 32-45. See also Erich Röhr, *Die Volkstumskarte. Voraussetzungen und Gestaltung* ("Volkstumsgeographische Forschungen. In Verbindung mit dem Atlas der deutschen Volkskunde," I; Leipzig, 1939).

[108] *Die Gedichte Reinmars von Zweter* (Leipzig, 1887), *passim*.

[109] In this instance, further investigation of the facts is desirable.

[110] Berlin, in progress.

has never been critically examined.[111] The matters which particularly call for examination are the relations to Danzig of one Hans Pantzer, who is said to have been a Meistersinger, and the significance of certain plays, which have been thought to be the work of Meistersinger. If the existence of Meistergesang in Danzig can be demonstrated, the influence of the schools extended much farther than we now believe. A discussion of the evidence for the practice of Meistergesang in Switzerland would also be pertinent to the investigation of the influence exerted by the schools. The evidence to be considered differs from that cited for Danzig. Goedeke[112] gives examples of verses written in the metres of the Meistersinger by Swiss authors; we should inquire whether these examples imply more than a superficial acquaintance with Meistergesang. Further study of these matters seems likely to add to our knowledge of Meistergesang.

29. *The City-Poem.*—Although many topographical poems were written in the fifteenth and sixtenth centuries in Germany and else-where, the origins, connections, and development of the genre are imperfectly known.[113] These poems belong to the encomiastic verse and prose familiar in the Renaissance. Eulogies celebrated everything con-ceivable: wine, gout, folly, rustic life,[114] printing, individuals, and places. An encomium exhibiting the humanistic associations of the genre is Richard Croke's *Achademiæ Lipsensis encomium congratulatorium* (1515).[115] The newly invited professor of Greek read this poem as an introduction to his lectures on Ausonius. In view of Ausonius' connec-tion with the beginnings of the city-poem, Croke's verses demonstrate both his good-will toward Leipzig and his knowledge of the tradition behind the city-poem. Croke was perhaps following a tradition exempli-fied by an earlier work. When appointed to a professorship of poetry at Leipzig, Priamus Capotius of Trapani (Sicily) composed *Fridericeidos Liber* (1488), a heroic poem on the exploits of Frederick I of Saxony

[111] See my *Literary History of Meistergesang* (New York, 1937), pp. 15-18; Taylor and Ellis, *A Bibliography of Meistergesang* ("Indiana University Studies," CXIII; Bloomington, Ind., 1936), p. 54.

[112] *Grundriss,* II, 257, no. 29.

[113] For works on the city-poem, see Appendix IV.

[114] See, e.g., H. Kier, *De laudibus vitae rusticae* (Diss.; Marburg, 1933). Here the connection with classical models was particularly close. See H. Böss, "Fischarts Bearbeitung lateinischer Quellen, 1, Fischarts Lob des Landlebens und sein Vorbild, die 2. Epode des Horaz," *Alemannia,* XLIV (1917), 125-137; A. Pfleger, "J. Fischarts 'Lob des Landlustes,'" *Elsassland,* V (1925), 303-305.

[115] J. Nadler, *Literaturgeschichte der deutschen Stämme* (3d ed.; Regensburg, 1929), II, 216. See J. G. Böhme, *De litteratura Lipsiensi opuscula* (Leipzig, 1779), pp. 191-205.

in his war against Adolph of Nassau and his Bohemian mercenaries (*ca.* 1420).

Although the city-poem is found in German-speaking regions from the beginning of humanistic influence, its great popularity came in the period of late humanistic writing after 1500. Such masters of humanism as Conrad Celtis and Helius Eobanus Hessus in Germany, Marcus Antonius Coccius Sabellius in Italy, Damião de Goes in Portugal, and Joachim du Bellay in France wrote city-poems. John of Jandun enjoyed the charms of Senlis and sketched vividly the Parisian scene.[116] Lorenzo Valla characterized Bruni's laudation of Florence succinctly: "plenam levitatis et supinitatis." In his handbook of poetics, the rule-giver J. C. Scaliger accepted the genre and described it.[117]

The city chosen as subject was that in which the author happened to be born, that in which he had had some pleasant experience, or that from which he expected a reward. Ordinarily the author did receive appropriate recognition from a patron or the municipal officials. Sannazaro's reward for a very brief epigram on Venice aroused the admiration and envy of his contemporaries. The contents of the city-poem include historical materials, descriptions of the landmarks, local peculiarities of dress, speech or customs. Naturally enough, the theme and the abilities of most authors of city-poems did not produce works of great artistic merit, but since the form was so popular at this time, a description of the genre is necessary to a full understanding of the age. Although the task demands familiarity with classical literature as well as acquaintance with the historical and geographical writings of the time, the student with few materials can do much to clarify the origin and development of the genre.

I shall discuss primarily the questions arising in connection with the beginning of the city-poem. The ultimate inspiration of the genre is to be found in classical literature, but the connections have not been worked out.[118] An enumeration of the conflicting origins suggested for the genre

[116] H. O. Taylor, *Thought and Expression in the Sixteenth Century* (New York, 1920), I, 77. For the reference to Valla see Taylor, I, 50.

[117] *Poetices libri septem* (Lyons, 1561), pp. 166-167 (III, c.cxxi, "Urbs"). See also pp. 86 (III, v), 160 (III, cx), 165 (III, cxx). Compare Hippolytis a Collibus (i.e., of Colli, 1561-1612), *Incrementa urbium sive de caussis* [sic] *magnitudinis urbium* (Hanover, 1600).

[118] Various dissertations have dealt with the methods of praising cities in classical literature. Of these W. Gernentz, *Laudes Romae* (Rostock, 1918) is especially useful for our purposes. G. G. Fraustadt, *Encomiorum in litteris graecis usque as Romanam aetatem historia* (Leipzig, 1909) gives us an exhaustive analysis of the classical rules. E. Kienzle, *Der Lobpreis von Städten und Ländern in der ältern griechischen Dichtung* (Basel diss.; Kallmünz, 1936) includes many casual encomiastic adjectives and phrases of little interest to us. See also S. Bauck, *De*

is instructive. According to Ellinger,[119] descriptions of cities appeared first in the fourteenth century in prose. Soon versifications followed, either as epigrams or as longer poems. All of these varieties—prose eulogy, epigram, and longer poem—continued to live side by side. The interrelations of these varieties are obscure and perhaps cannot be clarified. The genre developed, thinks Ellinger,[119] at first in French prose. Then came descriptions in verse, notably by Antonio Astesano, an Italian turned Frenchman. Later, he thinks, came the use of the genre in Italy and finally in Germany. Study of the origins of the genre will shake our faith in Ellinger's theories. Astesano's manner varies completely from that of the conventional city-poem. Neff[119] maintains that the genre originated in Italy. Werminghoff emphasizes the influence of Enea Silvio de Piccolomini in determining the content and style of city-poems written in Germany, and he might have noted that Max Herrmann found Albrecht von Eyb's eulogy of Bamberg—one of the earliest Latin examples of the form—to have been modelled on Balthasar Rasinus' eulogy of Pavia.[120] Classical Latin models existed in the verse celebrating the beauties of a province. Hermann Tiemann's interesting suggestion of Spanish influence can yield at best only a clue to one of the various influences which affected the development of the genre.[121] It belongs in the same class with Karl Wotke's suggestion of Byzantine origins—a suggestion which he supports with some striking examples.[122]

A particular variety of this regional encomiastic writing appears to be distinguished by the patriotic use of historical matter and the frequent references to allegorical figures representing river-gods.[123] This variety attained its highest development at the hands of Bembo and Sannazaro.

---

laudibus Italiae (Königsberg i. Pr., 1919) and Otto Schroeder, *De laudibus Athenarum a poetis tragicis et ab oratoribus epidicticis excultis* (Göttingen, 1914).

[119] For references, see Appendix IV.

[120] Herrmann, p. 109. J. W. Nagl and J. Zeidler, *Deutsch-österreichische Literaturgeschichte,* I (Vienna, 1899), 420-421, also find the origin of humanistic encomia of cities in the descriptions by Enea Silvio.

[121] *Das spanische Schrifttum in Deutschland von der Renaissance bis zur Romantik* ("Ibero-amerikanische Studien," VI; Hamburg, 1936), pp. 21-34.

[122] "Ueber den Einfluss der byzantinischen Literatur auf die älteren Humanisten Italiens," *Verhandlungen der 42. Versammlung deutscher Philologen und Schulmänner* (Leipzig, 1894), pp. 290-293.

[123] Spekke, pp. 11, 103-116 (citing M. Scherillo [ed.], J. Sannazaro, *Arcadia* [Turin, 1888]); Hilda Taylor, *Topographical Poetry in England During the Renaissance* (Manuscript diss.; Chicago, 1926). For the classical and early Christian background of these ideas see O. Waser, "Vom Flussgott Jordan und anderen Personifikationen," *Festgabe Adolf Kaegi . . . dargebracht zum 30. September, 1919* (Frauenfeld, 1919), pp. 191-217; E. Kienzle, *Der Lobpreis von Städten und Ländern in der älteren griechischen Dichtung* (Basel diss.; Kallmünz, 1926), p. 55, n. 1.

In an unpublished doctoral dissertation, Hilda Taylor shows that the personification of rivers—a device much favored in England—has classical origins and is connected with Tudor pageantry. Although Ausonius' *Mosella* (*ca.* A.D. 371-375) was highly esteemed in Germany, the personification of rivers seems not to have attained the same popularity as in England. In an elegy composed by Ermoldus Nigellus for Pippin, the figures of rivers do honor to a prince,[124] but this convention of early medieval Latin verse is not a direct influence on later writers. During the seventeenth century, the personification of rivers for this purpose becomes a convention in German opera; it is presumably of Italian origin and is connected also with pageantry.

Consideration of verse in which rivers are personified leads into the study of verse celebrating the beauties of a region or province.[125] Apparently these forms of verse—the personification of rivers and the regional eulogy—can be differentiated in their historical developments from the city-poem, but cross-influences were no doubt always present. Obviously the city-poem is closely allied to the critical and descriptive material in chronicles and geographical works and often draws upon them.[126] Chronicles and guides give the poet useful information.

Commercial reports and diplomatic papers often contain materials intimately related to the city-poem.[127] Modern consular reports are of the same species, but perhaps do not often make the same effort at literary style. In the sixteenth century, such documents appear to have had a wide circulation. They were often written by persons with a literary background. Models for the writing of these reports were found in the reports of the Venetian emissaries.[128]

[124] G. H. Pertz, *Monumenta Germaniae Historica, Scriptores,* II (Hanover, 1829), 517-518; E. Faral (ed.), Ermold le Noir, *Poême sur Louis le Pieux et épîtres au roi Pépin* ("Les classiques de l'Histoire de France au moyen-âge," XIV; Paris, 1932), pp. 208-213.

[125] See, e.g., Ellinger, "Städte- und Landschaftsgedichte," in *Reallexikon der deutschen Literaturgeschichte,* IV, 90; H. Meuss, "Des Vulturinus Lobgedicht auf Schlesien von 1506," *Mitteilungen der schlesischen Gesellschaft für Volkskunde,* XXVIII (1927), 38-81.

Compare Opitz's *Zlatna* (1623), *Vielgut* (1629), and *Vesuvius* (1633) as examples of compositions nearly related to the city-poem.

[126] See Werminghoff, p. 81, n. 4. For an introduction to the history of guides to cities see J. von Schlosser, "Materialien zur Quellenkunde der Kunstgeschichte, III, § 3, Die Kunsttopographie. Beginn der Guidenliteratur," *Sitzungsberichte der k. Akademie* (Vienna), *philosophisch-historische Klasse,* CLXXX, no. 5 (1916), 52-70. An important work in this connection is Ludwig Schudt, *Le guide di Roma. Materialien zu einer Geschichte der römischen Topographie* ("Quellenschriften zur Geschichte der Barockkunst in Rom"; Vienna and Augsburg, 1930).

[127] See examples in the list below, s.v. "Emden."

[128] Compare also the reports made to and by the Fuggers and the "Newe Zeitungen": Victor Klarwill, *Fugger-Zeitungen; ungedruckte Briefe an das Haus Fugger*

Although the question of the origin of the city-poem has not been answered and although the historian of literature should not seek a single origin for a genre drawing upon such various sources, a full discussion of the influences leading to its popularity is in order. Perhaps the first step in writing the history of the city-poem would consist in arranging the earliest examples in chronological sequence and in looking for interrelations among them. As early as the middle or end of the fourteenth century we find echoes of the city-poem in various places. Should we perhaps see one in Oswald von Wolkenstein's line, "Ich rüem dich Haidelberg?"[129] If so, we have evidence for the existence of the city-poem at a surprisingly early time. A passage in a Rhenish legend of the Three Magi begins "O Coellen, du edel krone" and extends to no less than 65 lines.[130] A much shorter passage of similar nature occurs in a Rhenish song about St. Ursula's ship; it begins "O coelne aller stede eyn blome."[131] This introductory formula appears to be conventional, but I have not traced its history. There is, for example, another instance in William Dunbar's "London Thow Art the Flowre of Cytes All."[132] Nor have I found the context of four lines celebrating Cologne which Norrenberg quotes from Ulrich von Hutten.[133] These Rhenish examples of formulas suggesting a familiarity with the city encomium may be grouped—at least for the present—with "Groningen is an edle stad" in the introductory stanza of a historical song[134] ascribed to about 1390 and with verses praising Brunswick from the same period.[135] It is very curious that these fragments belong to Northwestern Germany, where the city encomium is otherwise almost unknown. A detailed study of the geographical aspects of the genre is obviously called for.

Konrad Burdach and before him W. Wattenbach called attention to two very early examples of the *descriptio* and *laudatio urbis*, perhaps the earliest in German-speaking regions,[136] but did not fix the places of

---

aus den Jahren 1568-1605 (Vienna, 1923); Paul Roth, *Die 'Neuen Zeitungen' in Deutschland im 15. und 16. Jahrhundert* ("Preisschrift der fürstlich Jablonow-skischen Gesellschaft in Leipzig," XLIII; Leipzig, 1914).

[129] J. Schatz, *Die Gedichte Oswalds von Wolkenstein* (2d ed.; Göttingen, 1904), p. 230, no. 99.

[130] P. Norrenberg, *Kölnisches Literaturleben im ersten Viertel des 16. Jahrhunderts* (Vierson, 1873), p. 51, 11. 541 ff.

[131] Norrenberg, p. 9.

[132] See below p. 164.

[133] Norrenberg, p. ix.

[134] Liliencron, *Die historischen Volkslieder der Deutschen,* I (Leipzig, 1865), 155-156, no. 38; Goedeke, *Grundriss,* I, 460, II, 12.

[135] F. G. H. Culemann, "Lobgedicht auf die Stadt Braunschweig," *Jahrbuch des Vereins für niederdeutsche Sprachforschung,* I (1875), 56-57.

[136] *Vorspiel,* I, Part 2 (Halle, 1925), 260 (= *Deutsche Literaturzeitung,* XIX [1898], cols. 1964-65) and 162 (= "Eine Forschungsreise zum Ursprung der

these texts in the history of the genre. These texts occur in the *Candela rhetoricae* compiled by an unknown clerk at Iglau. Written between 1403 and 1418, they describe in prose and verse the city of Iglau. To be sure, Burdach considers a brief verse in praise of Vienna written in the thirteenth century to be perhaps the first suggestion of the genre, but he seems to assign little importance to it. The possible significance of the very early praise of Milan printed by F. Novati[137]—to which Burdach calls attention—has not been discussed. Georg Ellinger and others neglect the anonymous German eulogy of Nuremberg written in 1427. This must be almost the earliest German example of the genre. The use of German is striking, for the later examples are often in Latin and the form is conspicuously associated with humanism. Twenty years later, the barber and poet, Hans Rosenplüt, wrote a second German poem on Nuremberg. A form which was familiar to such writers as the anonymous eulogist of 1427 and Hans Rosenplüt must have been fairly well known.

In tracing the history of the city-poem, the student will point out changes in the aims and uses of the genre. The city-poem shifts from an encomium based on historical materials to a discussion of geographical and economic subjects and comes to include something about the language, customs, and even dress of the residents. A. Meinhard's verses on Wittenberg (1508) are sometimes considered to mark an advance in the use of materials from cultural history. The Meistersinger and particularly Hans Sachs, who wrote a dozen eulogies of cities, adapted the genre to the needs of their craft. The compositions of the professional versifiers called "Pritschmeister" celebrated athletic events, ordinarily a shooting contest. Although such compositions drew upon city-poems for information about the city where the event was held, they represent a distinct literary species.[138] In the latter part of the sixteenth century, much that is characteristic of the city-poem appears in topographical works. Such compendia as Sebastian Münster's *Cosmographey/ das ist/ Beschreibung aller Länder/ Herrschaften und fürnemesten Stetten des*

---

neuhochdeutschen Schriftsprache und des deutschen Humanismus," *Abhandlungen der k. preussischen Akademie der Wissenschaften* [1903], no. 1, p. 26) ; W. Wattenbach, "Candela rhetoricae," *Archiv für Kunde österreichischer Geschichts-Quellen,* XXX (1864), 181-202, especially pp. 186-97. Compare also the *Laudes Coloniae* (written *ca.* 1400) in J. F. Boehmer, *Fontes rerum Germanicarum,* IV (Stuttgart, 1898), 463-470 and the introduction, p. liv.

[137] "De magnalibus urbis Mediolani," *Bulletino dell' istituto storico italiano,* no. 20 (1898).

[138] Georg Baesecke (ed.), Johann Fischart, *Das glückhafte Schiff von Zürich (1577)* ("Neudrucke deutscher Literaturwerke des 16. und 17. Jahrhunderts," CLXXXII, Halle, 1901), pp. xiv-xxiv, especially pp. xxii-xxiii.

gantzen Erdbodens sampt ihren Gelegenheiten/ Eygenschafften/ Religion/ Gebräuchen/ Geschichten und Handtierungen (1598) and Daniel Meissner's *Thesaurus Philopoliticus* (1624-26), which appeared in later editions (1638-42, 1682) under the title *Scigraphia cosmica,* with 800 views of cities,[139] contain much material resembling that used in city-poems. The tradition of such works goes back through Glareanus, *Helvetiae descriptio* (1515) and *De geographia* (1527) to Strabo.[140] Perhaps the first printed book to include views of cities was Bernhard von Breidenbach's *Peregrinatio in terram sanctam* (1486). The topography of Matthaeus Merian (1642-61)—one of the showpieces of German printing in this period—contains copper-plates accompanied by a description in prose. The division of the city-poem into these two branches—the verses of the *Pritschmeister* and the topographical compendia—represents a convenient terminus in a historical account of the genre.

Among the best examples of the city-poem are Conrad Celtis' and Helius Eobanus Hessus' eulogies of Nuremberg, Hermann Buschius' eulogy of Leipzig and Philip Engelbrecht's eulogy of Freiburg i. B. All of these have been well edited. A review of the genre might disclose others worthy of an edition,[141] clarify the differences of opinion regarding origins, and reveal more fully the development of the genre. In the light of Ludwig Geiger's remarks,[142] I recommend an edition of Andreas Meinhard's *Dialogus illustrate ac augustissime urbis Albiorene vulgo Vittenberg dicte situm amenitatem ac illustrationem docens tirocinia nobilium artium jacentibus editus* (Leipzig, 1508). It is said to contain interesting materials for the student of cultural history. Meinhard's use of the dialogue, a form which is rare if not unique in city-eulogies, is of uncertain origin. William Hammer thinks the use of this form cannot have been suggested by Petrarch's *De remediis utriusque fortunae,* I, Dial. 118 (on ruins).[143] M. Rudthard's poem on Joachimsthal is said to be interesting for its linguistic peculiarities.[144]

---

[139] See a new edition by Fritz Herrmann and Leonhard Kraft (Heidelberg, 1927).

[140] See Hans Rupprich, *Humanismus und Renaissance in den deutschen Städten* ("Deutsche Literatur"; Leipzig, 1935), pp. 10, 51.

[141] Compare Hugh William Davies, *Bernhard von Breydenbach and His Journey to the Holy Land, 1483-84. A Bibliography* (London, 1911).

[142] *Renaissance und Humanismus in Italien und Deutschland* (Berlin, 1882), pp. 472, 578.

[143] See now W. S. Heckscher, *Die Romruinen. Die geistigen Voraussetzungen ihrer Wertung in Mittelalter und in der Renaissance,* (Hamburg diss.; Würzburg, 1936) and William Hammer's review, *Classical Philology,* XXXIII (1938), 433-435.

[144] R. Wolkan, *Böhmens Anteil an der deutschen Literatur des 16. Jahrhunderts* (Prague, 1890), III, 320.

CHAPTER IV

PROBLEMS IN THE HISTORY OF IDEAS

30. *Ideas of Marriage.*—As a first example of a problem in the literary history of ideas, I choose the post-medieval books on marriage. The study of such books leads us to the indistinct boundaries separating literary history from theology, law, sociology, medicine, and cultural history. Since time immemorial, books have given instruction in etiquette, morals, and the problems of life. Admonitory writing and the need for it is perennial. Only the other day Richard C. Cabot wrote *What Men Live By; Life Begins at Forty* is only a few years old, and *Wake Up and Live!* has yielded its place as a best seller to *Live Alone and Like It.* There are handbooks for rulers, of which the *Hitopadeça* exemplifies the Oriental and Niccolò Machiavelli's *Il Principe* or Thomas Elyot's *The Gouvernour* exemplifies the Occidental manner. Baldassare Castiglione's *Ill Cortegiano* is but one of the many guides for the courtier. There are handbooks to instruct us in rearing children, in marrying, and even in dying.[1] Treatises on marriage are perhaps the most interesting of all these guides. Their variety in the treatment of the subject, their freedom in the choice of sources, and their intimate connection with the ideals and the life of the age, all make them attractive subjects for investigation.

Our notions of the duties and rights, the joys and sorrows of marriage have descended to us from classical antiquity and the church in all its periods, from medieval dogmatists, knights, and wandering scholars, from foreign and native sources. The historian of marriage-books seeks to determine the contribution of each of these sources, to characterize the epochs in the development of the genre, and to interpret the changes which he finds. Long before its religious sanctions were discussed, marriage was a social problem. The Pauline epigram "It is better to marry than to burn" (1 Cor. 7:9) still colors writings on marriage. The Goliards and the humanists turned over in their minds the problem of marriage. When the venereal pestilence swept Europe in the sixteenth century, the ways of thinking about marriage necessarily altered. Apart from dogmatic dispute, Martin Luther considered the social, ethical, and physical aspects of marriage. The sources and connections of the many meditations on marriage, their relations to the religious doctrines of the

[1] On the *Ars moriendi,* see below, pp. 143-144.

124

time, and their reflection of contemporary social conditions are problems for investigation.

A satisfactory history of post-medieval German guides to marriage remains to be written. In Max Herrmann's brief sketch of such works,[2] we find a sufficient review of Oriental, Greek, and Roman guides to marriage, to provide a background. He continues with an account of the guides to marriage written in the fifteenth century in Germany. Waldemar Kawerau and Franz Falk have reviewed at greater length than did Max Herrmann the guides to marriage written before 1520. These writers have sought to provide an account of the background of Eyb's *Ehebüchlein* (Herrmann), or to prove the need for the Lutheran reformation of marriage (Kawerau), or to defend the state of marriage before Luther (Falk). Obviously, there is a place for a history which does none of these things but which traces the development of guides to marriage as an end in itself.

In the following statement of the problem, I indicate briefly the materials to be used in investigating the contribution of classical antiquity, Christianity, Germanic racial ideals, chivalry and the Courts of Love, ecclesiastical and scholastic anti-feminism, and the cultural ideals of the Renaissance. Then follows comment on the materials for the study of marriage found in literature and law. Literary monuments reflect an author's views on marriage and often exemplify the use of a theme which the age has associated with the discussion of marriage. Legal treatises are devoted to matrimonial affairs, and legal ideas connected with marriage appear in literary monuments. Study of these literary and legal problems fills in the background necessary for the appreciation of marriage-books. After these prefatory remarks, I take up typical problems in the history of German guides to marriage. Since the texts written before 1520 are for the most part brief documents which have not been reprinted, I have dealt with them at length as problems well suited to our circumstances. Since the texts written after 1520 are often lengthy treatises difficult of access to scholars outside Germany, I have surveyed them bibliographically. In doing so, I may have made errors in grouping and characterization, since few of these

[2] *Albrecht von Eyb und die Frühzeit des deutschen Humanismus* (Berlin, 1893), pp. 315-329. This section on marriage has been suggested by the comparison of Herrmann's survey with Waldemar Kawerau, *Die Reformation und die Ehe, ein Beitrag zur Kulturgeschichte des 16. Jahrhunderts* ("Schriften des Vereins für Reformationsgeschichte," XXXIX; Halle, 1892) and the answer from the Catholic side in Franz Falk, *Die Ehe am Ausgang des Mittelalters. Eine kirchen- und kulturgeschichtliche Studie* ("Erläuterungen und Ergänzungen zu Janssens 'Geschichte des deutschen Volkes,'" VI, 4; Freiburg i. Br., 1908).

books are within my reach and I have been forced to rely upon secondary sources. I have suggested problems in the religious and legal aspects of these books, in their form, and in the effect of foreign influences upon them.

Such classical writers as Plutarch, Theophrastus, Stobaeus, and Seneca (in a lost work) formulated their ideas on matrimony, and later ages often turned to them for guidance. The influence of the Old and New Testament, of the Greek reinterpretation of Christianity (notably in St. Paul's writings), and of the Church Fathers—Tertullian and St. Jerome on the side of asceticism and Clement of Alexandria and St. John Chrysostom on the other—has been continuous throughout the history of European culture.[3] Collections of sermons of illustrative stories for use in sermons show how these ideas and their later developments were communicated to the people of the Middle Ages. In any collection of exempla, the stories under such heads as *adulterium, castitas, femina, luxuria, mulier,* and the like illustrate the ideas preached far and wide in the Middle Ages.

A difficult problem lies in the oft-repeated claim that the Germanic-speaking peoples have displayed from the earliest times a peculiar respect and reverence for women.[4] Max Herrmann argues eloquently for the Germanic origin of a high morality in marriage, for the importance of woman's rôle, and for the persistence of these ideas in the fifteenth and sixteenth centuries. Gustav Roethe conjectures that the rhetorical contrast of *menlich wip, wiplich man* was already traditional in Middle High German times. Granted that a lofty conception of women can be found in Tacitus and that it is part of Germanic tradition, does it enter into the guides to marriage written in the fifteenth and sixteenth centuries? The emphasis placed on such matters in Germany of today does not appear to be an unbroken continuation of an ancient way of thinking, but rather an effort to regain the old ideals.

Chivalry and the Courts of Love are altogether more favorable to women than the Church Fathers. Although chivalric notions and even much of the medieval phraseology are found in our own day, these resemblances may have arisen in the romantic revival of the Middle Ages rather than by survival through a long period of time. The romanticists may have been led to take up these medieval ideas by the influence of a more nearly just and more generous conception of the place of women which had been created by Rousseau and by Storm and

---

[3] For reference to the discussion of treatises on marriage in classical antiquity and early Christianity, and the later subdivisions of this subject, see Appendix V, pp. 165-167.

[4] For references, see below, pp. 167-168.

Stress. These matters are yet to be investigated and need not concern us further here.

The allegorical verse of the later Middle Ages—notably Guillaume de Lorris's *Roman de la Rose* (*ca.* 1235) and its continuation by Jean de Meung (*ca.* 1277)—dealt at great length with the problems of love and marriage.[5] Embittered ascetism with antecedents in monastic hostility to women often found utterance; it was answered in such a work as Martin le Franc's *Champion des dames* (*ca.* 1485).[6] The wandering scholars of the Middle Ages had their own notions about marriage, and voiced their low esteem of the marital state in terms borrowed from the church and classical antiquity. They gave the famous verses "De conjuge non ducenda" (first printed *ca.* 1495) wide currency.[7]

New ideals of marriage came with the Renaissance, and they, too, have not lost their power over us.[8] In the handbooks on marriage and in contemporary literature the aims and principles of the Renaissance mingled with standards created by a bourgeois, commercial society. In the following pages I shall examine at some length the problems which

[5] See especially A. Wulff, *Die frauenfeindlichen Dichtungen in den romanischen Literaturen des Mittelalters bis zum Ende des 13. Jahrhunderts* ("Romanistische Arbeiten," IV; Halle, 1914); T. L. Neff, *La satire des femmes dans la poésie lyrique du moyen âge* (Paris, 1900).

[6] J. W. Spargo, *Virgil the Necromancer* ("Harvard Studies in Comparative Literature," X; Cambridge, Mass., 1934), p. 339, n. 55.

[7] They appeared under the title *Remedium contra concubinas et conjuges* (Memmingen, *ca.* 1495) published with J. Motis, *Invectiva cetus feminei contra mares*. See editions from manuscripts by Thomas Wright and E. du Méril. For discussion compare Paul Lehmann, *Die Parodie im Mittelalter* (Munich, 1922), pp. 165-168; and *Pseudo-antike Literatur des Mittelalters* ("Studien der Bibliothek Warburg," XIII; Leipzig, 1927), pp. 23-25; S. M. Tucker, *Verse Satire in England before the Renaissance* (New York, 1908), pp. 175-176; A. Wulff, *Die frauenfeindlichen Dichtungen in den romanischen Literaturen des Mittelalters bis zum Ende des 13. Jahrhunderts* ("Romanistische Arbeiten," IV; Halle, 1914), pp. 36-40. On the *Epistola Valerii ad Rufinum* see F. Tupper, Jr. and M. B. Ogle (transl.), *Courtier's Trifles* (Walter Map's *De nugis curialium*) (London, 1924), pp. 189-199, 366; D. M. Schullian, "Valerius Maximus and Walter Map," *Speculum*, XII (1937), 516-518.

[8] Since the discussion which follows is an elaboration of this sentence, I content myself with the indication of works which are valuable to us for particular purposes. The guides to marriage which won international recognition are easily identified in Louis B. Wright, *Middle-Class Culture in Elizabethan England* (Chapel Hill, 1935). Alice Clark, *Working Life of Women in the Seventeenth Century* (London, 1919) describes the social and economic background of a somewhat later time and suggests pertinent things to look for in our period. The significance of the religious element is well discussed in L. L. Schücking, *Die Familie im Puritanismus. Studien über Familie und Literatur in England im 16., 17. und 18. Jahrhundert* (Leipzig, 1929).

the study of marriage in Germany during our period offers. I shall mention first the literary sources of our knowledge, then the legal aspects of marriage, the handbooks on marriage before and after 1470, when Albrecht von Eyb's *Ehebüchlein* appeared, and shall take up finally the religious traditions, the literary conventions, and the foreign influences in the handbooks. My treatment of these subjects is necessarily cursory and is intended only to suggest the problem and the nature of the materials for its solution. A book is ordinarily mentioned only in a single connection and as an example of a particular aspect of the problem. Obviously, a satisfactory treatment of any problem will involve the discussion of texts supplementing those which I have cited.

From literary monuments we can learn much about the status of marriage at a particular time. In estimating the value of an author's remarks, we must consider his interests, his education, his social position, and the exigencies of his theme. The dissertations which have chosen as their subject marriage in German literature of the Renaissance are for the most part perfunctory pieces of work, chiefly useful as collections of material. They should have achieved something significant in the interpretation of the author, his idea of marriage, and the relations to the age. A model for emulation is C. H. Herford, *Shakespeare's Treatment of Love and Marriage*.[9] An investigation of this sort in German literature might deal with Hans Sachs. He had a long and happy married life and married a second time, he was interested in moralizing, and he was familiar with the ordinary books of advice on marriage.

In the fifteenth and sixteenth centuries, certain themes are conspicuously associated with the discussion of marriage. Thus, for example, the stories of Sigismund and Guiscarda, Griselda, Lucretia, and the marriage at Cana are used again and again.[10] It has been suggested that the marriage at Cana became a subject for literary and pictorial treatment because Lutherans interpreted Christ's presence at the wedding as evidence of His approval of marriage as a divine institution. From what has been said, it is clear that such themes as these should be

[9] London, 1920.

[10] On Sigismund and Guiscarda see A. C. Lee, *The Decameron: its sources and analogues* (London, 1909), pp. 116-123.—On Griselda see my collectanea in *Modern Philology*, XXXI (1933-34), 105; the forthcoming *Chaucer Analogues*. Stammler calls attention (pp. 464-465) to a problem in the relations of some German texts.—On Lucretia see G. Voigt, "Die Lucretia-Fabel und ihre literarischen Verwandten," *Berichte der k. sächsischen Gesellschaft der Wissenschaften, philosophisch-historische Klasse*, 1893, pp. 1-36; P. Strauch, *Zeitschrift für deutsches Altertum*, XXIX (1885), 431.—On the marriage at Cana see Kawerau, pp. 67-68 and 97, n. 115. Compare the use of the theme in plastic art.

studied historically in their various versions. Particularly interesting as an example of an investigation in the field of comparative literature is the problem offered by an aphorism widely used in the sixteenth century and later. This aphorism, which Basil L. Gildersleeve wittily called an ordnance-map of feminine charms, recites the various points of perfection in a woman.[11] The number ranges from seven to thirty. Particularly interesting and important is the influence exerted by collections of proverbs, epigrams, quotations, and sententious observations on life. For the sixteenth and seventeenth centuries, such works were guides to manners and morals as well as summaries of accepted ideas and ideals. The *Adagia* of Erasmus is the most conspicuous example of the species. Its significance in representing or forming the attitude of the age toward women might be investigated. Sebastian Franck's collection entitled *Sprichwörter: Schöne, weise, herzliche Clugreden* (1541)— which was widely circulated in an epitome bearing a very similar title— was condemned for its hostility to women. It was one of the sources of Johann Fischart's *Philosophisches Ehezuchtbüchlein* (1578).

31. *Handbooks on Marriage.*—German handbooks on marriage written before 1520 raise many questions. What guides to married life exist? What ones are accessible in modern editions? What characteristics do they display? Upon what sources do they draw? What influence do they exert upon one another? How well do they reflect contemporary conditions? To such questions we have no satisfactory answers. Those who have described these works have sought to demonstrate the low state of morals in the fifteenth century or to illustrate one or another religious doctrine in its relations to matrimony.

In the fifteenth century, the first treatise on marriage appears to be the still unpublished *Labyrinthus vitae conjugalis* or *De vita conjugali* (1432) by Konrad Bitschin.[12] Both the first draft and the finished form

---

[11] I have collected references in *The Proverb* (Cambridge, Mass., 1931), pp. 103-104, n. 1. See further G. Manacorda, "Zu dem volkstümlichen Motive von den weiblichen Schönheiten," *Zeitschrift des Vereins für Volkskunde,* XVIII (1908), 436-441 and "Beziehungen Hans Sachsens zur italienischen Literatur," *Studien zur vergleichenden Literaturgeschichte,* VI (1906), 228-230; W. Suchier, *L'enfant sage* ("Gesellschaft für romanische Literatur," XXIV; Dresden, 1910), pp. xiii, 393, 405, no. 16. Compare Reik's misconception of a passage in the *Comedy of Errors;* see *Internationale Zeitschrift für Psychoanalyse,* II (1914), 61. A vast deal of material has been assembled and some of it has been classified, but neither the collection nor the classification has thrown any light on such significant matters as the origin of the theme or the inferences to be drawn from its dissemination.

[12] Ziesemer in *Verfasserlexikon,* I, cols. 240-242; Stammler, p. 79; Herrmann, p. 424; F. Hipler, "Die Pädagogik des Konrad Bitschin," *Mitteilungen der Gesellschaft für deutsche Erziehungs- und Schulgeschichte,* II (1892), 1-10; R. Galle

of this guide to manners and morals in the married state are still in existence. Walther Ziesemer comments briefly on them and considers them worthy of investigation and perhaps even of publication. To be sure, the *De vita conjugali* appears to be merely a compilation of traditional phrases and ideas, but the procedure is characteristic of the age. We may perhaps credit Bitschin with a new idea in making marriage the center of his discussion of manners and morals.

In this first period of post-medieval guides to marriage, most of the works are juristic or theological, and apparently several interesting or typical ones are still unpublished. Some are shorter than Bitschin's guide and can be photographed cheaply, e.g., the *Epistola ad amicum de uxore non ducenda*[13] and a German essay bearing no title.[14] Like Bitschin's compendium, the German essay cites a number of illustrations from the Bible. These treatises deserve more careful examination than they have yet received. In some guides to marriage, the technicalities of canon law in respect to marriage are expounded at length, or a list of twelve reasons for marriage is given.[15] It would be interesting to know whether this list plays any part in later guides to marriage.

Even at the beginning of the fifteenth century, Theophrastus is a source, although indirectly, for reflections on marriage. The title of the Latin treatise which I have just quoted echoes an old question: "Should a scholar marry?" (An sapienti sit uxor ducenda?).[16] Through Petrarch, Francesco Barbaro, Poggio, and Albrecht von Eyb, the theme came into the hands of German humanists. Its history reaches back to St. Jerome, who is the source of the variations on the theme circulated by Abelard, by John Salisbury, by Vincent of Beauvais, and by many another. Nor was it original with St. Jerome, for he acknowledged his indebtedness to Seneca. Seneca's criticism of marriage is lost, but may have been ultimately derived from Theophrastus. Such is the outline of the history of the theme, but the details are yet to be investigated, the variations are yet to be accounted for, and their interpretation in the light of social, economic, and political history is yet to be given.

(ed.), *Konrad Bitschin's Pädagogik. Das 4. Buch des enzyklopädischen Werkes 'De vita conjugali'* (Gotha, 1905).

[13] *Cod. lat. mon. 7879,* fol. 140 ff.; cited by Herrmann, p. 327. No one has commented on the possible, nay probable, relation of this work to a composition with a similar title ascribed to Walter Map. On this latter work see above p. 127.

[14] *Cod. germ. mon. 737,* fol. 2. Cited by Herrmann, p. 329.

[15] *Cod. lat. mon. 5940,* fol. 6[b]. Cited by Herrmann, p. 328.

[16] K. Burdach, *Vom Mittelalter zur Reformation,* III, i (Berlin, 1917), pp. 294, 411. See also Landau, *Zeitschrift für vergleichende Literaturgeschichte,* N.F., X (1896), 285-286.

Still definitely in the medieval tradition is a small document, the so-called letter of St. Bernard, "De cura et modo rei familiaris," or, as it is variously called, "Epistola super gubernatione rei familiaris," on practical rather than religious aspects of matrimony.[17] Although ascribed to St. Bernard of Clairvaux and printed in his works, it is from the hand of his contemporary, Bernard Silvestris or Bernard of Chartres, who lived about 1150. Interesting as a medieval commentary on family life which gives attention to secular matters, it enjoyed a wide popularity, sixteen editions having appeared in Germany before 1511. Its wide distribution, special character, and the authority of the name which it bore assured it of a prominent place. A reprint of one of the German translations might throw light on the sources of the practical admonitions in marriage-books. Felix Hemmerlin's *Dialogus de matrimonio,* written before the middle of the fifteenth century, is said to be a predecessor of humanistic thinking about marriage,[18] but our information about the book is very scanty. A fuller discussion is in order.

For several reasons, a brief discussion of marriage entitled *Eine nützliche Lehre und Predigt wie sich zway menschen in dem Sacrament der heiligen Ee halten süllen* (*ca.* 1472)[19] is interesting. It enjoyed a notable success. The text, which has not been reprinted in modern times, occurs in the manuscripts *Cod. germ. mon. 638* and *4873* and no doubt elsewhere, finds a place in a volume of moralizing according to the Ten Commandments which was issued twice (1472, 1476), is rewritten and condensed (Augsburg, 1482), and has a surprising rebirth in five editions between 1513 and 1520. Concerning its sources we know nothing. Although the author makes strange mistakes—e.g. Ulixes (Ulysses) remains true to his wife Nawsica (Nausicaa) when a Trojan woman attempts seduction—he has distinct humanistic leanings. On the other hand, there are reminiscences of medieval notions such as the comparison of matrimony to an ecclesiastical order. This comparison is used in the still unpublished *Spiegel ehelichen ordens* (*ca.* 1487) by Marcus von Weida, in Johannes Spangenberg's *Des ehelichen ordens Spiegel und Regel* (1545), in Hans Sachs's Meisterlied (1550), and in Cyriacus Spangenberg's *Ehespiegel* (1561), which was enlarged and reissued in 1578.[20] A new edition of *Eine nützliche Lehre und Predigt* offers inter-

[17] Falk, pp. 33 ff.

[18] Samuel Singer, *Die mittelalterliche Literatur der deutschen Schweiz* ("Die Schweiz im deutschen Geistesleben," LXVI-LXVII; Frauenfeld, 1930), p. 129.

[19] See K. Sudhoff, *Deutsche medizinische Inkunabeln* ("Studien zur Geschichte der Medizin," II-III; Leipzig, 1908), pp. 46-47, nos. 49-50; Herrmann, p. 329; Falk, pp. 29 ff.; N. Paulus, *Historisch-politische Blätter,* CXLI (1908), 1017-1019.

[20] On the notion of marriage compared to an ecclasiastical order see G. Roethe,

esting problems in the constitution of a text, in its interpretation, and in placing it in relation to its age and to other works on the same subject.

A new spirit in guides to marriage appears in Albrecht von Eyb's *Ob einem Mann sei zu nehmen ein ehelich Weib* (*ca.* 1472), the so-called *Ehebüchlein*.[21] The title echoes the old question, "An sapienti sit uxor ducenda?" His work breaks with the earlier ecclesiastical and juristic traditions dominating the discussion of marriage, and calls attention to psyiological and ethical aspects hitherto unnoticed by writers of handbooks on marriage. Concerning it we are fairly well informed. We have a satisfactory modern edition of the text and an elaborate discussion of its sources and connections. To be sure, Albrecht von Eyb's earlier drafts of essays on marriage—a section of his *Margarita poetica* and two other essays—have never been reprinted,[22] and some problems in its

Die Gedichte Reinmars von Zweter (Leipzig, 1887), p. 225, N. Paulus, "Mittelalterliche Stimmen über den Eheorden," *Historisch-politische Blätter,* CXLI (1908), 1008-1024, and on the figurative use for other purposes see J. J. A. Frantzen and A. Hulshoff, *Drei Kölner Schwankbücher* (Utrecht, 1920), pp. xvi-xvii.

On Marcus von Weida see Falk, pp. 27-28, and "Der Unterricht des Volkes in den katechetischen Hauptstücken am Ende des Mittelalters," *Historisch-politische Blätter,* CVIII (1891), 553-560, 682-694, especially pp. 682-689; Franz Breitkopf, *Marcus von Weida, ein Prediger und theologischer Volksschriftsteller des ausgehenden Mittelalters* (Diss.; Greifswald, 1932). On Hans Sachs, see A. Dreyer in *Analecta germanica Hermann Paul dargebracht* (Amberg, 1906) citing (p. 373, n. 1) the "Allerley örden des Ehstandes" or "Die acht verendrung im ehstand"; and Keller-Goetze, XXV, 337, no. 3256. On the Spangenbergs see Kawerau, p. 81.

[21] See Max Herrmann's edition ("Schriften zur germanischen Philologie," IV, i; Berlin, 1890). For discussion compare Falk, p. 23; Herrmann, pp. 332-355; K. Sudhoff, *Deutsche medizinische Inkunabeln* ("Studien zur Geschichte der Medizin," II-III; Leipzig, 1908), pp. 43-46, nos. 46-48; K. Schottenloher, *Das Regensburger Buchgewerbe im 15. und 16. Jahrhundert* ("Veröffentlichungen der Gutenberg-Gesellschaft," XIV-XX; Mainz, 1920), p. 56; Stamminger in Wetzer and Welte's *Kirchenlexikon oder Encyclopädie der katholischen Theologie und ihrer Hülfswissenschaften* (2d ed.; Freiburg, i.B., 1882-1903), IV (1886), 1151. Possibly the significance of the *Ehebüchlein* has been overrated; see Wunderlich, *Literaturblatt für germanische und romanische Philologie,* XV (1894), cols. 292-294.

An anonymous condensation of the *Ehebüchlein* in 8 leaves (Augsburg, *ca.* 1516) calls for a brief characterization. The ascription to a mysterious Martin von Eyb appears to be without foundation. Although humanism had been extending its influence in Germany for more than two generations, this editor of the *Ehebüchlein* omitted all of the significant humanistic elements. Compare Proctor, 10379; Emil Weller, *Repertorium,* p. 90; Herrmann, p. 423. For comment on the contemporary interest of the age in the physiological aspects of marriage see G. Schneider (ed.), M. Luther, *Sexualethische Anweisungen* ("Sexualpsychologie," II; Kandern, 1926).

[22] Herrmann, pp. 266 ff.; Karstien, *Germanisch-Romanische Monatsschrift,* XI (1923), 217-225, 278-288. Unfortunately there is no modern edition of the *Margarita poetica,* an epochmaking humanistic treatise.

sources remain to be investigated. In the essay "Clarissimarum feminarum laudacio," utilized in the *Ehebüchlein*, Albrecht gave a variety of illustrations of the virtue of chastity, but we do not know where he found his materials.[23] The question is a small one, but an answer to it will reveal something of his background and his way of writing. Herrmann also finds it impossible to name Albrecht's sources for the illustrative examples of the literary and artistic achievements of women.[24]

The circumstances in which the *Ehebüchlein* came to be written and the relations of the work to the more important earlier treatises on marriage are not entirely clear. Albrecht von Eyb was interested in marriage during his years of study in Italy. His miscellanea dating from this period are still available in a copy made by Hartmann Schedel,[25] but no one has discussed their value in explaining the composition of the *Ehebüchlein* or in rounding out the picture of postmedieval ideas of marriage derived from Italy. Again and again,[26] we are told that Albrecht did not find his inspiration in the epochmaking *De re uxoria* (1415-16) of Francesco Barbaro. Karl Goedeke[27] throws out the suggestion that Albrecht has much in common with Johann Hartlieb's translation (1440) of Andreas Capellanus' *Liber de honeste amandi*. Although this suggestion is not very apposite, it must be disposed of. Furthermore, the *Ehebüchlein* has been said to contain medical and physiological information and therefore to be the beginning of a new sort of marriage-book. Max Herrmann, who is responsible for these opinions, does not support them with sufficient evidence and consequently leads the reader to form an erroneous idea of Albrecht von Eyb's position in the history of guides to marriage.[28] It remains to be established when and where comment on the medical and physiological aspects of marriage—aspects which are extensively dealt with in modern treatises—was introduced into the tradition of handbooks on marriage.

Returning to the chronological arrangement of guides to marriage,

[23] Herrmann, p. 268.

[24] Herrmann, p. 269, n. 2.

[25] *Cod. lat. mon. 504.* See Herrmann, p. 158, n.

[26] See, e.g., Herrmann, p. 325. A German translation of *De re uxoria* was published at Hagenau in 1583. J. Cluten's edition (Strassburg, 1612) is in the University of Chicago Library.

[27] *Grundriss,* I, 371.

[28] I am grateful to Rev. Joseph A. Hiller of the Catholic University for warning me against this error, into which I had fallen. His forthcoming study *Albrecht von Eyb, A Mediaeval Moralist* will set right this and other matters and will be a basis for further study of an important figure in the didactic tradition.

we come to an uninspired set of admonitions entitled *Frauenspiegel*.[29] Since this title was applied to at least two different works at about the same time, careful distinctions must be drawn. A bit of moralizing under this title was published four times between 1520 and 1522 at Augsburg and Strassburg. It seems not to have been particularly influenced by the growing interest in the religious aspects of matrimony. We know nothing about its sources and connections. There is, furthermore, a curious problem in its relation to *Ein spruch genant der Brüde büchlin* (1520) in ten quarto sheets preserved in a single copy in the cantonal library of Lucerne.[30] Possibly the *Brüde büchlin* is worth reprinting. These works must be differentiated from a *Frawen Spiegel* printed at Vienna in 1553.[31] It, too, is worthy of a fresh examination. A dull "Spruch vom ehelichen Stand" by Kunz Has, a Meistersinger of Nuremberg, must have been written before 1525, by which date Has is known to have died.[32] The "schon new lied von dem heiligen Ehstandt" (1550) by the Meistersinger Johannes Kauffungen[33] reflects no doubt the Lutheran doctrines prevailing in the schools of the Meistersing. Since it has been printed—and a few Meisterlieder of this period have been printed,—it might be worth republishing as an example of what the Meistersinger wished to be known by.

In the first twenty years of the sixteenth century, a flood of pamphlets on marriage appeared. These pamphlets reflected the attitudes and ideas of various classes of society. A fuller description and interpretation of these pamphlets are needed as a background for the controversies begun by Martin Luther. Hieronymus Emser's *Ein deutsche Satyra vnd straffe des Eebruchs vnd in was würden vnnd erenn der Eelichen stand vorczeiten gehalten, mit erclarung vil schoner historien* (1505)[34] is interesting as the work of a man who was later to oppose Luther. It represents the old tradition of the use of illustrative stories. Johannes Murner, the brother of Thomas, wrote *Von ehelichen Stands Nutz und*

---

[29] K. Sudhoff, *Deutsche medizinische Inkunabeln* ("Studien zur Geschichte der Medizin," II-III; Leipzig, 1908), pp. 47-48, nos. 51-52, cites a work probably printed after 1500. It may be different from the book cited in Falk, p. 35, and Goedeke, II, 282, no. 41, and reprinted in E. Weller, *Dichtungen des 16. Jahrhunderts* ("Bibliothek des Literarischen Vereins," CXIX; Tübingen, 1874), pp. 78-93, no. 9.

[30] E. Weller, *Annalen*, I, 297, no. 27. I have not found Falk's reference (p. 35) to Weller, 1385.

[31] A. Hauffen, *Zeitschrift für deutsche Philologie*, XXVII (1895), 341.

[32] Matthias, *Mitteilungen des Vereins für die Geschichte der Stadt Nürnberg*, VII (1888), 209-233.

[33] Goedeke, II, 263, no. 53.

[34] In 11 fol. See Kawerau, pp. 65, 96, no. 108.

Beschwerden (ca. 1510).[35] The verses entitled "Von der Ehe," which the Strassburg humanist and doctor Johann Adelphus Muling appended to his edition of Hermann von Sachsenheim's *Die Möhrin* (1512), are interesting because of the author's position as a mediator between the late mystics and the humanists.[36] The couplets of *Ein schoner spruch von Eelichen standt (ca.* 1515) by the Meistersinger Martin Maier of Reutlingen comprise the familiar rules.[37] An anonymous work gives general advice: *Wie ein junger Gesell weiben soll* (1515).[38] Not very different is *Ich will haushalten, vnd wil ein Weib nehmen. Ein schön Büchlein allen Geistlichen vñ weltlichen, Jungen und Alten nützlich und kurtzweylig zu lesen* (1529).[39]

The most important works of the decade 1520-30 came from the pens of Desiderius Erasmus and Martin Luther. The former—a bachelor—expressed his ideas about marriage in the *Encomium matrimonii* (1518), the *Conjugium* (1524), the *Uxor* Μεμψιγαμος, a colloquy reprinted from the *Colloquia familiares* (1516) and circulated in English, French, and German, and at greater length in the *Matrimonii Christiani institutio* (1526). These were widely read and often reprinted. Their influence must have been considerable. For example, the translator Johannes Herold, a defender of Lutheranism, based his treatise *Vom loblichen herkommen . . . der hayligen Eh* (1542) on Erasmus. The influence exerted by Erasmus's *Adagia* in its rapidly enlarged editions from 1500 on is also to be taken into account. Martin Luther's observations on marriage—which begin at least as early as 1519—are of course a storm-center of doctrinal disputes.[40] From almost the beginning of the Refor-

[35] F. Rödiger, *Johannes und Thomas Murner: ein sprachlicher Vergleich* (Diss.; Greifswald, 1925).

[36] J. Knepper, " Beiträge zur Würdigung des elsässischen Humanisten Adelphus Muling," *Alemannia,* XXX (1903), 143-192, especially pp. 176-192; J. Nadler, *Literaturgeschichte der deutschen Stämme und Landschaften* (3d ed.; Ratisbon, 1929), I, 290-291.

[37] Kawerau, p. 66; Weller, *Dichtungen,* pp. 33-36, no. 5; Weller, *Annalen,* I, 293, no. 17; E. Hofmann, *Martin Maier aus Reutlingen* (Diss.; Greifswald, 1930), p. 32.

[38] Kawerau, p. 66; Weller, *Dichtungen des 16. Jahrhunderts* ("Bibliothek des Literarischen Vereins," CXIX; Tübingen, 1874), pp. 22-32, no. 4.

[39] Goedeke, II, 282, no. 41, 2.

[40] For a convenient bibliography of Luther's writings on marriage and the works dealing with them see Schottenloher, I, 523, nos. 12330-42, and 590-591, nos. 13765-65a, and above, p. 226, n. 1. For the Catholic attitude toward Luther's ideas of marriage, see S. Baranowski, *Luthers Lehre von der Ehe* (Münster i. W., 1913). The most recent interpretations of Luther's views that I have noted are Lilly Zarncke, "Der Begriff der Liebe in Luthers Aeusserungen über die Ehe," *Theologische Blätter,* X (1931), 45-49 and "Die naturhafte Eheanschauung des

mation, writings on marriage increased by leaps and bounds. These books and pamphlets are always tinged with controversy. They often deal with the controversial doctrinal questions of the celibacy of the clergy and the position of marriage as a sacrament. For the purposes of the literary historian, brief characterizations and summaries will suffice in describing these works. Except for the few works of cardinal significance, reprints are probably unnecessary.

The following treatises appear to illustrate primarily the religious aspects of the sixteenth-century interest in marriage: J. Brenz, *Wie in Eesachen und den fellen so sich derhalben zu tragen nach Göttlichem billichem rechten zu handeln sey* (ca. 1530);[41] Leonhart Culmann, *Jungen Gesellen, Jungfrauen und Witwen . . . , ein Unterrichtung* (1531), which was soon translated into Low German;[42] a chapter "Von dem Ehlichen Standt" was inserted in the edition of Sebastian Brant's *Freidank* issued in 1538;[43] Heinrich Bullinger, *Der christliche Ehestand* (1540), which Miles Coverdale translated (1543) into English, became in the opinion of L. B. Wright[44] the typical English work of the period and passed through at least nine editions before 1575; Andreas Lucas, *Kurtzer und warhafftiger Bericht von dem heyligen Ehestande* (ca. 1540), J. Flinner, *Ein christlicher sendtbrieff darinnen er einem s. freund, so zu heyraten bedacht, wes sich zu erinnern von noeten, fuer helt u. zu bedencken gibt. Umb Hurerey willen habe ein jedlicher sein eygen Weyb* (ca. 1545); Erasmus Alberus, *Ein Predigt vom Ehestand* (1546), K. Bienemann, *Ehebüchlein für christliche Eheleute* (1552),[45] Erasmus Sarcerius, *Buch vom heiligen Ehestand* (1553),[45] Johannes Mathesius, *Vom Ehestand und Hauswesen* (1563), Johannes Ursinus, *Psalmus 112. Vom Gottseligen Haushalten Wie es Gott segnet, mit Kindern, Gütern, und Frewde, n. s. reichen verheissung* (1568), and Gregorius Marspach, *Commendatio conjugii* (1586).

The legal aspects of marriage are occasionally important for the

---

jungen Luther," *Archiv für Kulturgeschichte*, XXV (1934-35), 281-305. For the background see Hans Hartmann, *Kirche und Sexualität. Der Wandel der Erotik* (Rudolstadt, 1929).

[41] See Johannes Luther, *Die Titeleinfassungen der Reformationszeit* (Leipzig, 1909-13), Plate 122. Martin Luther wrote a preface to a pamphlet with the same title; see Köhler, no. 44; Luther, Plate 48.

[42] Goedeke, II, 282, no. 43. The edition of 1532 seems to have disappeared; see C. Borchling and B. Claussen, *Niederdeutsche Bibliographie* (Neumünster, 1932), cols. 499-500, no. 1119. The edition of 1534 is in the Hamburg Stadtbibliothek; see Borchling and Claussen, col. 533, no. 1188.

[43] W. Grimm (ed.), *Freidanks Bescheidenheit* (2d ed.; Göttingen, 1860), p. v.

[44] Pp. 205-206.

[45] Copies in the University of Chicago Library.

historian of literature and even more so for the historian of culture.[46] Legal considerations play a large rôle in handbooks of marriage, and must not be neglected in the interpretation of the origins and relations of such works. Long ago, Gustav Ehrismann called attention to the legal aspects of love and marriage in the *De amore libri tres* of Andreas Capellanus. Although the author was not a lawyer, his codification of the rules of the Court of Love should be interpreted in the light of contemporary legal practise.

The widely known *Silva nuptialis* (Lyons, 1521) by Giovanni Nevizzani, who was the first to compile a legal bibliography, was perhaps the most familiar of legal treatises. This whimsical work of a misogynist[47] went through a number of editions and was considerably altered in the process. A. Tiraquellus' serious work *De legibus connubialibus et iure maritali* reached a fifth edition (Lyons, 1554). Popular German legal works are K. Huber's *Spiegel des Hausrechts* (1565) and Huldericus Therander's (i.e., Johann Sommer's) *Bul- oder Bindbrieff auss H. Schrifft, göttlichen, natürlichen vnd weltlichen Rechten das ehelich Leben herrlich bewiesen* (1606). Analysis of these works in the light of the revision and codification of German law under Charles V—the so-called *Carolina*—is perhaps the task of the legal historian rather than the student of literature. In a historical account, the influence of Lutheranism must also be defined and estimated. On the hotly waged dispute over the celibacy of the clergy I need only touch here. Involving primarily theological doctrine and canon law, it has a history and literature of its own.[48] Bigamy is also a problem which concerns the historians of law and culture much more closely than the historian of literature.[49] It was freely discussed in Germany.

The literary convention[50] of the dialogue, popular in the controversies of the Reformation, recurs in Johann Freder's *Dialogus dem Ehestand zu Ehren* (1545), directed against Sebastian Franck's proverbs on women.[51] Dedicated to Queen Dorothea of Denmark, this *Dialogus* was

[46] See below, Appendix V.

[47] Michaud, *Biographie universelle* (2d ed.; Paris, n.d.), XXX, 355-356. The University of Chicago Library has the following editions: Lyons, 1526; Lyons: A. Vincentius, 1556; Lyons: I. Frellonius, 1556; Lyons, 1572; Frankfurt am Main, 1647.

[48] Fundamental to the study of this subject is H. C. Lea, *History of Sacerdotal Celibacy in the Christian Church* (3d ed., New York, 1907). See below p. 172.

[49] See below, p. 172.

[50] I deal here with literary conventions in the *form* of the guides to marriage and not with literary conventions in marriage itself. For a study of the latter sort see, e.g., Lu Emily Pearson, *Elizabethan Love Conventions* (Berkeley, 1923). This is a good survey of Petrarchan conventions.

[51] Kawerau, p. 58; Goedeke[2], II, 274, no. 75.

translated into Low German and Latin. Since the Latin translation is dated 1544, the date of the German original seems uncertain but must be earlier than 1545. The form of a dialogue is used again by Zacharias Zymmer in *Ein sehr schönes vnd gar lustiges Gesprech, zwischen zweyen Weybern, den Ehestand betreffende* (1577).[52] The encomium of marriage becomes a genre with several notable representatives.[53] Religious versifying of the sixteenth century turned discourses on marriage into rhyme and set them to music: Ludwig Helmbold, *Vom H. Ehestand: Viertzig Liedlein* (1583), enlarged in 1595 to *41 Liedlein.*[54] The Devil-literature, which dominated Protestant didactic writing in the middle of the sixteenth century, appears to have left a mark on the books dealing with marriage. Andreas Musculus, a Lutheran pastor in Frankfurt an der Oder, wrote an *Eheteufel* (1556) which was reissued at least eight times before the end of the century.[55] This work, it is said, influenced Adam Schubart's good-humored *Hausteuffel* (1565). The influence of the genre persists beyond the turn of the century in Georg Schwaneberger's rhymed comedy, *Der Engel Raphael wider den Eheteufel Asmodeum* (1615)[56] and Tobias Wagner's sermon, *Siebenfältiger Ehehalten-Teuffel* (1651).[57]

Just at the end of the sixteenth century, there was a short-lived fashion of dramatized admonitions on marriage; Thomas Birck's *Ehespiegel* (1593) and J. Bütow's *Heiratsspiegel* (1602), which have parallels in such dramatizations of advice on rearing children as Michael Druida's *Spiegel gottseliger Eltern und frommer Kinder* (1572), Johann Rasser's *Kinderzucht* (1573), and Arnold Quiting's *Kinderzucht* (1591). The suggestion of such didactic dramas[58] seems to have come from Martin

[52] Goedeke,[2] II, 368, no. 191a. This may be identical with *Ein schön lustig Gespräch zweyer Weibsbilder von der Ehe* (1565), which deals with the nature of marriage, the qualities which make a woman suited to marriage, the desirability of a mother's nursing her children, and the problems of disciplining children.

[53] A. Hauffen, *Vierteljahrschrift für Litteraturgeschichte,* VI (1893), 165, n. 6.

[54] Goedeke[2], II, 195, no. 100, 7.

[55] R. Grümmer, *Andreas Musculus: sein Leben und seine Werke* (Jena diss.; Eisenach, 1912), pp. 39-44, 56-89. For the influence of the *Eheteufel* on the *Hausteuffel* see G. Roethe, *Allgemeine deutsche Biographie,* XXXII (1891), 587-588.

[56] Stammler, pp. 449, 541.

[57] A copy in the University of Chicago Library.

[58] Stammler, pp. 353, 354; Kawerau, pp. 99, n. 126; Goedeke, II, 359-360, 387, no. 292; P. B. Raché, *Die deutsche Schulkomödie und die Dramen vom Schul- und Knabenspiegel* (Diss.; Leipzig, 1891); G. Binz, "Johann Rassers Spiel von der 'Kinderzucht,'" *Zeitschrift für deutsche Philologie,* XXVI (1894), 480-493; E. Schwabe, "Johann Rassers Schuldrama von der 'Kinderzucht,'" *Neue Jahrbücher für das klassische Altertum,* XV (1912), 196-206. On Martin Hayneccius'

Hayneccius' *Almansor* (1582) rather than from the first example of dramatized advice on marriage: Paul Rebhun's *Hausfried, was Ursach den christlichen Eheleuten zu bedenken, den lieben Hausfrieden in der Ehe zu erhalten* (1546). Probably Maturnus Steyndorffer's *Comedia lectu utilis et jucunda tractans de matrimonio aliisque rebus scitu dignis* (1540) should also be examined in that connection.[59] Unfortunately, few of these writings are accessible in America, and we cannot appraise them or estimate their relations to earlier writings or to their own age.

One might continue the history of German marriage-books down to the appearance of a new pattern. Quite in the baroque style are P. H. F., *Epithalamion von der heiligkeit nutz vnd noht dess Ehstandes* (1579), and Adelarius Rhote (or Roth), *Der Eheleute Lustgarten: Darinn der heilige Ehestand gar Artlich gepflantzet vnd abgebildet ist* (1600).[60] Abraham Hosemann's *Warhaftige gewisse und eygentliche Beschreibung der rechten ehelichen Liebe zwischen zweyer Ehegatten* and its two following parts entitled *Wahre Abkontrafactur der rechten hertzbrennenden Liebe abgebildet* and *Apologia conjugalis amoris* (1642-51) or the comprehensive instructions for confessors by T. Sanchez, *De sancto matrimonio disputationes* (Lyons, 1625)—so comprehensive, and so circumstantial, in fact, that the church placed the work on the index— might be taken to mark the end of an epoch in the history of books on marriage.

I have thus far considered books about marriage primarily in chronological order. One may ask, however: What was the influence of writings in other languages?[61] How much do the German handbooks of marriage owe to Xenophon's treatise on the household or to Theophrastus' *De nuptiis liber aureolus* preserved to us only in quotations made by St. Jerome?[62] Was the influence of St. Jerome's *Adversus*

Almansor (1582) see Goedeke, II, 353, no. 100. Compare also Johannes Rudolphus Klauser's *Almansor sive de disciplina puerili* (1590), which is cited in J. Spath, *Nomenclator* (1598), p. 213.

[59] Goedeke, II, 137, no. 16.

[60] Goedeke, II, 284, nos. 69, 70.

[61] The present question is limited to an inquiry into the specific dependence of Renaissance moralists, humanists, and theologians on classical and other sources. The interpretation of the answer to this question will lead to matters of much larger import than the establishment of specific connections. As we know, the humanists—Erasmus and Vives—and the moralists—Calvin and Beza—resorted to Tertullian, St. Ambrose, St. Augustine, St. Gregory, and other early fathers for the standards of domestic morals.

[62] See Hieronymus, *Adversus Jovinianum libri duo* in Migne (ed.), *Patrologia, series latina,* XXIII, 276, and the critical edition by F. Bock, *Leipziger Studien zur klassischen Philologie,* XIX (1899), 1-72. For discussion see R. Koebner, *Die*

Jovinianum (derived in part from Theophrastus) direct or indirect? Christopher Flurheym von Kytzingen issued *Eyn Epistel des heyl. Hieronymi von dem ampt eyner Haussmutter . . . Ynn der vorrede wird gemelt, was die Ehe sey, Wo und von wem sie yhren anfang hab, Wie man sich dartzu schicken sol* (1528) and added a condemnation of the Lutheran attacks on the celibacy of the clergy. The contribution of Stobaeus might be estimated, and that of Boccaccio in *De claris mulieribus* and other writings. The epochmaking work of the Italian Renaissance on the subject of marriage—Francesco Barbaro's *De re uxoria* (1415-16)—was not important north of the Alps for some time. At least for the beginnings of the German guides to marriage, we do not need to take it into consideration as a direct source. Ercole Tasso's declamation against women and his brother Torquato's defense, which were issued together as *Dello ammogliarsi piacevolei contesa fra i due moderni Tassi* (Bergamo, 1594), found a translator in England. Were these works known in Germany? In the *Underweysung eyner christlichen Frawen* (1544), Christoph Bruno translated the treatise *De institutione foeminae christianae* (1524) by Juan Luis Vives and issued in the same year the companion-piece, *De officio mariti,* under the title *Von gebirlichem Thun und Lassen aynes Ehemanns.*[63] *De re uxoria* (1415-16) of Francesco Barbaro, published at Hagenau in 1533 and

---

Eheauffassung des ausgehenden Mittelalters (Berlin diss.; Breslau, 1911), pp. 59 ff.; P. Strauch, *Zeitschrift für deutsches Altertum,* XXIX (1885), 385; K. Burdach, *Der Ackermann aus Böhmen,* p. 294 (note on Ch. XX); E. Wiessner, *Kommentar zu Heinrich Wittenwiler's 'Ring'* ("Deutsche Literatur"; Leipzig, 1936), p. 114.

[63] J. Nadler, *Literaturgeschichte der deutschen Stämme* (3d ed.; Regensburg, 1929), I, 383-384; J. Bolte, *Zeitschrift des Vereins für Volkskunde,* XXXVII-XXXVIII (1927-28), 103.

Compare such bibliographical guides as T. Musper, *Die Holzschnitte des Petrarkameisters. Ein kritisches Verzeichnis mit Einleitung und 28 Abbildungen* (Munich, 1927), L, 181 and L, 210; Campbell Dodgson, *Catalogue of Early German and Flemish Woodcuts* (London, 1903-11), II, 157, no. 70; R. Muther, *Die deutsche Bücherillustration der Gothik und Frührenaissance* (Munich, 1884, reprinted 1920), 1125; H. Hayn and A. N. Gotendorf, *Bibliotheca Germanorum erotica et curiosa* (Munich, 1912-29), VIII (1914), 135, and the works cited above (p. 10, nn. 1, 2). See the lists of editions and translations of works by Vives in A. Bömer, *Neue Jahrbücher für das klassische Altertum,* XIV (1904), 256-262.

On Vives and his influence see, e.g., Foster Watson (ed.), *Vives and the Renascence Education of Women* (New York, 1912); J. Wychgram, *Juan Luiz Vives' Schriften über weibliche Bildung* (Vienna, 1883); Otto Bürger, *Erasmus von Rotterdam und der Spanier Vives; eine pädagogische Studie* (Munich diss.; Kempten, 1914). For a superficial introduction to the background in pedagogical history see B. May, *Die Mädchenerziehung in der Geschichte der Pädagogik von Plato bis zum achtzehnten Jahrhundert* (Diss.; Erlangen, 1908).

often reprinted, gave Erasmus Alberus material for *Eyn gut Buch von der Ehe* (1536).[64] This he followed with *Das Ehebüchlein* (1539) translated from Erasmus Roterodamus and *Ein Predigt vom Ehstand* (1546) utilizing the marriage at Cana as text. Andreas Camutius, an Italian physician at the court of Maximilian II, drew on foreign sources for his *De amore et felicitate* (1574), we must suppose; but no one has stopped to identify them. Johann Fischart's *Philosophisches Ehezuchtbüchlein* (1578) rests largely on Latin and Greek sources and the task of identifying them has been accomplished. No doubt the grim and embittered pedant Aegidius Albertinus, who translated from Spanish sources at the beginning of the seventeenth century, drew on Spain or Italy for his *Hauspolicey* (1602), but the details are unknown.[65] It is one of the few contributions to the discussion of marriage by a Catholic. Outside our limits lie Johannes Olorinus Variscus (= Johann Sommer), *Ethographiæ Mundi Vierter Theil. Darin der Rechte Rathgeber zum Frewen* [i.e. Freien], *alle die so mit Liebesbanden verhafftet, richtig vnterweiset werden. Das ist: Ein Politischer Discurs vom heiligen Ehestande* (1612),[66] probably a spurious substitute for the true fourth part entitled *Geldtklage,* and Hippolytus Guarinoni, *Spiegel christlicher Eheleute* (1613), which may be mentioned as an example of a German guide to marriage of probably foreign origin. As a last example of these marriage-books at the beginning of the seventeenth century, I shall mention Henricus Salmuth's attractive little volume entitled *Gamologia* (1617).[67] All of these works need further characterization, the more important ones for their own sakes and the less important ones for their significance in the historical development. In ways not yet fully understood, foreign influences shaped the later course of books on marriage and overpowered the once-dominant Lutheran tradition in the genre.

32. *Devil-Literature.*—The Devil-literature which dominated German literature from 1540 to 1580 appeared in various forms and culminated in an encyclopedic *Theatrum diabolorum* (1569) compiled by the enterprising publisher Sigmund Feyerabend. Although there is an excel-

[64] Kawerau, p. 77. See also E. Körner, "D. Erasmus Albers Lehre von der Ehe," *Neue kirchliche Zeitung,* XXV (1914), 75-84, 130-156; Goedeke, II, 443-445, nos. 7-9, 19. On Francesco Barbaro see P. Gothein, *Francesco Barbaro* (Freiburg i. Br., 1932); Herrmann, pp. 323-325; and Attilio Gnesotto's edition of *De re uxoria* (Padua, 1915).

[65] Kawerau, p. 36. See N. Paulus, "Aegidius Albertinus über die Frau und die Ehe," *Historisch-politische Blätter,* CXXXIII (1904), 589-604, 648-655.

[66] See W. Kawerau's characterization of this book in "Johann Sommers 'Ethographia Mundi,'" *Vierteljahrschrift für Litteraturgeschichte,* V (1892), 161-201.

[67] A copy in the University of Chicago Library.

lent introduction to this genre, much remains to be made clear in its literary history.[68] Did Chryseus's *Hofteufel* (1545) set the fashion, as is generally assumed? This derivation of the genre needs investigation in the light of Jakob Wimpfeling's *Epistola de miseria curatorum seu plebanorum* (1489), a humorous description of the nine devils that annoy the clergy.[69] The text is easily accessible and raises only the minor question of the relation of the German translation to the printed Latin text. The *Epistola* did not fall on deaf ears. A connection with [Johannes Romer's] *Ein schöner Dialogus von den vier grössten Beschwernissen eines jeglichen Pfarrers* (1521)[70] is suggested by the titles. In 1540, five years before the appearance of the *Hofteufel*, Luther himself wrote a preface to a new edition of the *Epistola*. The *Hofteufel* by Johann Chryseus, one of the best polemic dramas of the age,[71] deserves more attention than it has received and may possibly merit an edition. It was printed at least five times in the sixteenth century and was a source of Franciscus Omichius' *Comœdia von Dionysii Syracusani* (1578). Its origins, style, and influence should be examined. Did the popularity of Luther's doctrines regarding the Devil interrupt the de-

[68] M. Osborn, "Die Teufelliteratur des 16. Jahrhunderts," *Acta Germanica*, N.F., III, no. 3 (Berlin, 1893). For a brief survey see M. Osborn (ed.), *Andreas Musculus, Vom Hosenteufel* (1555) ("Neudrucke deutscher Literaturwerke des 16. und 17. Jahrhunderts," CXXV; Halle, 1894), pp. xvii-xix. Compare further R. Newald, "Die Teufelliteratur und die Antike," *Bayerische Blätter für das Gymnasial-Schulwesen*, LXIII (1927), 340-347; H. Zieren, *Studien zum Teufelsbild in der deutschen Dichtung, 1050-1250* (Diss.; Bonn, 1937); G. Bebermeyer, "Teufelliteratur," in *Reallexikon der deutschen Literaturgeschichte*, IV, 90-93; Goedeke, 11, 479-483, no. 161. There is a copy of the *Theatrum diabolorum* (1575) in the University of Chicago library.

[69] Copy in the Newberry Library. See particularly the edition in A. Werminghoff, "Die 'Epistola de miseria curatorum seu plebanorum,'" *Archiv für Reformationsgeschichte*, XIII (1916), 200-227, and an anonymous note, *ibid.*, p. 305. On Wimpfeling see Goedeke, I, 406-412; Charles Schmidt, *Histoire littéraire de l'Alsace* (Paris, 1879), I, 1-188; J. Knepper, *Jakob Wimpheling* ("Erläuterungen und Ergänzungen zu Janssens 'Geschichte des deutschen Volkes,'" III; Freiburg i. Br., 1902). Compare also the biographical and bibliographical materials and editions of texts in [J. A. Riegger], *Amoenitates literariae friburgenses* (Ulm, 1776). A large paper copy of this work formerly in the library of Eduard Böcking, the editor of Ulrich von Hutten, is now in the University of Chicago Library.

[70] O. Clemen, *Flugschriften aus den ersten Jahren der Reformation*, III, ii (Leipzig, 1908), and A. Götze's review, *Neue Jahrbücher für das klassische Altertum*, XXIII (1909), 72-75.

[71] See, e.g., Holstein, *Zeitschrift für deutsche Philologie*, XVII (1886), 437; Stammler, p. 334; Goedeke, II, 361, no. 149. It is most easily accessible in the *Theatrum diabolorum* (1569), fol. 415[b]-430[a], which I have not seen, and ed. 1575, pp. 442-455.

velopment of the fool-literature, as some have said, and turn the current into the Devil-literature? The fact that the Devil-literature seems to have been particularly favored by East-German Protestants might support this suggestion. We are easily led to ask other questions about the history of the idea Devil-literature: What can we learn about the origin and development of Luther's ideas of the Devil? Why did Devil-literature flourish in Eastern Germany? Do the few Devil-books written by Catholics exhibit any unusual features? How did they come to be written?

33. *The History of Literature and the History of Art.*—The historian of literature often comes into contact with subjects dealt with by the historian of art. In the books of the sixteenth century the illustrations frequently present historical problems. Thus, for example, the woodcuts in Sebastian Brant's *Narrenschiff* (1494) have been ascribed to Albrecht Dürer, to a member of the school of Dürer, and to Brant himself. Although we shall probably never know who designed and cut them, we can reject Dürer with reasonable safety. It would enlarge our knowledge of the *Narrenschiff* if we could identify the artist responsible for the woodcuts. Since the blocks were a valuable piece of property, the printer did not discard them after using them once. He used them again as illustrations for Thomas Murner's satires on fools and in one of the editions of Geiler's sermons on the *Narrenschiff*. In this instance, the history of the illustrations has perhaps been clarified as far is it can be.[72]

Occasionally, a traditional series of illustrations accompanies the various revisions and redactions of a book through a long history. Probably the illustrations in the *Ars moriendi* are traditional, but the matter is yet to be carefully examined. An anonymous *Ars moriendi* (ca. 1509)[73] contains illustrations derived from those traditional in the fifteenth century and representing a comparatively primitive conception of the theme.[74] The most curious and interesting example of

[72] Stammler, p. 485 (note on p. 199).

[73] R. Muther, *Die deutsche Bücherillustration der Gothik und der Frührenaissance* (Munich, 1884; reprinted 1920), 1204; G. W. Panzer, *Annales,* IX, 550, no. 342 e; Robert Proctor, *An Index to the Early Printed Books in the British Museum,* II, i (1903), 101, no. 11057.

Compare L. Crust, *The Master E. S. and the 'Ars Moriendi'; a chapter in the history of engraving during the fifteenth century* (Oxford, 1898); Ernst Weil (ed.), *Ars Moriendi* (Munich, 1922), a facsimile of the German translation by Meister Ludwig (Ulm, ca. 1470). See a comparison of literary and plastic treatments of the *Ars moriendi* in H. Henze, *Die Allegorie bei Hans Sachs* ("Hermaea," XI; Halle, 1912), p. 93.

[74] On the *Ars moriendi* see F. Falk, *Die deutschen Sterbebüchlein von der ältesten*

traditional illustrations is the series of pictures accompanying the *Fables of Aesop* or the *Pañchatantra*. A generation ago, Joseph Jacobs pointed out that these pictures can be traced back, at least in some instances, to Sanskrit sources.[75] In other words, the illustrations in a cheap modern collection of didactic tales may have a history of more than a thousand years behind them. This subject needs more careful examination than it has yet received. Perhaps the most comprehensive and luxurious account of a pictorial tradition with literary connections is Aldred Scott Warthin's *The Physician of the Dance of Death;*

Zeit des Buchdrucks bis zum Jahre 1520 ("Vereinsschriften der Görres-Gesellschaft," 1890, no. 2; Cologne, 1890) ; Herrmann, p. 417; E. Döring-Hirsch, *Tod und Jenseits im Spätmittelalter* ("Studien zur Geschichte der Wirtschaft und Geisteskultur," II; Berlin, 1927) ; Paul de Keyser (ed.), *Colijn Caillieu's Dal sonder wederkeeren of pas der doot* ("Universiteit te Gent; Werken uitgegeven door de faculteit der wijsbegeerte en letteren," LXXIII; Antwerp, 1936).

Apart from the problems considered here, the *Ars moriendi* offers others worthy of investigation. On the relations of certain texts, see A. Burssens, "Verhouding van de Nederlandse sterfboeken tot 'L'Art de bien mourir,' " *Leuvensche bijdragen,* XVI (1924), 150-152. Further investigations into such problems and a survey of the ascertainable facts are no doubt desirable. A certain Einhard, a Dominican monk at Nuremberg, left a Latin treatise which no one has examined; see St[ammler] in *Verfasserlexikon,* I, col. 525. The Meistersinger often dealt with the art of holy living and holy dying; see Jacob Grimm, *Ueber den altdeutschen Meistergesang* (Göttingen, 1811), p. 158, n. 176. The extent of their interest and its characteristic features and its sources might be briefly studied. Johannes Dugo Philomius, a late humanist at Nuremberg, treated the subject of the *Ars moriendi* in a dialogue—the conventional literary form of the Reformation—and added humanistic ideas. His dialogue would be a starting-point for the investigation of the attitudes of the humanists toward a characteristically medieval ecclesiastic notion. Possibly [Jacob Cammerlander's] *Vom Todten Schifflein* (ca. 1530) belongs to this genre; see F. Zarncke (ed.), *Sebastian Brants Narrenschiff* (Leipzig, 1854), p. cxxxviii. The *Todten Schifflein* appears to be interesting for other aspects than its possible relations to the *Ars moriendi*. At a time when his revolutionary ideas had taken shape, Luther dealt with the subject in *Sermon von der Bereytung zum Sterben* (1519). Protestants continued to use the theme, e.g. F. Spitta, "Wie die Konstanzer Reformatoren A. Blaurer und J. Zwick über rechte Vorbereitung auf den Tod gepredigt und gedichtet haben [1541]," *Monatsschrift für Gottesdienst,* XIX (1914), 333-336.

[75] *The Earliest English Version of the 'Fables of Bidpai'* (London, 1888), pp. ix, lxiv. For the Fables of Aesop see Dora Lämke, *Mittelalterliche Tierfabeln und ihre Beziehungen zur bildenden Kunst in Deutschland* ("Deutsches Werden," XIV; Greifswald, 1937) ; G. Thiele, *Der illustrierte lateinische Aesop in der Handschrift des Ademar* (Leiden, 1905). I have not seen Sirarpie der Nersessian, *L'illustration du 'Roman de Barlaam et Joasaph'* (Paris, 1937), which seems to be an iconographic history of the sort suggested above. Sirarpie der Nersessian's work consists of a text-volume of 250 pages and an album of 250 plates.

a historical study of the Dance of Death mythus in art.[76] The disputed questions of the origin and history of the Dance of Death are too complicated to unroll here. An iconographic history of the Devil—a figure of many shapes—would yield interesting and important results for students in many disciplines.[77] A minor problem involving the iconographic history of a theme is the proverb "March comes in like a lion and goes out like a lamb."[78] In this form, the proverb is merely an augury con-

[76] New York, 1931. Warthin's book is a reprint (with some additions) of articles published in *Annals of Medical History,* n.s., II (1930), III (1931). On the Dance of Death see above pp. 110-111. I have not seen A. Behne, *Läkaren i konsten. En medicinisk bildatlas med beledsagande konsthistorisk text* (Stockholm, 1937), which might contain pertinent additions.

Consider the need for a study of the pictorial and poetic tradition of Death. See, e.g., Rudolf Helm (b. 1899), *Skelett- und Todesdarstellungen bis zum Auftreten der Totentänze* ("Studien zur deutschen Kunstgeschichte," CCLV; Strassburg, 1928) ; Peter Johansen, *Dødens billede, Et Udsnit af kunstens og kulturens historie* (Copenhagen, 1917), and Jan Vanderheijden, "Het thema en de uitbeelding van den Dood in de poëzie der late middeleeuwen en der vroege renaissance in de Nederlanden," *Koninklijke Vlaamsche Academie, Uitgaven,* 6. reeks, XLVII; Ghent, 1931).

[77] J. E. Wessely's inadequate *Die Gestalten des Todes und des Teufels in der darstellenden Kunst von den Anfängen bis zum Zeitalter Dantes und Giottos* (Leipzig, 1876) may serve as a starting-point. A. Köppen, *Der Teufel und die Hölle in der darstellenden Kunst* (Diss.; Berlin, 1895), O. A. Erich, *Die Darstellung des Teufels in der christlichen Kunst* ("Kunstwissenschaftliche Studien," VIII; Berlin, 1931), and Jacques Levron, *Le diable dans l'art* (Paris, 1935), have not exhausted the subject. Interesting materials will be found in Paul Sébillot, "Le diable et l'enfer dans l'iconographie," *Revue des traditions populaires,* V (1890), 20-28 (and in other articles belonging to this series) ; P. Danielsson, *Djävulsgestalten i Finlands svenska folktro* ("Bidrag till kännedom of Finlands natur och folk," LXXXIII, no. 5, LXXXIV, no. 2; Helsingfors, 1930-32) ; M. J. Rudwin, *The Devil in Legend and Literature* (Chicago, 1931) ; M. Garçon and J. Vinchon, *The Devil; an historical, critical, and medical study* (transl. S. H. Guest; New York, [ca. 1930]) ; and in Scheible's *Kloster* (Stuttgart, 1845 ff.).

[78] See my *Proverb* (Cambridge, Mass., 1931), p. 111, and *Index to the 'Proverb'* ("FF Communications," CXIII; Helsinki, 1934), p. 47. For references to German verses on the months see Ehrismann, pp. 650-651. For iconographic materials see A. Riegl, "Die Holzkalender des Mittelalters und der Renaissance," *Mitteilungen des Instituts für österreichische Geschichtsforschung,* IX (1888), 82-103, and "Die mittelalterliche Kalenderillustration," *ibid.,* X (1889), 1-74; R. Tuve, *Seasons and Months; studies in a tradition of Middle English poetry* (Paris, 1933) ; D. de Vries, *Some Suggestions Concerning Regular Seasons in Art with Special Reference to English Literature* (Diss.; Amsterdam, 1933). For the pictorial branch of the tradition see C. F. Miller, "Zu den Monatszyklen der byzantinischen Kunst," *Rheinisches Museum,* L (1895), 301-4 (with useful references). Olga Koseleff's dissertation, *Die Monatsdarstellungen der französischen Plastik des 12. Jahrhunderts* (Marburg, 1934), contains only the chapter "Ikonographie." See also Ernst Buchner, "Monats- und Jahreszeitenbilder Hans Wertingers," *Zeitschrift*

cerning the weather. It has not always been an augury. If we look at the earlier forms, we find in them references to "March, black ram" and the like. Even more curious is the Scottish "March comes in with an adder's head and goes out with a peacock's tail."[79] Some of these references are to be explained, I believe, by the conventional series of pictorial representations of the months and of the signs of the zodiac, but such an explanation is yet to be given.

THE INTERRELATIONS OF ART AND LITERATURE

Many themes appear in both plastic art and literature and the two modes of treatment react upon each other.[80] Jörg Wickram hoped that

für bildende Kunst, LXI (1927-28), 106-112. A recent book which is essential in all further study of the subject is J. C. Webster, *The Labors of the Months in Antique and Mediaeval Art to the End of the Twelfth Century* ("Northwestern University Studies in the Humanities," IV; Evanston and Chicago, 1938). For the suggestion of some very curious connections which need further discussion see M. R. James, *Marvels of the East* ("Roxburghe Club';' Cambridge, 1929).

[79] D. Grewar, "Scottish Proverbial Weather Lore, III, March," *Scottish Notes and Queries*, 3d ser., II (1924), 38; various, *Notes and Queries*, 7th ser., XI (1891), 287, 393.

[80] See some general remarks and pertinent references in Kurt Schmidt, *Der lüstliche Würtzgarte* (Diss.; Griefswald, 1932), p. 74; K. Burdach, *Vorspiel*, I (Halle, 1925), 58 ff., 78 ff.; and especially the references collected in Wackernagel, *Geschichte der deutschen Literatur* (2d ed.; Basel, 1879), I, 476, *s.v.* "Bildende Kunst," and Max Krüger, *Ueber das Verhältnis von Bühne und bildender Kunst* (Münster diss.; Vienna, 1911). W. Stammler surveys the publications and comes to very discouraging conclusions about their value; see *Die Totentänze des Mittelalters* ("Einzelschriften zur Bücher- und Handschriftenkunde," IV; Munich, 1922), pp. 47-48, n. 5. Friedrich von der Leyen's "Deutsche Dichtung und bildende Kunst im Mittelalter," *Abhandlungen zur deutschen Literaturgeschichte Franz Muncker zum 60. Geburtstage dargebracht* (Munich, 1916), pp. 1-20, suggests an abundance of problems and gives excellent bibliographical materials. For more recent discussions see G. Bebermeyer, "Die deutsche Dicht- und Bildkunst im Spätmittelalter, Ein Durchblick auf ihre Wechselbeziehungen," *Deutsche Vierteljahrsschrift für Literaturwissenschaft*, VII (1929), 305-328; F. Panzer, "Wort und Bild in der Ueberlieferung altdeutscher Dichtung," *Dichtung und Volkstum*, XXXVI (1935), 1-21; Albert Rapp, *Studien über den Zusammenhang des geistlichen Theaters mit der bildenden Kunst im ausgehenden Mittelalter* (Munich diss.; Kallmünz, 1936).

For typical studies see L. van Puyvelde, *Schilderkunst en tooneelvertooningen op het einde der middeleeuwen* ("Koninklijke Vlaamsche Academie; Uitgaven," IV, 10; Ghent, 1910); W. Hitzig, *Zur Geschichte der Wechselwirkung zwischen der geistlichen Bühne und der bildenden Kunst*, I, *Das Problem und die Grundlagen* (Programm; Mannheim, 1914); Hugo Beck, *Das genrehafte Element im deutschen Drama des 16. Jahrhunderts; ein Beitrag zu den Wechselbeziehungen zwischen Dichtung und Malerei* ("Germanische Studien," LXVI; Berlin, 1929).

The transfer of critical generalizations from one field to another as is illus-

his adaptation of a translation of Ovid's *Metamorphoses* would suggest themes to artists. Stammler finds that the results of comparisons between drama and plastic art have been unimportant and the possibilities of studies in the interrelations of mysticism and art have been neglected.

In studying, for example, the themes of Susanna and the unjust judges or the marriage at Cana, the student cannot neglect Rembrandt's paintings and the artistic tradition behind them.[81] In such studies, the historian of art joins hands with the historian of literature. The community of interests may extend even farther. Kaarle Krohn illustrates the distortions of Christian story from pictures in manuscripts and on the walls of medieval churches and supports by such comparisons his argument for the borrowing of German materials in Germanic myth.[82] The vivid descriptions of the sufferings of Jesus as found in the literature of the late fifteenth century contrast sharply with the vague generalities of medieval writers. Perhaps realistic paintings of the Crucifixion inspired the descriptions of Hans Folz, and Neil C. Brooks shows that the Corpus Christi procession at Ingolstadt took suggestions from the pictures in a household book of the day, the *Biblia pauperum*.[83] It is neither necessary nor possible to differentiate the influence of plastic

---

trated by the current borrowing of ideas from the history of art to interpret literary movements seems to me a procedure likely to be dangerous. Compare, e.g., Oskar Walzel, *Wechselseitige Erhellung der Künste; ein Beitrag zur Würdigung kunstgeschichtlicher Begriffe* (Berlin, 1917), and *Gehalt und Gestalt im Kunstwerk des Dichters* ("Handbuch der Literaturwissenschaft"; Berlin-Neubabelsberg, 1923-25).

[81] For references to the use of a theme by artists consult such works as Adam Bartsch, *Le peintre-graveur* (3d ed. with supplements by J. Heller and R. Weigel; Würzburg, 1920-22); J. D. Passavant, *Le peintre-graveur contenant l'histoire de le gravure sur bois, sur métal et au burin jusque vers la fin du 16e siècle* (Leipzig, 1860-64); W. L. Schreiber, *Manuel de l'amateur de la gravure sur bois et sur métal au 15e siècle* (Berlin, 1891-1911), and the much enlarged edition in 8 vols., *Handbuch der Holz- und Metallschnitte des 15. Jahrhunderts* (Leipzig, 1926-30). M. Lehr's standard work, *Geschichte und kritischer Katalog des deutschen, niederländischen und französischen Kupferstichs im 15. Jahrhundert* (Vienna, 1908-34), was published in so few copies and at so high a price that very few libraries could acquire it. See also F. Sauerhering, *Vademecum für Künstler und Kunstfreunde; ein systematisches nach Stoffen geordnetes Vademecum der bedeutendsten Malerwerke aller Zeiten* (Stuttgart, 1896-1904).

[82] *Skandinavisk mytologi* (Helsingfors, 1922).

[83] "An Ingolstadt Corpus Christi Procession and the 'Biblia pauperum,'" *Journal of English and Germanic Philology*, XXV (1936), 1-16. For the background see Theodore Spencer, *Death and Elizabethan Tragedy* (Cambridge, Mass., 1936), pp. 14-20.

art from that of dramatic representations.[84] One reacted on the other and both on literature. Nor need we limit our studies to the influence of plastic art on literature. Carl Giehlow's commentary on Albrecht Dürer's "Melancholy" is a brilliant example of the services which a student of literature can render to the student of art.[85]

*   *

*

Here I shall stop, not because the material is exhausted but because I hope that I have given the discerning reader a sufficient idea of the problems in German literature of the fifteenth and sixttenth centuries and of the ways and means to solve them. That discerning reader will understand how to satisfy not only his own desire for knowledge but also the desire of his fellows. He will know that, if he would accomplish his own desire, he must regard his research as the lesser part of his labors and the greater part as the effective communication of his results in a style at once cogent and appropriate. Here indeed the best possible comment is, *Finis coronat opus.*

[84] Emil Mâle, *L'art religieux de la fin du moyen âge en France* (3d ed.; Paris, 1925), *passim.*

[85] "Dürers Stich 'Melencolia I' und der Maximiliansche Humanistenkreis," *Mitteilungen der Gesellschaft für vervielfältigende Kunst, Beilage der graphischen Künste,* 1903, pp. 29-41, 1904, pp. 6-18, 57-78. See the rich literature cited in Schottenloher, I, 187, nos. 4649-70. Notable is the recent study by E. Panofsky and F. Saxl, *Dürer's 'Melencolia I', eine quellen- und typengeschichtliche Untersuchung.* ("Studien der Bibliothek Warburg," II; Leipzig, 1923).

APPENDICES

APPENDIX I

CRITICAL BIBLIOGRAPHY OF THE CULTURAL AND LITERARY HISTORY OF STRASSBURG i. E.

GENERAL BIBLIOGRAPHY

Catalogue of Printed Books in the British Museum, "Periodical Publications" (London, 1899), cols. 1590-1592, *s.v.* "Strassburg."

A useful list of periodicals dealing with Strassburg.

Cl. Baeumker, *Der Anteil des Elsass an den geistlichen Bewegungen des Mittelalters* (Strassburg, 1912).

Ulysse Chevalier, *Répertoire des sources historiques du moyen-âge, topo-bibliographique* (Montbéliard, 1903), cols. 3009-3016.

F. C. Dahlmann and G. Waitz, *Quellenkunde zur deutschen Geschichte* (9th ed.; Leipzig, 1931), p. 55, no. 961 and *passim.*

The reference to bibliographies of Alsace-Lorraine is cited. Since there is no index of subjects, references to Strassburg are not immediately available. This fundamentally important work is cited again and again in the following notes.

Ernst Markwald, Ferdinand Mentz, and Ludwig Wilhelm, *Katalog der Universitäts- und Landesbibliothek Strassburg: Katalog der elsass-loth-ringischen Abteilung* (1908-23).

Karl Schottenloher, *Bibliographie zur deutschen Geschichte im Zeitalter der Glaubensspaltung 1517-1585* (Leipzig, 1935), II, 691-699, nos. 20961-27038.

Contains primarily references to discussions of religious, economic, and political matters. See also the references on Alsace in *ibid.,* III, 168-170, nos. 30076a-30091b.

Gustav Wolf, *Quellenkunde der deutschen Reformationsgeschichte,* I (Gotha, 1915), 571-578, §59.[1]

An admirable survey covering the period of the Reformation.

POLITICAL HISTORY (INCLUDING PERIODICALS)

Dahlmann-Waitz, pp. 61-62, no. 1074 (periodicals concerned with the history of Alsace-Lorraine), 81, nos. 1378-1379 (bibliography of charters), 109, no. 1941 (compare nos. 1936-1940 on the history of Alsace-Lorraine), 498-499, nos. 7843-7844, 641, no. 10136.

O. Lorenz and W. Scherer, *Geschichte des Elsasses* (Berlin, 1871).

GENERAL HISTORICAL PERIODICALS

Beiträge zur elsass-lothringischen Geschichte und Landeskunde, I-LIII (Strassburg, 1887-1918).

Elsass-Lothringisches Jahrbuch, I (1922 ff.).

[1] This will be referred to as Wolf.

Vol. II (1923) contains a useful bibliography of publications dealing with Alsace-Lorraine issued between 1919 and 1923. The bibliography is continued in later volumes.

Jahrbuch für Geschichte, Sprache und Literatur Elsass-Lothringens, I-XXXIV (1885-1918).

Contains a useful annual bibliography.

Zeitschrift für die Geschichte des Oberrheins, I (1850) ff.

An indispensable annual bibliography of Alsace-Lorraine.

BIOGRAPHY

E. Sitzmann, *Dictionnaire de biographie des hommes célèbres de l'Alsace,* I-II (Rixheim, 1910).

P. A. Grandidier, *Fragment d'une Alsatia litterata ou dictionnaire biographique des littérateurs et artistes alsatiens* ("Nouvelles œuvres inédites," II; Colmar, 1897).

ECONOMIC HISTORY[2]

Wolf, I, 571-572 and *passim.*

An excellent survey in brief space.

ECCLESIASTICAL HISTORY

Dahlmann-Waitz, pp. 109, no. 1936, 184, no. 3223, 563, no. 8810, 618-19, no. 9829.

Indispensable bibliography. A selection of the periodicals given in the first reference is listed below.

Wolf, I, 577.

A good brief survey with bibliography.

J. Adam, *Evangelische Kirchengeschichte der Stadt Strassburg bis zur französischen Revolution* (Strassburg, 1922).

E. Köthe, *Kirchliche Zustände Strassburgs im 14. Jahrhundert* (Freiburg i. Br., 1903).

F. Landtmann, "Zum Predigtwesen der Strassburger Franziskaner-Provinz in der letzten Zeit des Mittelalters," *Franziskanische Studien,* XIV (1927), 317-332.

L. Pfleger, "Beiträge zur Geschichte der Predigt und des religiösen Volksunterrichts in Elsass während des Mittelalters," *Historisches Jahrbuch,* XXXVIII (1917), 661-717.

———, "Zur Geschichte des Predigtwesens in Strassburg vor Geiler von Kaisersberg," *Strassburger Diözesanblatt,* XXVI = 3. Folge IV (1907), 248-268, 298-314, 344-360, 392-416.

O. Winckelmann, "Zur Kulturgeschichte des Strassburger Münsters im 15. Jahrhundert," *Zeitschrift für die Geschichte des Oberrheins,* LXI = N.F. XXII (1907), 247-290, LXIII = N.F. XXIV (1909), 302-323.

[2] The investigation of the economic history of the medieval guilds at Strassburg was epoch-making in German historical study.

Compare the many articles and books on such figures as Johannes Tauler, the Gottesfreunde (notably Ruolman Merswin), and Johannes Geiler von Kaisersberg.

PERIODICALS

Archiv für elsässische Kirchengeschichte, I (1926) ff.

Includes many important articles on the ecclesiastical history of Strassburg.

Bullétin ecclésiastique de Strasbourg, I (1882)—VI (1887); *Ecclesiasticum argentinense; Strassburger Diözesanblatt,* VII (1888)—XVII (1898); *Strassburger Diözesanblatt; kirchliche Rundschau,* XVIII (1899)—XXIII (1904); *Strassburger Diözesanblatt in Verbindung mit der katholisch-theologischen Fakultät und dem Priesterseminar zu Strassburg,* ed. A. Lang, XXIV (1905)—XXIX (1910; *Strassburger Diözesanblatt; Monatsschrift für amtliche Mitteilungen,* . . . *religiöse Wissenschaft,* ed. I. Fahrner, XXX (1911)—XXXVII (1918); *Bullétin ecclésiastique de Strasbourg,* XXXVIII (1919) ff.

Contains official publications of the Roman Catholic church. Only the issues from 1899 to 1918 are important for us.[3]

EDUCATIONAL HISTORY[4]

Dahlmann-Waitz, pp. 212, no. 3568, 213, no. 3592, 583, no. 9107.

Wolf, I, 577-578.

Compare the abundant articles on Johann Sturm, the University of Strassburg, and the school at Schlettstadt. A typical example is W. Sohm, *Die Schule Johann Sturms und die Kirche Strassburgs in ihrem gegenseitigen Verhältnis* (Munich, 1912). Compare also such a figure as Jakob Wimpfeling, on whom see J. Knepper, *Jakob Wimpfeling* ("Erläuterungen und Ergänzungen zu Janssens 'Geschichte des deutschen Volkes,'" III, 2-4; Freiburg i. Br., 1902).

MUSICAL HISTORY

J. F. Lobstein, *Beiträge zur Geschichte der Musik im Elsass und besonders in Strassburg von den ältesten Zeiten bis auf die neuste Zeit* (Strassburg, 1840).

M. Vogeleis, *Quellen und Bausteine zu einer Geschichte der Musik und des Theaters im Elsass 500-1800* (Strassburg, 1911).

THEATRICAL HISTORY

A. Jundt, *Die dramatischen Aufführungen im Gymnasium zu Strassburg* (Programm; Strassburg, 1881).

M. Vogeleis, see above "Musical History."

---

[3] I am indebted to the Wissenschaftliches Institut der Elsass-Lothringer im Reich (Frankfurt a. M.) for this description and information. There appears to be no copy of this journal in America.

[4] A valuable brief introduction to this field is Friedrich Roth, *Der Einfluss des Humanismus und der Reformation auf das gleichzeitige Erziehungs- und Schulwesen bis in die ersten Jahrzehnte nach Melanchthon's Tod* ("Schriften des Vereins für Reformationsgeschichte," LX; Halle, 1898).

HISTORY OF ART

Archives alsaciennes de l'histoire de l'art, I (1922) ff.

The chief artistic monument of Strassburg—the cathedral—has been often discussed. Compare, for example, Goethe's enthusiasm for it. There is a large literature on the clock in the cathedral; see Schottenloher, II, 696, nos. 27002 a-f. For discussion of the history of illustrations in books see the works on books and printing.

A. Woltmann, *Geschichte der deutschen Kunst im Elsass* (Leipzig, 1876).

HISTORY OF PRINTING AND BOOKS

F. J. Ritter, *Gesamtkatalog der elsässischen Drucke des 16. Jahrhunderts der Universitäts- und Landesbibliothek Strassburg* (Strassburg, 1934 ff.).

Charles Schmidt, *Répertoire bibliographique strasbourgeois jusque vers 1530,* I-VIII (Strassburg, 1893-96).

——, *Zur Geschichte der ältesten Bibliotheken und der ersten Buchdrucker zu Strassburg* (Strassburg, 1882).

LITERARY HISTORY

F. Behrend, "Die deutsche Literatur im Elsass," *Deutsche Studien* (1936), I, 10-27.

Charles Schmidt, *Histoire littéraire de l'Alsace,* I-II (Paris, 1879).

O. Hubert, *Zur Geschichte des Deutschtums im Elsass; eine literarisch-historische Studie.* Programm. Landsberg a.W., 1904.

Ernst Martin (ed.), *Elsässische Literatur-Denkmäler aus dem 14.-17. Jahrhundert,* I-V (Strassburg, 1878-88).

—— and W. Wigand (eds.), *Strassburger Studien; Zeitschrift für Geschichte, Sprache und Litteratur des Elsasses,* I-III (Darmstadt, 1883-88).

LINGUISTIC HISTORY

E. Halter, *Die deutsche Sprache im Elsass auf historischer Grundlage* (Jena, 1914).

Ernst Martin and H. Lienhart, *Wörterbuch der elsässischen Mundarten* (Strassburg, 1899-1907).

See E. Martin, "Die deutsche Lexikographie im Elsass," *Strassburger Festschrift zur 46. Versammlung deutscher Philologen und Schulmänner* (Strassburg, 1901), pp. 29-38 and "Nachträge und Berichtigungen zum 'Wörterbuch der elsässischen Mundarten,'" *Jahrbuch für Geschichte, Sprache und Literatur Elsass-Lothringens,* XXIII (1907), 159-64; M. Koehnlein, F. W. Ander, and E. Martin, "Zum 'Wörterbuch der elsässischen Mundarten,'" *ibid.,* XXV (1909), 214-237.

Virgil Moser, *Die Strassburger Druckersprache zur Zeit Fischarts, 1570-90* (Munich, 1920).

Charles Schmidt, *Historisches Wörterbuch der elsässischen Mundart* (Strassburg, 1901).

——, *Wörterbuch der Strassburger Mundart* (Strassburg, 1896).

APPENDIX II

CATALOGUES OF PRIVATELY OWNED GERMAN LIBRARIES OF THE FIFTEENTH AND SIXTEENTH CENTURIES

Princes of Anhalt. K. Haebler, *Deutsche Bibliophilen des 16. Jahrhunderts. Die Fürsten von Anhalt, ihre Bücher und ihre Bucheinbände* (Leipzig, 1923). P. Wahl, "Fürst Georgs-Bibliothek," *Zentralblatt für Bibliothekswesen,* XLIV (1927), 359.

Herren von Berlichingen. A. Schmidt, "Aus eine alten Bibliothek der Herren von Berlichingen," *Zeitschrift für Bücherfreunde,* N.F., IX, i (1917), 41-53.

Sebastian von Beroldingen. Gabriel Meyer, "Sebastian von Beroldingens Bibliothek nebst einem Anhang über die Bücherzensur in Uri," *Historisches Neujahrsblatt des Vereins für Geschichte und Altertümer von Uri,* X (1904), 1-12.

Tycho Brahe. W. Prantl, *Die Bibliothek des Tycho Brahe* (Vienna, 1933), which is a reprint of an article in *Philobiblion,* V (1932), 291-299, 321-329. See also W. Norlind, "Ex 'Bibliotheca Tychoniana'; några anteckningar," *Nordisk tidskrift för bok- och biblioteksväsen,* XIII (1926), 211-218.

Citizens of Brunswick. O. Schütte, "Vom Büchernachlass einiger Braunschweiger Bürger aus den Jahren 1585-1639," *Braunschweigisches Magazin,* XVI (1910), 145-146.

Doctors at Cracow. J. Lachs, "Die Lektüre der Krakauer Ärtze und Studierenden im 16. Jahrhunderts," *Archiv für die Geschichte der Medizin,* VII (1914), 206-217.

Nicolaus von Cues. W. Stockhausen, "Die Cusanus-Bibliothek [in Cues]," *Sankt Wiborada,* V (1938), 1-9.

Johannes von Dalberg. K. Hartfelder, "Zur Gelehrtengeschichte Heidelbergs, §3: Johannes von Dalberg, gen. Camerarius," *Zeitschrift für die Geschichte des Oberrheins,* XLV (N.F. VI; 1891), 150-152. Addenda to the list in K. Morneweg, *Johannes von Dalberg, ein deutscher Humanist und Bischof* (Heidelberg, 1887), pp. 236-239.

Nikolaus von Ebeleben. J. Hoffman, "Die Bibliothek des Nikolaus von Ebeleben," *Zeitschrift für Bücherfreunde,* XVIII (1926), 82-91.

Oswald von Eck. O. Hartig, "Der Katalog der 'Bibliotheca Eckiana,'" *Beiträge zur Geschichte der Renaissance und Reformation; Joseph Schlecht . . . als Festgabe dargebracht* (Munich, 1917), pp. 162-168. K. Löffler, "Die Bibliiotheca Eckiana,'" *Zentralblatt für Bibliothekswesen,* XXXVI (1919), 195-210.

Georg Eder. L. F. Stelzhammer, "Die Bibliothek eines Landpfarrers am Ende des 16. Jahrhunderts," *Heimatgaue,* VI (1925), 203-206.[1]

[1] Compare this library with the suggestions for such a library in J. C. Siebenkees,

Desiderius Erasmus. F. Husner, "Die Bibliothek des Erasmus," *Festschrift zum 400. Todestage des Erasmus von Rotterdam* (ed. by the Historische und Antiquarische Gesellschaft zu Basel; Basel, 1936), pp. 228-259. F. Ritter, "Die Bibliothek des Erasmus, Johannes a Lasco und Gerhard Montaigne in Emden," *Upstalsboomblätter,* XIII (1927), 108-114. D. J. H. ter Horst, "Nog enkele aanteekeningen over de bibliotheek van Erasmus," *Het boek,* N.R., XXIV (1936-37), 229-234. H. Zehnter, "Die Bibliothek des Erasmus," *Der schweizerische Sammler,* XI (1937), 187-190.

Peter Falck. W. J. Meyer, "Der Freiburger Peter Falck (†1519) als Bibliophile und Humanist," *Schweizerische Rundschau,* XXV (1925-26), 53-56.

Sebastian Franck. A. Bruckner, "Verzeichnis der hinterlassenen Bücher Sebastian Francks, *"Zentralblatt für Bibliothekswesen,* LIV (1937), 286-289.

Herren von Frundsberg. F. Zoepfl, "Die Bibliothek der Herren von Frundsberg," *Zeitschrift des historischen Vereins für Schwaben und Neuburg,* LII (1936), 61-84.

Johann Jakob Fugger. Otto Hartig, "Die Gründung der Münchner Hofbibliothek durch Albrecht V. und Johann Jakob Fugger," *Abhandlungen der königlich bayerischen Akademie der Wissenschaften, philosophisch-philologische und historische Klasse,* XXVIII, no. 3 (1917), pp. 193-276.

Martin Futterer. G. Liebe, "Die Bibliothek eines Eichsfelder Pfarrers in der Zeit der Gegenreformation," *Zeitschrift des Vereins für Kirchengeschichte in der Provinz Sachsen,* IV (1907), 263-269.

Théodore Gaudanus. J. Gass, "Théodore Gaudanus," *Anzeiger für elsässische Altertumskunde,* IV (1922-26), 268-271.

Dr. Adolf von Glauben. H. Traut, "Dr. Adolf von Glauben und seine Bibliothek," *Festgabe für Friedrich Clemens Ebrard* (Frankfurt a.M., 1920), pp. 1-34.

Sigismund Gossembrot. P. Joachimsohn, "Aus der Bibliothek Sigismund Gossembrots," *Zentralblatt für Bibliothekswesen,* XI (1894), 249-268, 297-307.

Sigmund Gotzkircher. Paul Lehmann, "Haushaltungsaufzeichnungen eines Münchner Arztes aus dem 15. Jahrhundert," *Sitzungsberichte der k. bayer-*

Materialien zur Nürnbergischen Geschichte, I, (Nuremberg, 1792), 54-55, "Worin musste 1546 die Bibliothek eines Nürnbergischen Landgeistlichen bestehen?" See also "Ordnungen deutscher Kirchen- und Pfarrbibliotheken des 16. Jahrhunderts . . . ," *Anzeiger der Bibliothekswissenschaft,* 1846, pp. xlvii-l; W. Diehl, "Bibliothek eines Studenten der Theologie aus der Zeit um 1590," *Beiträge zur hessischen Kirchengeschichte,* III (1908), 80-87; Wolters, "Pastoren-Büchereien 1572," *Zeitschrift des Vereins für niedersächsische Kirchengeschichte,* XLII (1937), 289-301; and the references below to the libraries of Martin Futterer, Georg Haschka, Théodore Gaudanus, Conrad Hatter, Johannes Mendlein, Johannes Murer, Rudolph Noviomagus, Gregor Ramyng, and Marcus Wagner.

ischen Akademie, philosophisch-philologische und historische Klasse, 1909, no. 5.

Contains instructive comment on the methods of describing a private library. See also the addenda in his "Aus einer Münchner Büchersammlung des ausgehenden Mittelalters," *Festschrift für Georg Leidinger* (Munich, 1930), pp. 157-164.

Blasius Grunwald. O. Meltzer, *Aus der Bibliothek eines Leipziger Studenten und Docenten im ersten Viertel des 16. Jahrhunderts* (Dresden, 1878).

Georg Haschka. W. von Boetticher, "Hausrat und Bibliothek eines oberlausitzischen Geistlichen zu Ende des 16. Jahrhunderts," *Neues lausitzisches Magazin,* LXXVII (1901), 271-276.

Conrad Hatter. "Bibliothek eines Geistlichen im 16. Jahrhundert," *Archiv für hessische Geschichte und Alterthumskunde,* XI (1867), 429-431.

Hans Hattstatt. C. Wittmer, "Ein Buchvermächtnis des Hans Hattstatt vom 28. August 1493 an die Dominikaner zu Colmar," *Annuaire de Colmar (Colmarer Jahrbuch),* III (1937), 47-61.

Caspar Hilspach. P. Keiper, "Catalogus librorum Caspari Hilspachii ludimoderatoris Hornbacensis (1580)," *Blätter für das Gymnasial-Schulwesen,* XXXV (1899), 50-55.

Johannes von Kreuzlingen. A. Werminghoff, "Die Bibliothek eines Konstanzer Officials aus dem Jahre 1506," *Zentralblatt für Bibliothekswesen,* XIV (1897), 290-298.

Ludwig Graf zu Stolberg. E. Jacobs, Die ehemalige Büchersammlung Ludwigs, Grafen zu Stolberg im Königstein (Wernigerode, 1868). Cited from Wieland Schmidt, *'Die vier und zwanzig Alten' Ottos von Passau* ("Palaestra," CCXII; Leipzig, 1938), p. 219, n. 1.

Kaiser Maximilian. T. Gottlieb, *Die Büchersammlung Kaiser Maximilians I., Part I: Die Ambraser Handschriften, I* (Leipzig, 1920).

Joh. Mendlein. K. Schornbaum, "Die Bibliothek des letzten katholischen Pfarrers von Ansbach Joh. Mendlein," *Jahresbericht des historischen Vereins für Mittelfranken,* LVI (1909), 163-167.

Sebastian Mieg. J. Rathgeber, "Die Schicksale einer Strassburger Bibliothek," *Jahrbuch für Geschichte, Sprache und Literatur Elsass-Lothringens,* IV (1888), 63-71.

Hieronymus Muenzer. E. P. Goldschmidt, *Hieronymus Muenzer und seine Bibliothek* (London, 1938).

Johannes Murer. G. Happeler, "Aus der Bibliothek eines Züricherischen Geistlichen aus dem Jahre 1528," *Züricher Taschenbuch auf das Jahr 1926,* N.F., XLVI (1925), 241-243.

Rodolphus Noviomagus. G. Ficker, "Die Büchersammlung eines evangelischen Predigers aus dem Jahre 1542," *Schriften des Vereins für schleswig-holsteinische Kirchengeschichte,* 2. Reihe, VII (1918), 1-85.

Count Wilhelm von Oettingen. G. Grupp, "Eine gräfliche Bibliothek im 15. Jahrhundert," *Centralblätt für Bibliothekswesen,* IX (1892), 484-490.

Bischof Otto III of Constance. A. Werminghoff, "Die schriftstellerische Thätigkeit des Bischofs Otto III. von Konstanz," *Zeitschrift für die Geschichte des Oberrheins,* LI (N.F., XII; 1897), 3-12.

Duke Philip I of Pomerania. J. Deutsch, "Die Bibliothek Herzog Philipps I. von Pommern," *Pommersche Jahrbücher,* XXVI (1931), 1-45.

Johannes Poliander. C. Krollmann, *Geschichte der Stadtbibliothek zu Königsberg* (Königsberg i. Pr., 1929). Containing pp. 5-20 and "Appendix," pp. 1-66, "Die Bibliothek des M. Johannes Poliander, 1560."

Wilibald Pirkheimer. H. F. Massmann, "Wilibald Pirkheimers Bibliothek in England," *Bayerische Annalen für Vaterlandskunde,* III (1835), 61-63. F. Homeyer, "Pirckheimers Bibliothek," *Monatshefte für Bücherfreunde,* I (1925), 358-359.

Jakob Püterich. Arthur Goette, *Der Ehrenbrief des Jakob Püterich von Reichertshausen an die Erzherzogin Mechthild* (Diss.; Strassburg, 1899). F. Behrend and R. Wolkan (eds.), *Der Ehrenbrief des Püterich von Reichertshausen* (Weimar, 1920). See useful notes in Wilhelm Scherer, *Die Anfänge des deutschen Prosaromans und Jörg Wickram von Colmar* ("Quellen und Forschungen zur Sprach- und Culturgeschichte der germanischen Völker," XXI; Strassburg, 1877), pp. 16 ff.; Konrad Burdach, *Vorspiel,* I. 2. ("Deutsche Vierteljahrsschrift für Literaturwissenschaft, Buchreihe," II; Halle, 1925), 79 ff. Eduard Sievers' copy of the edition of the *Ehrenbrief* by T. G. Karajan, *Zeitschrift für deutsches Altertum,* VI (1848), 31-48 is in the University of Chicago Library; it contains notes which could be consulted in any future study of the *Ehrenbrief.*

Gregor Ramyng. O. Glauning, "Das Bücherverzeichnis eines Geistlichen aus der ersten Hälfte des 16. Jahrhunderts," *Jahrbuch des historischen Vereines für Nördlingen und Umgebung,* VI (1917), 19-72.

Heinrich Rantzau. Isak Collijn, "Neue Beiträge zur Geschichte der Bibliothek des Heinrich Rantzau," *Zentralblatt für Bibliothekswesen,* L (1933), 111-120.

Thomas Rehdiger. A. W. J. Wachler, *Thomas Rehdiger und seine Büchersammlung in Breslau* (Breslau, 1828).

Johannes Reuchlin. Karl Christ, *Die Bibliothek Reuchlins in Pforzheim* ("Zentralblatt für Bibliothekswesen, Beiheft," LII; Leipzig, 1924).

Beatus Rhenanus. A. Horawitz, "Die Bibliothek und Korrespondenz des Beatus Rhenanus zu Schlettstadt," *Sitzungsberichte der philosophisch-historischen Classe der kaiserlichen Akademie der Wissenschaften* (Vienna), LXXVIII (1874), 313-340. Compare also G. C. Knod, "Aus der Bibliothek des Beatus Rhenanus. Ein Beitrag zur Geschichte des Humanismus," *Die Stadtbibliothek zu Schlettstadt. Festschrift zur Einweihung des neuen Bibliotheksgebäudes am 6. Juni,* 1889 (Strassburg, 1889); Knod's essay is Part II (Schlettstadt, 1889), pp. i-xii, 1-85. See also Schottenloher, II, 176, no. 17975.

Count Johann von Rietberg. E. Friendländer, "Hinterlassenschaft eines Kölner Studenten und Bücherpreise aus der Mitte des 16. Jahrhunderts," *Zeitschrift für deutsche Kulturgeschichte,* N.F., II (1873), 126-128.

Georg Sabinus. F. Schillmann, "Die juristische Bibliothek des Georg Sabinus," *Zentralblatt für Bibliothekswesen,* XXVIII (1911), 487-495.

Hans Sachs. Schottenloher, II, 201, nos. 18535-18537 (A bibliography of articles on Hans Sachs's library).

Hartmann Schedel. See above, pp. 12-13, and Otto Hartig, "Die Gründung der Münchener Hofbibliothek durch Albrecht V. und Johann Jakob Fugger," *Abhandlungen der königlich bayerischen Akademie der Wissenschaften, philosophisch-philologische und historische Klasse,* XXVIII (1917), no. 3, pp. 261-266.

Paul Schleiffer. [Max Perlbach], "Paul Schleiffer aus Zerbst und seine Bücher," *Aus alten Büchern der Hallischen Universitäts-Bibliothek* (Halle a. S., 1900), pp. 53-63.

Jakob Spiegel. A. Semler, "Die Bibliothek des Humanisten Jakob Spiegel," *Zeitschrift für die Geschichte des Oberrheins,* LXXI (N.F., XXXII; 1917), 84-97.

Dr. Blasius Spiess. W. Beemelmans, "Dr. Blasius Spiess und seine Bücher," *Jahrbuch für Geschichte, Sprache und Literatur Elsass-Lothringens,* XXX (1914), 252-281.

Johannes Trithemius. "Nachrichten von der Sponheimer Bibliothek des Abtes Johannes Trithemius," *Festgabe zum 7. September 1910 . . . Hermann Grauert . . . gewidmet* (Freiberg i. Br., 1910), pp. 205-220.

Elspet Volkenstorferin. K. Schorbach, *Studien über das deutsche Volksbuch Lucidarius* ("Quellen und Forschungen zur Sprach- und Culturgeschichte der germanischen Völker," LXXIV; Strassburg, 1894), p. 58 (the library of an Elspet Volkenstorferin, fl. *ca.* 1400).

Johann Wachsring. Dekan Breining, "Bücherei eines schwäbischen Präzeptors am Ende des 16. Jahrhunderts," *Württembergische Vierteljahrshefte für Landesgeschichte,* N.F., XXI (1912), 317-324.

Marcus Wagner. Walther Schmidt-Ewald, "Die Bibliothek eines thüringischen Gelehrten aus dem 16. Jahrhundert," *Beitrage zur thüringischen und sächsischen Geschichte; Festschrift für Otto Dobenecker* (Jena, 1929), pp. 343-360. For some interesting details about Wagner and a valuable reference see H. Schneider, "Die Bibliotheksreisen des Marcus Wagner," *Zentralblatt für Bibliothekswesen,* L (1933), 678-683.

Dr. Johannes Weidemann. H. Herbst, "Dr. Johannes Weidemann (1470-1520) und seine Bibliothek," *Sachsen und Anhalt,* VII (1931), 341-359.

Johann Albrecht Widmannstetter. Otto Hartig, "Die Gründung der Münchener Hofbibliothek durch Albrecht V. und Johann Jakob Fugger," *Abhandlungen der königlich bayerischen Akademie der Wissenschaften, philosophisch-philologische und historische Klasse,* XXVIII, no. 3 (Munich, 1917), pp. 9-18, and 170-193, §3, "Die Bibliothek Johann Albrecht Widmannstetters."

APPENDIX III

BIBLIOGRAPHY OF THE LANGUAGE OF GERMAN HUNTERS

GENERAL WORKS

Paul Lembke's *Studien zur deutschen Weidmannssprache* (Rostock diss.; Dresden, 1898) is a satisfactory introduction to the field of hunter's language. Friedrich Seiler's *Entwicklung der deutschen Kultur im Spiegel des deutschen Lehnworts* (Halle, 1924 ff.) is less helpful than one might expect. Fundamental to further study is Raoul Ritter von Dombrowski and others, *Allgemeine Encyklopädie der gesammten Forst- und Jagdwissenschaften*, I-VIII (Vienna, 1886-94). This is excellent for historical lexicography to the letter "G"; after that letter, the Middle High German citations fall off sharply and as the work progresses, it gives fewer and fewer of the words known only in Middle High German. Compare also the most recent enterprises of this sort: B. Hilf and F. Röhrig, *Wald und Weidwerk in Geschichte und Gegenwart* (Potsdam, 1936 ff.), and K. Lindner, *Geschichte des deutschen Weidwerks* (Berlin, 1937 ff.), which is planned to extend to six volumes. As examples of reprints of old texts compare F. Pomay, *Ein sehr artig Büchlein von dem Weydwerck und der Falcknerey. Wortgetreuer Abdruck der Original-Ausgabe, Lyon 1671* (Stuttgart, n.d.); J. Täntzer, sächs. Wildmeister, *Geheime und gar rare Jägerkünste oder 70 Arcana ... Nürnberg 1631* (Stuttgart, n.d.); Eberhardus Tappius, *Waidwerck und Federspiel. Strassburg 1542* (Stuttgart, n.d.).

DICTIONARIES ON THE LANGUAGE OF GERMAN HUNTERS

The German dictionaries, of which J. Kehrein, *Wörterbuch der Weidmannssprache für Jagd- und Sportfreunde* (Wiesbaden, 1871), is probably the best, give little or nothing about the origin and history of the technical terms. A special study, which may serve in some ways as a model, is Hermann Schmidt, *Die Terminologie der deutschen Falknerei* (Diss.; Freiburg i. Br., 1909). In the absence of a bibliography of German dictionaries of hunting terms the following list of books and pamphlets will suggest the variety of available lexical works: G. L. Hartig, *Anleitung zur Forst- und Weidmanns-Sprache oder Erklärung der älteren und neueren Kunstwörter beym Forst- und Jagdwesen* (2d ed.; Tübingen, 1821) and *Lexikon für Jäger und Jagdfreunde* (2d ed.; Berlin, 1861); J. G. T. Grässe, *Jägerbrevier* (2d ed.; Berlin, 1885), which has no index; H. W. von Schuckmann, *Waidmanns-Wörterbuch, zu Nutz und Frommen für Dianen's junge Schüler* (Leipzig, 1879) and *Waidmanns-Wörterbuch, ... für Diana's angehende Jünger* (Leipzig, 1882); Ernst Ritter von Dombrowski, *Deutsche Weidmannssprache* (2d ed.; Neudamm, 1897 = 3d ed.; Neudamm, 1913); L. E. Fritsche, *Die Weidmannssprache unter Berücksichtigung des gesammten Weidwerks* ("Für den deutschen Jäger," XIV; Berlin-Schöneberg, 1914); Erich Bischoff, *Wörter-*

buch der wichtigsten Geheim- und Berufssprachen. Jüdisch-Deutsch, . . .
Weidmanns-, . . . und Komödiantensprache (Leipzig, [1916]) ; *Rosenthals*
Jagdlexikon (2d ed.; Neudamm, 1916) ; E. Teuwsen, *Einführung in die*
Weidmannssprache (Neudamm, 1927) ; K. Zeiss, *Deutsche Weidmanns-*
sprache (Vienna, 1932) ; H. Kautzsch, *Die Jägersprache in ihren zumeist*
verkommenden, der Zugehörigkeit nach geordneten Ausdrücken (Neudamm,
1935).

THE BIBLIOGRAPHY OF BIBLIOGRAPHIES ON HUNTING

For the biliography of hunting see R. F. Souhart, *Bibliographie générale*
des ouvrages sur la chasse, la vénerie et la fauconnerie (Paris, 1886) ; Anon.,
"List of Works in the New York Public Library on Sport in General, and on
Shooting in Particular," *Bulletin of the New York Public Library,* VII
(1903), 164-186, 201-234; J. Thiébaud, *Bibliographie des ouvrages français*
sur la chasse (Paris, 1934) ; and the costly *Hunting, Hawking, Shooting Il-*
lustrated in a Catalogue of Books, Manuscripts, Prints, and Drawings Col-
lected by C. F. G. R. Schwerdt (London, 1928-37). The fourth volume of
the catalogue of Schwerdt's collection is about to appear; it will contain
additions and indexes. For similar German bibliographical works see Arnold,
p. 234; Dahlmann-Waitz, pp. 125, no. 2214, and 576, no. 8953.

BOOKS AND ARTICLES ON HUNTING, PARTICULARLY MEDIEVAL HUNTING

The essays and books on hunting are of very unequal value. Perhaps the
best general discussion in German is U. Wendt, *Kultur und Jagd,* I, *Das*
Mittelalter (Berlin, 1907). D. H. Madden, *A Chapter of Medieval History;*
the Fathers of the Literature of Fieldsport and Horses (London, 1924), is a
pleasant introduction. Even better for our purposes is H. L. Savage, "Hunting in the Middle Ages," *Speculum,* VIII (1933), 30-41. See also the excellent
essay, "The Latin Literature of Sport," in C. H. Haskins, *Studies in Medi-*
aeval Culture (Oxford, 1929), pp. 105-23. An exhaustive, special study is
P. Sahlender, *Das englische Jagdwesen in seiner geschichtlichen Entwicklung*
("Neusprachliche Abhandlungen," VI; Dresden, 1898). For an introduction
to medieval French sources—the basis of so many works on hunting—see
H. Werth, *Altfranzösische Jagdlehrbücher, nebst Handschriftenbibliographie*
der abendländischen Jagdliteratur überhaupt (Halle, 1889),—which mentions
nothing in German manuscripts. Typical studies of hunting in medieval
French literature are F. Borchert, *Die Jagd in der altfranzösischen Literatur*
(mit Ausschluss der Artus- und Abenteuerromane) (Diss.; Göttingen, 1909) ;
E. Bormann, *Die Jagd in den altfranzösischen Artus- und Abenteuerromanen*
("Ausgaben und Abhandlungen aus dem Gebiete der romanischen Philologie,"
LXVIII; Marburg, 1887). Similar studies in German literature are largely
lacking. See the notes on the hunt in the *Nibelungenlied* (see E. Matthias,
"Die Jagd im Nibelungenlied," *Zeitschrift für deutsche Philologie,* XV
[1883], 471-501 and the additional references in Ehrismann, p. 140) and the
breaking of the deer in Gottfried von Strassburg's *Tristan* and compare the
collections of metaphors from hunting in K. Matthaei, *Das weltliche Klöster-*

lein (Diss.; Marburg, 1907), pp. 44-45, 47; E. Nickel, *Studien zum Liebes-problem bei Gottfried* ("Königsberger deutsche Forschungen," I; Königs-berg i. Pr., 1927), p. 15.

K. Taut's *Die Anfänge der Jagdmusik* (Leipzig, 1926), which also ap-peared as a dissertation, *Beiträge zur Geschichte der Jagdmusik* (Leipzig, 1927), are incidentally useful and deal with a subject which, according to Savage, has been neglected.

BOOKS AND ARTICLES ON HUNTERS' WORDS OF FRENCH ORIGIN

Much of the vocabulary of hunting is derived from French, and a con-venient source of information is G. de Marolles, *Langage et termes de vénerie. Étude historique, philologique et critique* (Paris, 1906). For German words of French origin see E. Öhmann, *Studien über die französischen Worte im Deutschen des 12. und 13. Jahrhunderts* (Diss.; Helsinki, 1918); Hugo Suolahti, *Der französische Einfluss auf die deutsche Sprache im 13. Jahrhundert* ("Mémoires de la société néo-philologique," VIII, X; Helsinki, 1929, 1933); A. Rosenqvist, *Der französische Einfluss auf die mittelhoch-deutsche Sprache in der ersten Hälfte des 14. Jahrhunderts* ("Mémoires," IX [1932], 1-277.

The bibliographical indications given here are necessarily incomplete, but will suggest lines of attack.

APPENDIX IV

THE CITY-POEM

The best introductions to the literary history of the city-poem are J. Neff's preface to his edition of Helius Eobanus Hessus' *Noriberga illustrata* ("Lateinische Literaturdenkmäler des 15. und 16. Jahrhunderts," XII; Berlin 1896) and William Hammer, *Latin and German Encomia of Cities* (University of Chicago diss.; Chicago, 1937). See also G. Ellinger, "Städte-und Landschaftsgedichte," in *Reallexikon der deutschen Literaturgeschichte*, IV, 89-90; A. Werminghoff, *Conrad Celtis und sein Buch über Nürnberg* (Freiburg i. Br., 1921), pp. 80-85. See also some interesting suggestions regarding the importance of the city-poem as a source for the history of culture in Arthur Haberlandt, *Volkskunde* ("Volk," I; Halle, 1935), pp. 11-12. Neff, Ellinger, and Werminghoff give many important references to discussions of the literary history of the genre. Compare further Stammler, pp. 133-134; G. Voigt, *Die Wiederbelebung des classischen Altertums,* II (3d ed.; Berlin, 1893), 505-510, which treats primarily the geographical works of the humanists (see a fuller bibliography in V. Hantzsch, "Die landes-kundliche Literatur Deutschlands im Reformationszeitalter," *Deutsche Geschichtsblätter,* I [1900], 18-22, 41-47); L. Geiger, *Renaissance und Humanismus in Italien und Deutschland* (Berlin, 1892), pp. 471-473; K. Goedeke, *Dichtungen von Hans Sachs* ("Deutsche Dichter des 16. Jahrhunderts," IV; 2d ed.; Leipzig, 1883), I, p. xliii; W. Nagel, *Studien zur Geschichte der Meistersänger* (Langensalza, 1909), p. 187; P. Lehmann, "Mitteilungen aus Handschriften," *Sitzungsberichte der philosophisch-philologischen und der historischen Klasse der bayerischen Akademie . . . zu München,* 1929, no. 1, p. 28, n. 1; A. Spekke, *Alt-Riga im Lichte eines humanistischen Lobgedichts vom Jahre 1595* (Riga, 1927); and the collection of references in R. Bethge (ed.), *Ergebnisse und Fortschritte der germanischen Philologie* (Leipzig, 1902), p. 307. A few city-poems by German writers celebrated cities outside of Germany. For examples see Schottenloher, I, 54, nos. 1352-53, and 271, no. 6640; Johannes Bochius, *Panegyrici in Antwerpiam sibi et regi obsidione restitutam* (Antwerp, 1587).

Compare also the verses celebrating a list of cities. See J. Bolte, "Ein Lobspruch auf die deutschen Städte aus dem 15. Jahrhundert," *Zeitschrift des Vereins für Volkskunde,* XVIII (1908), 300-304, XIX (1909), 206-207; K. Euling, *Kleinere mittelhochdeutsche Erzählungen, Fabeln und Lehrgedichte* ("Deutsche Texte des Mittelalters," XIV; Berlin, 1908), pp. 93-94, no. 557. Jacobus Caviceo's *Urbium dicta* (n.p., 1491; a photostat in the University of Chicago Library) contains speeches addressed by the great cities to the victorious Maximilian. A modern example of these pedestrian eulogies is Max von Schenkendorf, *Die deutschen Städte* (1814).

See also a brief introduction to the city-poem in R. A. Aubin, *Typographi-*

cal Poetry in Eighteenth-Century England ("Modern Language Association, Revolving Fund Series," VI; New York, 1936) and especially the bibliographies, pp. 333-350, 392-394. William Dunbar's "London, thou art the flower of cities all" is an early example of the English genre. Compare C. F. Bühler, " 'London Thow Art the Flowre of Cytes All,' " *Review of English Studies,* XXII (1937), 1-10.

Wouter Nijhoff's list of descriptions of places in the Netherlands gives a notion of the variety of such works and includes a few examples of descriptions praising a city; see *Bibliographie van Noord-Nederlandsche plaatsbeschrijvingen tot het einde der 18ᵉ eeuw* ("Bijdragen tot eene Nederlandsche bibliographie," IV; Amsterdam, 1894). The early appearance of city-poems in Germanic countries and the intimate connection of verse and pictures are seen in J. D. Rutgers van der Loeff, *Drie Lofdichten op Haarlem* (Haarlem, 1911),—one is a poem by Dirk Mathijszen of 1483 and the other two, which are by Karel van Mander, poet and historian of art, are somewhat later.

The history of the *veduta,* the pictorial representation of a city, runs parallel to that of the city-poem; see Valentin von Loga, "Die Städte-Ansichten in Hartmann Schedels 'Weltchronik,' " *Jahrbuch der königlich preussischen Kunstsammlungen,* IX (1888), 93-107, 184-196. Schultheiss's more general essay, "Das Geographische in H. Schedels Weltchronik," *Globus* LXV (1894), 6-11, contains nothing pertinent here. Compare also a sumptuously printed collection of views of Rome in H. Egger, *Römische Veduten; Handzeichnungen aus dem 15. bis 18. Jahrhundert* (Leipzig, 1911-31). Many articles deal with the old views of German cities, e.g., K. Gebhardt, "Conrad Faber und die ältesten Ansichten von Frankfurt," *Alt-Frankfurt,* IV (1912), 104-114. A work belonging to this tradition which interests both the historian of literature and the historian of art is Philip von Zesen's *Beschreibung der Stadt Amsterdam* (Amsterdam, 1664).

APPENDIX V

THE HISTORY OF MARRIAGE

GENERAL WORKS

The anthropological and sociological treatises on marriage contain comparatively little for the student of German post-medieval handbooks on marriage. Consult for incidental information such works as R. Briffault, *The Mothers* (New York, 1928); E. Crawley, *The Mystic Rose; a Study of Primitive Marriage and of Primitive Thought in its Bearing on Marriage* (2d ed.; New York, 1927); W. Goodsell, *A History of Marriage and the Family* (New York, 1934), which should be compared with the first edition entitled *The Family as a Social Institution* (New York, 1915); G. E. Howard, *A History of Matrimonial Institutions* (Chicago, 1904); E. A. Westermarck, *History of Human Marriage* (5th ed.; New York, 1922). Chiefly erotica are the works of F. von Reitzenstein; they begin with the prehistory of marriage (*Urgeschichte der Ehe, ihre Bildung und ihr Entwicklungsgang* [Stuttgart, 1905]), and deal with the ancient Orient, classical and medieval Europe, Eastern Asia, and the American aborigines. Georg Steinhausen collects many more titles—some of them important in this connection and others pertinent to the later history of marriage—in a bibliographical survey in *Archiv für Kulturgeschichte*, XIII (1917), 352-374, XXIII (1935), 392-401. A noteworthy collection of pertinent books is G. E. Howard's library at the University of Chicago. See also the Gerritson library now in the John Crerar Library (Chicago). Compare further such standard bibliographical works as [Jules Gay, sometimes ascribed to the Comte d'Imbert], *Bibliographie des ouvrages relatifs à l'amour, aux femmes, au mariage et des livres facétieux etc.* (4th ed., enlarged by J. Lemonnyer; Paris, 1894-1900); [A. Laporte], *Bibliographie cléricogalante; ouvrages galants ou singuliers sur l'amour, les femmes, le mariage, le théâtre, etc. écrits par des abbées, ... papes* (Paris, 1879); H. Hayn and A. N. Gotendorf, *Bibliotheca Germanorum erotica et curiosa* (Munich, 1912-29). These deal with works more interesting to the collector of facetious and obscene literature than to the scholar.

MARRIAGE IN CLASSICAL ANTIQUITY AND EARLY CHRISTIAN TIMES

For a good introduction see Kunkel, "Matrimonium," in Pauly, Wissowa, and Kroll (eds.), *Real-Encyclopädie der classischen Altertumswissenschaft*, XIV (Stuttgart, 1930), cols. 2259-2286. Compare also N. Geurts, *Het huwelijk bij de Griekse en Romeinse moralisten* (Diss.; Amsterdam, 1928); P. E. Corbett's account of the legal background in *The Roman Law of Marriage* (Oxford, 1930); and J. Donaldson's book cited below. Some works which display a keen interest in the erotic aspects of sexual life, love, and marriage are Otto Kiefer, *Sexual Life in Ancient Rome* (London, 1934); H. Licht,

Sittengeschichte Griechenlands: I, *Die griechische Gesellschaft;* II, *Liebe und Ehe in Griechenland* (Berlin, 1925). Licht's second volume has been translated by F. H. Freese as *Sexual Life in Ancient Greece* (London, 1933).

For marriage in early Christian times see a comprehensive treatment in Godefroy's and Le Bras's articles on marriage in the *Dictionnaire de théologie catholique,* IX, ii (Paris, 1927), cols. 2044-2317 and the supplementary article by H. Leclercq in the *Dictionnaire d'archéologie chrétienne et de liturgie,* X, ii (Paris, 1932), cols. 1843-1982. Brief and authoritative are the pertinent articles in the *Catholic Encyclopedia,* IX (New York, 1910), 691-715. General works which are more readable than these very learned surveys are J. Donaldson, *Woman: Her Position and Influence in Ancient Greece and Rome and Among the Early Christians* (London, 1907); George H. Joyce, S.J., *Christian Marriage, an historical and doctrinal study* (London, 1933); D. A. Lougee, *The Status of Woman in the Earlier Latin Patristic Writers* (Diss.; University of Illinois, 1926. Only an abstract of 6 pp. was published); Ralph de Pomerai, *Marriage, Past, Present, and Future* (London, 1930); F. Freiherr von Reitzenstein, *Die Entwicklungsgeschichte der Liebe* (Stuttgart, 1908), which covers the historical development in Western Europe in 111 pages and makes some interesting suggestions; K. A. Wieth-Knudson, *Frauenfrage und Feminismus vom Altertum bis zur Gegenwart* (Stuttgart, 1926).

For the pertinent early Christian texts see in general Alexander Roberts (ed.), *The Ante-Nicene Christian Library* or *The Ante-Nicene Fathers* (various eds.). Convenient editions of a fundamental work are Septimius Tertullian, *De cultu feminarum libri II* ("Corpus scriptorum latinarum Paravianum," LIV; Turin, 1930) and W. Kok (ed.), Tertullian, *De cultu feminarum* (Dokkum, 1934).

General studies of early Christian ideas regarding women and marriage are Wilhelm Braun (b. 1873), *Die Frau in der alten Kirche* ("Zeit- und Streitfragen des Glaubens, etc. . . ," XIII, 5-6; Berlin, 1919); A. C. E. Gerlings, *De vrouw in het oud-christelijke gemeenteleven* (Diss.; Groningen, 1913. The edition circulated in the book-trade contains 30 additional pages); Elfriede Gottlieb, *Die Frau im frühen Christentum* (Leipzig, 1928); Hermann Jordan, *Das Frauenideal des Neuen Testaments und der ältesten Christenheit* (Leipzig, 1909); J. P. Kirsch, *Charakterbilder der katholischen Frauenwelt,* I, Part 2, *Die Frauen des kirchlichen Altertums* (Paderborn, 1912; 2d ed., n.d. [1920]); H. Preisker, *Das Christentum und die Ehe in den ersten Jahrhunderten* ("Neue Studien zur Geschichte der Theologie und Kirche," XXIII; Berlin, 1927).

Special works dealing with particular figures are Gerhard Delling, *Paulus' Stellung zur Frau und Ehe* ("Beiträge zur Wissenschaft vom Alten und Neuen Testament," IV, 5; Stuttgart, 1931); A. Michel, "Wie spricht Paulus über Frau und Ehe?," *Theologische Studien und Kritiken,* CV (1933), 215-225; H. Schumacher, *Das Eheideal des Apostels Paulus* (Munich, 1932); Bernard Alves Pereira, *La doctrine du mariage selon S. Augustine* (Paris,

1930) ; H. Arendt, *Der Liebesbegriff bei Augustin* ("Philosophische Forschungen," IX ; Berlin, 1929),—compare R. Seeberg's review, *Deutsche Literaturzeitung,* LI (1930), cols. 2114-16 ; J. Peters, *Die Ehe nach der Lehre des hl. Augustinus* ("Veröffentlichungen der Görresgesellschaft, Sektion für Rechts- und Sozialwissenschaft," XXXII ; Paderborn, 1918) ; Geneviève Serrier, *De quelques recherches concernant le mariage contract-sacrement et plus particulièrement de la doctrine augustinienne des biens du mariage* (Paris, 1928) ; A. Moulard, *St. Jean Chrysostome, le défenseur du mariage et l'apôtre de la virginité* (Diss.; Paris, 1923).

As an example of the information to be gleaned from the collections of exempla see Hjalmar Crohns, *Die Bewertung der Frau unter dem Einfluss der Cölibatsidee im Ms. lat. 15970 der Bibliothèque nationale (Stephanus de Borbone, De diversis materiis predicabilibus)* (Helsingfors, 1913), and "Legenden och medeltidens latinska predikan och 'exempla' i deras värdesättning av kvinnan," *Öfversigt af Finska Vetenskaps-Societens Förhandlingar,* LVII (1914-15), Afdelning B, no. 1 and "Några 'Scripta suppositis' i deras betydelse för värdesättningen av kvinnan," *ibid.,* no. 2. See also A. Broil, *Der erzieherische Gehalt der mittelalterlichen Exempelliteratur* (Cologne diss.; Altenkirchen, 1928).

GERMANIC IDEALS OF WOMAN AND MARRIAGE

See, e.g., Karl Weinhold, *Die deutschen Frauen im Mittelalter* (3d ed. in 2 vols.; Vienna, 1897). Perhaps the latest discussions of the subject are G. Neckel, *Liebe und Ehe bei den alten Germanen* (Leipzig, 1932), and the review in *Anzeiger für deutsches Altertum,* LI (1932), 161-170 ; G. Neckel, "Zur Stellung der Frau im germanischen Altertum," *Zeitschrift für deutsches Altertum,* LXX (1933), 197-205 ; K. Burdach, *Vorspiel,* I, Part 1 (Halle, 1925), 261-262. For the condemnation of effeminacy see G. Roethe, *Die Gedichte Reinmars von Zweter* (Leipzig, 1887), p. 235, n. 291. See also the parallels in Bruder Wernher und Pseudo-Gervelin cited in Alfons Weber, *Studien zur Abwandlung der höfischen Ethik* (Bonn diss.; Würzburg, 1936), p. 95.

WOMEN AND MARRIAGE IN THE MIDDLE AGES

See E. L. Linton, "The Women of Chivalry," *Fortnightly Review,* XLVIII (1887), 559-579 ; E. Wechssler, "Frauendienst und Vassalität," *Zeitschrift für französische Sprache und Literatur,* XXIV (1902), 159-190 ; P. Hermant, "Le sentiment amoureux dans la littérature medievale ; étude psychologique et sociale," *Revue de synthèse historique,* XII (1906), 152-181 ; Myrrha Lot Borodine, *La femme et l'amour au XIIe siècle d'après les poèmes de Chrétien de Troyes* (Paris, 1909).

For studies of conditions in Germany see R. Götte, "Liebesleben und Liebesdienst in der Liebesdichtung des deutschen Mittelalters," *Zeitschrift für Kulturgeschichte,* 4. Folge, I (1894), 426-466 ; Reinhold Becker, *Der mittelalterliche Minnedienst in Deutschland* (Halle, 1897) ; Elsbet Kaiser,

Frauendienst im mittelhochdeutschen Volksepos ("Germanistische Abhandlungen," LIV; Breslau, 1921); Lilli Seibold, *Studien über die Huote* ("Germanische Studien," CXXIII; Berlin, 1932), which offers, the reviewers point out, opportunities for further investigation; H. Langenbucher, *Das Gesicht des deutschen Minnesangs und seine Wandlungen* (Heidelberg, 1930); R. Haller, *Der wilde Alexander* (Bonn diss.; Würzburg, 1934), pp. 66-87; Alfons Weber, *Studien zur Abwandlung der höfischen Ethik* (Bonn diss.; Würzburg, 1936), pp. 88-98, "Die Frau und die Minne in der Spruchdichtung." Compare the discussion of plastic representations of married couples in H. Goern, *Das Ehebild im deutschen Mittelalter* (Halle, 1936).

For the Courts of Love, see F. Trojel, *Middelalderens Elskovshoffer* (Copenhagen, 1888); L. F. Mott, *The System of Courtly Love studied as an introduction to the 'Vita nuova' of Dante* (Boston, 1896).

For general treatises on women in the Middle Ages see K. Weinhold, *Die deutschen Frauen im Mittelalter* (3d ed. in 2 vols.; Vienna, 1897); Alwin Schultz, *Das höfische Leben zur Zeit der Minnesinger* (2d ed.; Leipzig, 1889) and *Deutsches Leben im 14. und 15. Jahrhundert* (Grosse Ausgabe; Vienna, 1892); H. Finke, *Die Frau im Mittelalter* ("Sammlung Kösel," LXII; Kempten, 1913), and K. Wenck's review, *Deutsche Literaturzeitung*, XXXVI (1915), cols. 2156-2161; E. Power, "The Position of Women," in C. G. Crump and E. F. Jacob, *The Legacy of the Middle Ages* (Oxford, 1926), pp. 401-433; Blanche H. Dow, *The Varying Attitude Toward Women in French Literature of the Fifteenth Century* ("Institute of French Studies"; New York, 1937).

For discussion of certain special aspects touching women see, e.g., Alice Hentsch, *De la littérature didactique du moyen âge s'addressent spécialement aux femmes* (Halle diss.; Cahors, 1903); E. R. Goddard, *Women's Costume in French Texts of the XIth and XIIth Centuries* ("Johns Hopkins Studies in Romance Literatures and Languages," VII; Baltimore, 1927). One or another of such special treatises (which are often limited to a comparison of English and French conditions) may suggest the need of a companion-piece for German literature. See, e.g., E. Meyn- von Westenholz, *Frauenbildung im Mittelalter* ("Quellenhefte zum Frauenleben in der Geschichte," IX a; Berlin [1930]), and the other volumes in this series; W. Ruhmer, *Pädagogische Theorien über Frauenbildung im Zeitalter der Renaissance; nebst einer kritischen Würdigung der Leistungen mittelalterlicher Theoretiker* (Diss.; Bonn, 1915).

Many works which do not deal directly with the problem of marriage will throw light on the background. See, e.g., on morality—including more than sexual morals—such popular erotica as Rudolph Quanter, *Sittlichkeit und Moral im heiligen römischen Reich deutscher Nation* (2d enl. ed.; Berlin-Lichterfelde, 1911), F. Freiherr von Reitzenstein, *Liebe und Ehe im Mittelalter* (Stuttgart, 1912), and Gustav Jung, *Die Geschlechtsmoral des deutschen Weibes im Mittelalter* (Leipzig, n.d. [1921]), on the economic position of women see W. Behagel, *Die gewerbliche Stellung der Frau im mittelalter-*

lichen Köln ("Abhandlungen zur mittleren und neueren Geschichte," XXIII; Berlin, 1910); H. Wachendorf, *Die wirtschaftliche Stellung der Frau in den deutschen Städten des späteren Mittelalters* (Hamburg diss.; Quakenbrück i. H., 1934); H. Triebel, *Die wirtschaftliche Stellung der deutschen Ehefrau in Vergangenheit, Gegenwart und Zukunft* (Diss.; Halle, 1936). The dissertations—especially the second one—fall far short of their titles. Such a lecture as Carl Bücher, *Die Frauenfrage im Mittelalter* (Tübingen, 1882; 2d ed., Tübingen, 1910) is a better introduction to the problem than these dissertations.

TREATISES ON MARRIAGE IN THE RENAISSANCE: GENERAL WORKS AND WORKS DEALING WITH COUNTRIES OTHER THAN GERMANY

For Italy see, e.g., *Year's Work in Modern Languages,* 1933, p. 11; P. Lorenzetti, "La donna presso gli scrittori del Cinquecento," *Rivista d'Italia,* July 15, 1914; G. Rossi, "La collezione Giordani della biblioteca communale di Bologna," *Giornale storico della letteratura italiana,* XXVII (1896), 372-390 (an illustration of the books which one might collect on the subject); P. Lorenzetti, "La bellezza e l'amore nei trattati del Cinquecento," *Annali della r. scuola normale superiore,* XXVIII (Pisa, 1917); G. Zonta, *Trattati del cinquecento sulla donna* ("Scrittori d'Italia," LVI, 1; Bari, 1913) and *Trattati d'amore del cinquecento* ("Scrittori d'Italia," XXXVIII, 1; Bari, 1912); E. Rodocanachi, *Le femme italienne avant, pendant et après la renaissance* (Paris, 1922), pp. 303-322 (compare especially the bibliographical references in the notes); A. P. Molmenti, *La storia di Venezia nella vita privata* (6th ed.; Bergamo, 1925), II, 267-360; N. Tamassia, *L'amore nella poesia e nel pensiero del rinascimento* (Florence, 1933) and *La famiglia italiana nei secoli decimoquinto e decimosesto* (Milan, n.d. [1910]). Many of these references I owe to the kindness of my friend and former colleague W. L. Bullock. Stammler's reference (p. 462, note on p. 16) to Wenck, *Mitteilungen des Instituts für österreichische Geschichtsforschung,* XVIII, 101 ff., 123 ff., appears to be an error.

Comparison with English treatises and editions is helpful and may be a guide to the discussion of the development in Germany. See Routh, "The Progress of Social Literature in Tudor Times," in the *Cambridge History of English Literature,* III (Cambridge, 1918), Ch. V, pp. 83-114. Essential works are Chilton Powell, *English Domestic Relations, 1487-1653* (New York, 1917), and L. B. Wright, *Middle-Class Culture in Elizabethan England* (Chapel Hill, N.C., 1935). See further such editions of sixteenth-century texts with important introductions and editorial comment as R. W. Bond (ed.), William Bercher (or Barker), *The Nobility of Women* ("Roxburghe Club," CXL-CXLI; London, 1904-5; F. P. Wilson (ed.), *The Batchelars Banquet* (Oxford, 1929), a translation of *Les quinze joies de mariage.* See incidentally H. Stein, "Six Tracts About Women: a Volume in the British Museu," *The Library,* 4th ser., XV (1935), 38-48; B. White, "Two Tracts on Marriage," *Bulletin of the Huntington Library,* I (May, 1931), 205-207.

A pertinent dissertation on Dutch literature is A. L. A. Roessingh, *De vrouw bij de dietsche moralisten* (Diss.; Groningen, 1914).

The abundant literature on *Les quinze joies de mariage* will lead the student into the discussion of the subject in France. See, e.g., F. Fleuret (ed.), *Les quinze joies de mariage* (Paris, 1936); Blanche H. Dow, *The Varying Attitude Toward Women in the French Literature of the Fifteenth Century* ("Institute of French Studies"; New York, 1937).

TREATISES ON MARRIAGE IN THE RENAISSANCE: WORKS DEALING WITH GERMAN CONDITIONS

See, e.g., Franz Falk, *Die Ehe am Ausgang des Mittelalters. Eine kirchen- und kulturgeschichtliche Studie* ("Erläuterungen und Ergänzungen zu Janssens 'Geschichte des deutschen Volkes,'" VI, 4; Freiburg i. Br., 1908. Compare the brief notice in *Zeitschrift des Vereins für Volkskunde*, XIX [1909], 240-241); Waldemar Kawerau, *Die Reformation und die Ehe, ein Beitrag zur Kulturgeschichte des 16. Jahrhunderts* ("Schriften des Vereins für Reformationsgeschichte," XXXIX; Halle, 1892); A. Bömer, "Die deutschen Humanisten und das weibliche Geschlecht," *Zeitschrift für Kulturgeschichte*, 4. Folge, IV (1897), 94-112, 117-197; R. Koebner, "Die Eheauffassung des ausgehenden Mittelalters," *Archiv für Kulturgeschichte*, IX (1911), 136-198, 279-318 (an additional chapter, *Die religiöse Beurteilung des ehelichen Lebens*, was issued as a Berlin dissertation [Breslau, 1911]). I have not seen N. Paulus, "Gedruckte und ungedruckte Ehebüchlein des ausgehenden Mittelalters," *Kölnische Volkszeitung*, 1903, no. 20. Waldemar Kawerau provides an entertaining introduction in "Lob und Schimpf des Ehestandes in der Literatur des sechzehnten Jahrhunderts," *Preussische Jahrbücher*, LXIX (1892), 759-781. See also Max Herrmann's bibliographical survey in a dozen lines: *Albrecht von Eyb*, pp. 329-330, n. 2.

MARRIAGE IN MEDIEVAL AND RENAISSANCE LITERATURE

See, e.g., B. Barth, *Liebe und Ehe im altfranzösischen Fabel und in der mittelhochdeutschen Novelle* ("Palaestra, XCVII; Berlin, 1910); T. Krabbes, *Die Frau im altfranzösischen Karlsepos* ("Ausgaben und Abhandlungen aus dem Gebiete der romanischen Philologie," XVIII; Marburg, 1884); A. Preime, *Die Frau in den altfranzösischen Fabliaux* (Göttingen diss.; Cassel, 1901); Blanche H. Dow, *The Varying Attitude Toward Women in French Literature of the Fifteenth Century* ("Institute of French Studies"; New York, 1937); Bertha M. van der Stempel, *De vrouw in onze Britische romans* (Diss.; Amsterdam, 1910). The best of the German studies is F. Brietzmann, *Die böse Frau in der deutschen Literatur des Mittelalters* ("Palaestra," XLII; Berlin, 1912). See also W. Berger, *Das Ehebruchsmotiv im älteren deutschen Drama* (Würzburg diss.; Heppenheim, 1912); H. Gattermann, *Die Frau in den Fastnachtspielen* (Diss.; Greifswald, 1911); Rudolph Schmidt, *Die Frau in der deutschen Literatur des 16. Jahrhunderts* (Diss.; Straussburg, 1917).

THE LEGAL ASPECTS OF MARRIAGE

See a general treatise by E. Friedberg, *Das Recht der Eheschliessung in seiner geschichtlichen Entwicklung* (Leipzig, 1865). Convenient introductory lectures and essays are L. Wahrmund, *Ehe und Eherecht* ("Sammlung gemeinverständlicher wissenschaftlicher Vorträge," CXV; Leipzig, 1906); Marianne Weber, *Ehefrau und Mutter in der Rechtsentwicklung* (Tübingen, 1907); and G. Merschberger, *Die Rechtsstellung der germanischen Frau* ("Mannusbücherei," LVII; Leipzig, 1937). The following titles are arranged according to the periods with which they deal: P. Wilutzky, *Vorgeschichte des Rechts*, I, *Die Eheverfassungen* (Berlin, 1903); P. E. Corbett, *The Roman Law of Marriage* (Oxford, 1930); K. Frölich, "Die Eheschliessung des deutschen Frühmittelalters im Lichte der neueren rechtsgeschichtlichen Forschungen," *Hessische Blätter für Volkskunde*, XXVII (1928), 144-195, 285-286 (an admirable introduction to the problems as well as a survey of recent discussion); Hans Fehr, *Die Rechtsstellung der Frau und der Kinder in den Weistümern* (Jena, 1912); W. Plöchl, *Das Eherecht des Magisters Gratianus* ("Wiener staats- und rechtswissenschaftliche Studien," XXIV; Leipzig, 1935); Joseph Freisen, *Geschichte des canonischen Eherechts bis zum Verfall der Glossenliteratur* (2d ed., Tübingen, 1893); F. Rodeck, *Beiträge zur Geschichte des Eherechts deutscher Fürsten bis zur Durchführung des Tridentinums* ("Münstersche Beiträge zur Geschichtsforschung," N.F., XXVI; Münster, 1910); A. Leinz, *Der Ehevorschrift des Concils von Trient Ausdehnung und heutige Geltung* (Freiburg i. Br., 1888).

The bibliography of canon law regarding marriage is very extensive. In addition to the titles already cited, consult G. Le Bras, "La doctrine du mariage chez les théologiens et les canonistes depuis l'an mille," *Dictionnaire de théologie catholique*, IX, ii (Paris, 1927), cols. 2123-2317 (a compact and authoritative statement); J. M. O'Hara and F. Brennan (transl.), A. C. Cigognani, *Canon Law* (Philadelphia, 1934), an introduction to the subject of canon law; A. Esmein, *Le mariage en droit canonique* (Paris, 1891. Reissued in one vol.; Paris, 1929); Hildegard Borsinger, *Rechtsstellung der Frau in der katholischen Kirche* (Zürich diss.; Borna-Leipzig, 1930), and the discussion of special points in the "Canon Law Studies" of the Catholic University of America (Washington, D.C.).

For general works and bibliographies see H. Brunner and Claudius Freiherr von Schwerin, *Deutsche Rechtsgeschichte* (Munich, 1906, 2d ed. of vol. II, 1928); L. J. Paetow, *A Guide to the Study of Mediaeval History* (2d ed.; New York, 1931), pp. 189-194; Dahlmann-Waitz, pp. 140-141, no. 2445, and 203, no. 3462; Müller-Bergstrom, *Handwörterbuch des deutschen Aberglaubens*, VII (Berlin, 1935), col. 568.

For discussion of the legal aspects of a marriage described in a literary monument see such essays as O. Zahlinger, "Die Eheschliessung im 'Nibelungenlied' and in der 'Gudrun,'" *Sitzungsberichte der Akademie der Wissenschaften in Wien, philosophisch-historische Klasse*, CXCIX (1923), no. 1, and "Die Ringgaben bei der Heirat und das Zusammengeben im mittelalterlich-deutschen Recht," *ibid.,* CCXII (1931), no. 4; H. Meyer, "Die Ehe-schliessung im 'Ruodlieb' und das Eheschwert," *Zeitschrift der Savigny-Stiftung für Rechtsgeschichte, Germanistische Abteilung,* LII (= *Zeitschrift für Rechtsgeschichte,* LXV; 1932), 276-293. For mention of the problem offered by the legal aspects of Andreas Capellanus see G. Ehrismann, *Zeitschrift für deutsches Altertum,* LXIV (1927), 306. There is a similar problem in Martial d'Auvergne's *Les arrêts d'amour* (ed. Luise Götz; "Frankfurter Quellen und Forschungen zur germanischen und romanischen Philologie," I; Frankfurt a. M., 1932).

DISCUSSION OF CELIBACY, BIGAMY, AND POLYGAMY

The discussion of celibacy, bigamy, and polygamy does not play a very large rôle in writings which concern the historian of literature. As examples of the nature and currency of books on the celibacy of the clergy see Hainrich Schratt von Rubi, *Das priester ee nit wider das Göttlich, gaystlich vnnd weltlich recht sey* (1523), cited from Goedeke, II, 279, no. 16, 2; Leonhard Jacobi, *Von uneinigkeit der Concilien, der Priester Ehe, und das hochwidrige Sacrament des Leibs und Bluts Christi belangende* (1546); Marquis de Susanis, *Tractatus de coelibatu sacerdotum non abrogando* (Vience, 1565); J. Lorichius, *De ecclesiastico coelibatu, adversus sacrilegos nuptiatores et infamos* (1584); Michael Küblin, *Vom heiligen Ehstande, Catholische Antwort u. bericht, ob deshalb, zu diesen zeiten auch ein heilig Sacrament seye* (1597).

Although at least one Reformation pamphlet—an Anabaptist tract by Bernt (or Bernhart) Rotmann—has found its way into the "Neudrucke deutscher Literaturwerke des 16. und 17. Jahrhunderts," the discussion of bigamy and polygamy is not particularly important for students of literature. For an introduction to the subject see, e.g., W. W. Rockwell, *Die Doppelehe des Landgrafen Philipp von Hessen* (Marburg, 1904), Hastings Eells, *The Attitude of Martin Bucer toward the Bigamy of Philip of Hesse* ("Yale Historical Publications. Miscellany," XII; New Haven, 1924); Bernt Rotmann. *Restitution rechter und gesunder christlicher Lehre* ("Neudrucke deutscher Literaturwerke des 16. und 17. Jahrhunderts," LXXVII-LXXVIII; Halle, 1888) can be understood in the light of such interpretative studies as H. P. A. Detmer, *Bilder aus den religiösen und sozialen Unruhen in Münster während des 16. Jahrhunderts* (Münster i. W., 1903-4), III (1904), "Ueber die Auffassung von der Ehe und die Durchführung der Vielweiberei in Münster während der Täuferherrschaft" and R. H. Bainton, *David Joris, Wiedertäufer und Kämpfer für Toleranz im 16. Jahrhundert* ("Archiv für Reformationsgeschichte. Ergänzungsband," VI; Leipzig, 1937).

INDEX OF SUBJECTS

INDEX OF PROPER NAMES[1]

Abelard, 130.
Abels, H., and B. Graupe, 82, n.24.
Achor, 71, n.80.
Adam, J., 152.
Adolph of Nassau, 117.
Aesticampanius, 47.
Agricola, Johann, 21.
Albertinus, Aegidius, 53; 141.
Albertus Magnus, 90; 91, n.49.
Alberus, Erasmus, 9; 65; 136; 141.
Albrecht V., 13, n.39; 156; 159.
Alciati, Andreas, 28; 86, n.37; 87.
Alker, E., 1, n.1.
Alpers, Paul, 30; 30, n.89.
Ambrose, St., 139, n.61.
Amman, Jost, 41; 58, n.33; 88, n.38.
Ammianus Marcellinus, 20.
Amos, Flora Ross, 36, n.104
Amrain, K., 96, n.64.
Amram, D. W., 25, n.75.
Ander, F. W., E. Martin, and M. Koehnlein, 154.
Anderson, M. D., 82, n.25.
Andreas Ornithoparchus, 43, n.118.
Andreas Capellanus, 133; 137; 172.
Andree, R., 16, n.45.
Anrich, G., 75, n.7.
Apollinaris, see Sidonius.
Appel, M., 42, n.118.
Arendt, H., 167.
Arigo, 61.
Aristophanes, 33.
Arlt, Gustave Otto, xi; 45, n.128; 46, n.130; 69.
Arndt, E. M., 23, n.66.
Arnold, August, 14, n.41.
Arnold, R. F., 3, n.10; 4, nn.11, 14; 5, n.15; 26, n.81; 37, n.106; 78, n.15; 161.
Arnswaldt, A. von, 18, n.49.
Astesano, Antonio, 119.

Aubin, H., 116, n.107.
Aubin, R. A., 163.
Aue, Karl, 78, n.15.
Augustine, St., 139, n.61; 167.
Ausonius, 117; 120.
Avé-Lallemant, F. C. B., 40, n.115; 41.

Bacchus, 80, n.20.
Bacon, Francis, 104.
Bächtold-[Stäubli], Hanns, 16, n.45.
Baer, Leo, 89, n.44.
Baesecke, Georg, 122, n.138.
Baeumker, C., 17, n.47; 151.
Bahder, Karl von, 37, n.106.
Bainton, Roland H., xi; 172.
Baldensperger, F., 26, n.81.
Bang, A. C., 91, n.51.
Barack, K. A., 15, n.43.
Baranowski, S., 135, n.40.
Barbaro, Francesco, 130; 133; 140.
Barlandus, Adrian, 85.
Barth, B., 170.
Bartsch, Adam, 147, n.81.
Bartsch, K., 18, n.49; 19, n.53; 81, n.24; 109, n.90.
Basilikus, Heraklid, 15, n.43.
Baskervill, C. R., xi.
Basler, Otto, 10.
Bataillon, M., 65, n.53.
Bauch, Gustav, 11; 33, n.98; 70, n.74.
Bauck, S., 118, n. 118.
Baudet, F. E. J. M., 42, n.117.
Baudoin, Jean, 87, n.37.
Bauer, A., 34, n.100.
Bauer, K. F., 78, n.15.
Bauer, Ludwig, 23, n.66.
Bayley, Harold, 86, n.37.
Bebel, Heinrich, 84; 100; 103; 109, n.90.

[1] The names of fifteenth- and sixteenth-century authors and of a few others for whom subjects are suggested are italicized.

GENERAL SERIES

Address orders to the Executive Offices.—Orders from abroad should be addressed to Humphrey Milford, Oxford University Press, Amen Corner, London, E.C. 4.

I. THE SUBLIME: A STUDY OF CRITICAL THEORIES IN
XVIII-CENTURY ENGLAND
By Samuel Holt Monk
Published 1935 (vii + 252 pp.). Price $2.50.

II. VOLKSSPRACHE UND WORTSCHATZ DES BADISCHEN
FRANKENLANDES DARGESTELLT AUF GRUND
DER MUNDART VON OBERSCHEFFLENZ
By Edwin Carl Roedder
Published 1936 (xxvi + 606 pp.). Price $5.00.

III. CAVALIER DRAMA
By Alfred Bennett Harbage
Published 1936 (ix + 302 pp.). Price $2.50.

IV. THE LITERARY HISTORY OF MEISTERGESANG
By Archer Taylor
Published 1937 (x + 144 pp.). Price $2.00.

V. FRENCH REALISM: THE CRITICAL REACTION, 1830-1870
By Bernard Weinberg
Published 1937 (vii + 259 pp.). Price $2.50.

VI. SHAKESPEARE'S SEVENTEENTH-CENTURY
EDITORS, 1632-1685
By Matthew W. Black and Matthias A. Shaaber
Published 1937 (xi + 420 pp.). Price $3.00.

VII. LETTERS OF LUDWIG TIECK, HITHERTO
UNPUBLISHED, 1792-1853
By Edwin H. Zeydel, Percy Matenko, and Robert Herndon Fife
Published 1938 (xxx + 581 pp.). Price $5.00.

VIII. PROBLEMS IN GERMAN LITERARY HISTORY OF
THE FIFTEENTH AND SIXTEENTH CENTURIES
By Archer Taylor
Published 1939 (xviii + 212 pp.). Price $2.00.